EYES to SEE

EYES

TO

SEE

APPROACHING THE SPIRITUAL IN WORLD ART

ROGER LIPSEY

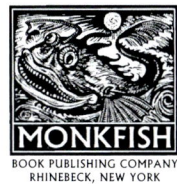

MONKFISH

BOOK PUBLISHING COMPANY
RHINEBECK, NEW YORK

Paperback ISBN 9781966608097
eBook ISBN 9781966608103

Library of Congress Cataloging-in-Publication Data
Names: Lipsey, Roger, 1942- author
Title: Eyes to see : approaching the spiritual in world art / Roger Lipsey.
Description: Rhinebeck, New York : Monkfish Book Publishing Company, [2026]
  | Includes bibliographical references.
Identifiers: LCCN 2025019712 (print) | LCCN 2025019713 (ebook) | ISBN
  9781966608097 paperback | ISBN 9781966608103 ebook
Subjects: LCSH: Art--Psychology | Art appreciation
Classification: LCC N71 .L5953 2026 (print) | LCC N71 (ebook) | DDC
  701/.18--dc23/eng/20250516
LC record available at https://lccn.loc.gov/2025019712
LC ebook record available at https://lccn.loc.gov/2025019713

Book design by Colin Rolfe

Monkfish Book Publishing Company
22 East Market Street, Suite 304
Rhinebeck, New York 12572
(845) 876-4861
monkfishpublishing.com

For Setsuya Kotani
and in memory of Erik Koch (1933 – 2024)
artists, teachers, friends

CONTENTS

Acknowledgments

This book is in a category we have come to know too well: written during the height of the Covid pandemic when authors could turn to projects that needed little personal outreach, much reflection. During that year and more of confinement, my wife Susan encouraged this book, read entries as they appeared, and understood. All my thanks, as you know.

A number of friends told me what this book is when they read it as an illustrated typescript. I'm especially grateful to David Appelbaum and Didier Mouturat for their insight that it's similar to a Book of Hours, best read from day to day, no rush.

At Monkfish Books, I am grateful to Paul Cohen, publisher, Jon Sweeney, and the designer Colin Rolfe for welcoming this book and marshalling the resources needed to let it be beautiful.

A first French edition was published by Philippe Muller in his series *Vivre l'Art* and translated by my friend Frédéric Blanc. What we learned preparing that edition has enhanced this one. All my thanks to you both.

Patty Villanova proved, not for the first time, to be a persevering assistant as we sought art resources and permissions.

About the dedications: Setsuya Kotani and his wife Yoko Yoshimatsu helped us to connect with art resources in Japan. Kotani-san has shown me through the decades of our friendship that traditional Japanese aesthetics and craftsmanship continue to move and amaze, today and always.

The second dedication: to the late Erik Koch, Danish by birth, living in France for much of his life. He was, I have long thought, the last representative of the Constructivist school in the art of our time. An extraordinary artist, he was the best of friends. I visited him last spring; that was good.

ROGER LIPSEY

Art contains in itself the deepest principles of life.

ANANDA K. COOMARASWAMY,
20TH-CENTURY POLYMATH

Whenever I encountered someone of genius,
I wrote about it in order to tell my friends.

BASHO,
17TH-CENTURY JAPANESE POET AND TRAVELER

Walk in the royal way, measuring
the milestones without meanness.

ABBA BENJAMIN,
5TH-CENTURY DESERT FATHER

INTRODUCTION

I began collecting icons—works of art that meant the world to me—at the time I began collecting a life: a life of challenge and reasonable promise, with as many tracks toward the future as a railroad yard. In early years I had the good fortune of meeting people who could "read" images, who—for reasons unclear to me at the time—approached images of rich cultural content as if they were texts endowed with voice and meaning. Inspired by their knowing love of visual art, I began to be populated inside with images of paintings, sculpture, ceramics, all manner of things, which vividly reminded me of what I was learning to care about as I grew up. More compact than nearly any text, they delivered messages about how to live and why—the "look", energies, and potential grace of that kind of living. The images I began to collect weren't prayer cards as in the Roman Catholic and Hindu traditions, though often all I had was a postcard of a work I had never seen or a memory imprinted like a prayer card in my mind. It was a student art collection but enough; later I would travel. The images or icons were from cultures, eras, and religions worldwide, and they played for me a role quite like prayer cards in the settled traditions. I would feel their force, their beauty, and what they point toward. Texts move through time, they are scrolls to be unwound. Images occupy space and shine toward us in a moment. Eyes and mind move over them, but they are still. That stillness is part of their magic.

Later I learned about the circulation of images from worlds of art into the inner life of reflection, feeling, and direction-finding, mainly through the writings of Ananda K. Coomaraswamy, the scholar whose brilliant studies and sensibility were shaped equally by Asian and Western cultures.[1] He was the first to speak of significant art as "a reminder and a support of contemplation."

These pages explore an approach to the many worlds of art from a spiritual or religious perspective: as if certain works of art and craft, at the height of religious and aesthetic tradition but equally from the realm of useful and decorative objects, can nourish a sense of direction and a growing soul. Texts are irreplaceable; they teach. Everyone with an inquiring temperament and the blessing of at least a little time for self-education knows the teachings of Moses and Jesus, the surpassing power of the biblical psalms, the deep chagrin of "The Preacher" Ecclesiastes, the heroic concentration of the *Bhagavad Gita*, the unfathomable depth of the *Tao Te Ching* and enlightening wit of Chuang Tzu, the lucidity and basic friendliness of Confucius, the penetrating simplicity of Heraclitus, the majestic teachings and life of Socrates, the barbed truths of Epictetus, the enduring wisdom of His Excellency Marcus Aurelius. There are so many texts, so much food for mind and heart. But images are there for us also when we welcome them with a little knowledge, a little love. By and large, texts are easier to approach; they take us in hand. But this is a book about images.

A personal icon collection tends to restock over time as some become important while others fade. There are wonders to be discovered in virtually all times and places. We humans, especially the artisans and makers, have been industrious for millennia. May we remain so for millennia more; we have barely begun. It would be good to illustrate at once the diversity of origins and meanings from which, each of us for our own reasons, can draw. I remember, for example, a color postcard of an Etruscan wall painting— sixth century BCE, central Italy before the Roman conquest—showing the

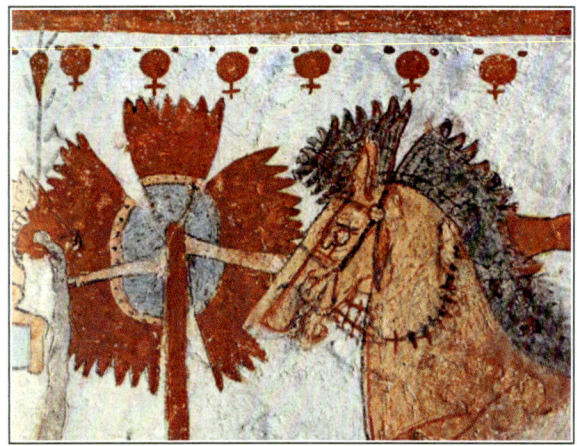

hero Troilus astride a horse with a spiky mane: the vision of a horse and its energy.

That image meant the world to me for a time. It was a sign of sheer joy, of the promise and even duty of exuberance. Marking another time in my life, I remember the simplest possible stone carving of the Buddha seated in meditation—from Sri Lanka, fourth to sixth centuries of our era. No ornament, no symbolic apparatus, just a young man readying to awaken (see p. 92). That image, too, has stayed with me for a lifetime, though I associate it especially with younger years when I was searching for the bare version of everything. Images can have that kind of staying power. Then they are icons.

For all this to work out well, there needs to be a core inside us—steady, thoughtful values supporting a dynamic life on the move. That is the magnet, the attractive force that brings icons together over a lifetime. They find their place, their spiritual home. They become the signs and symbols of a life in search of its meaning: the iconography of a self.

But what is an icon? How can we use this ancient term without abusing it? If you have had occasion to visit or attend services in an Orthodox Christian church, you will recall that it is a sheltered world of painted, sometimes carved, often richly framed icons on subjects sacred to that tradition. The light of flickering candles and oil lamps typically casts a dusky half-light on traditional images of Christ, the Theotokos or Mother of God, the Apostles, John the Baptist, saints sacred to a particular locale or congregation. There are images throughout the sanctuary, often at large size on the walls and overhead; such spaces mean to be another world, separate from the everyday. Traditional Christian icons where they belong, in church, offer a fixed community of meanings. They define a tradition, people it with holy figures and incidents from scripture and religious history. The custom of the faithful is to approach and kiss or otherwise acknowledge the icons intended for individual prayer, passing from icon to icon in a miniature pilgrimage.

The collection of icons offered in these pages does not have the fixity or boundary of a specific tradition, Orthodox Christian or other. It draws from worldwide sources, and in my experience, as noted a little earlier, such a collection changes over time, some images passing into a half-forgotten archive, others still fresh and inspiring. Yet there is a fixed point, an organizing principle. It isn't outward; It is situated within each of us who has learned to care for art and knows how to gather it in as guide, inspiration, solace, companion. The organizing principle is our own developing being, hungry for proofs and for company. The companionship offered particularly by portraits from ancient times is notable: in the crowd of surviving art, you sometimes come upon a face, a look in the eyes, that proves beyond doubt that others have lived as you live, with something like your concerns. Thanks to those encounters, we are for a time less lonely, and that is good. There is a long, long continuum; we note and feel that we are part of it.

All of us are aware of occupying a little shoal of time: it is our time, there isn't much of it, we'll soon be gone. Yet the presence of art in our lives from many different, often distant times and places widens that shoal into a condominium with all peoples everywhere. We share with them our paradox: to be time-bound and mortal but to feel that we belong here all the same, that our minds and hearts—against all proof to the contrary—are permanently alive. And even if my metaphysic here is wrong, the discovered company of an ancient metalworker's jewelry (p. 51) creates the strong encouragement of community. I keep on my desk a fossil icon from some four hundred million years ago, the accurate impress of a fern in sandstone—a beautiful thing, orderly, diminutive, complete. As much as any work of art from centuries ago, it speaks to survival and shared experience. Knowing art reasonably well, one cannot be alone. There is and has been life everywhere, and art is its record. There is even an irrational shred of logic, scarcely disclosed to oneself: if *this* has survived, then I shall survive. For some people—I hear my name being called—antiques are insurance policies.

We should look at the experience of encounter. I don't know that it makes sense to set out deliberately to assemble a personal icon collection. The enterprise is spontaneous by nature. Icons of the kind I have in mind are encountered unexpectedly; they emerge from the fog of things and make themselves known. You have no initial idea that you will cherish one work of art or another—until the moment of recognition, when light flashes into some little known or vital corner of self. The encounter engages not just the mind but also feeling and body in a moment of knowing, of surprise and delight, of measuring both what one is today and one's sense of direction. The response is quite total, a memorable event. Adoption occurs: the image becomes part of oneself.

Coomaraswamy once modeled this encounter in terms of pilgrimage and successive recognitions. That passage from an essay of 1938 on Buddhist art should have its place here.

> In order to understand the nature of the Buddha image and its meaning for a Buddhist we must, to begin with, reconstruct its environment, trace its ancestry, and remodel our own personality. We must forget that we are looking at "art" in a museum, and see the image in its place in a Buddhist [sanctuary] or as part of a sculptured rock wall; and having seen it, receive it as an image of

what we are ourselves potentially. Remember that we are pilgrims come from some great distance to see God; that what we see will depend upon ourselves. We are to see, not the likeness made by hands, but its transcendental archetype; we are to take part in a communion. . . . The image is of one Awakened: and for our awakening, who are still asleep. The objective methods of "science" will not suffice; there can be no understanding without assimilation: to understand is to have been born again.[2]

In his writings Coomaraswamy waged a long-running war—decades long—against the casual appreciation of art. For him the best of art throws one into the role of pilgrim; it kindles a moment or more of awakening, of a deep though perhaps transient "revaluation of values." The encounter is more like a communion than a passing moment of appreciation. For him the great works of art pose questions; we are to understand those questions, make them our own, and respond. This is so for me also; this is in part what makes art interesting.

Though Coomaraswamy's devoted editor and biographer, I am more accepting. For example, I am content to see museum goers enjoy whatever it is they wish to enjoy, to take pleasure in brilliant color and design, to explore artists' lives and loves; all to the good. I don't necessarily perceive genre art—images of everyday life, of a window looking toward a garden that blurs with color, a boy scrupulously building a house of cards, a captive goldfish in a sunlit bowl—as secular or trivial. It all depends on the artist's attention, skill, and love, which can transform common into special, and plain things into sacred narratives that hum inside you. Somewhere, sometime in the course of casual encounters with art, an icon may emerge and claim its person: an image that startles and calls to you, that separates from its setting to inhabit your mind and heart. Many lives ago I was in the US Army Reserve attending the obligatory two-week summer camp of my battalion at a fort near Washington, D. C. Saturday off, a friend and I in uniform went to the National Gallery and walked uncertainly, nearly unseeing through the Dutch painting collection. There was such distance between routines at camp and the splendor all around. Unbridgeable? We stopped at a Rembrandt self-portrait and found ourselves drawn in: it depicted the artist in middle years, his sensitive, questioning face emerging from a dark background. Such inner life, such human presence. I was forcibly reminded of what I care for. Though a brave soldier, for a moment I wept.

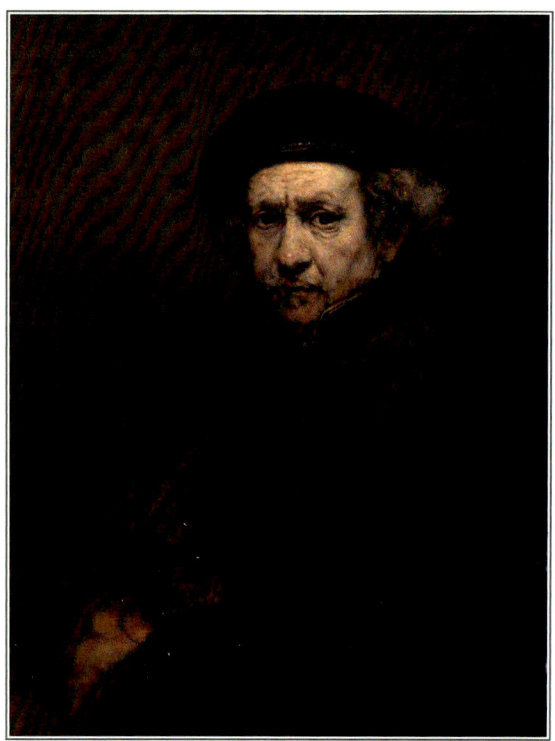

Such is the potential impact of an icon. No tears needed—my situation in passing from famine to feast was exceptional. But the shock of encounter is unmistakable.

Surely we are ready now to begin looking at a collection of icons that happens to be mine, ordered around and supporting the life that happens to be mine. The collection is meant only to model what your own collection might be. Explore the many worlds of art with innocent promiscuity: it is all potentially yours, collected in museums or remaining on site to brighten your mind. I will, however, say something about each work in these pages to do it honor and to translate from the silence of visual art into language we can share. Each work is a sign pointing toward the culture that made it. Following the direction indicated, you enter a world. One of the charms of each world is its proud boundaries, stating in effect that "this is the right way to see life and make things." Crossing those boundaries, we pass from world to world.

EYES TO SEE

The first need is to understand spiritual and sensual fundamentals. Early, sophisticated cultures with artists of genius offer visions of the essential human and of the youth of humanity. Dignity, self-possession, play and delight, knowing and serving God—it is all there in first versions. I didn't need art that reflects my day-to-day self—that was evident enough. No, I needed to know what I am, what we all are essentially. I needed to see that. I was patrolling the universe of images for clues to my identity and the identity we all share.

1. DIGNITY

Priestess known as Hera of Samos
The Greek Island of Samos, ca. 570 – 560 BCE
Height: 75.6 inches
The Louvre Museum, Paris
Source: Alamy

It is as if an upright column, pristinely abstract, perfectly vertical, has incorporated the human presence, yielding just enough of its remoteness for us to recognize ourselves. This is a figure of great dignity. Standing before her, even seeing the image on the page, you can't help but feel addressed. Long ago she was part of a row of similar figures at the temple of Hera, queen of the gods, on the island of Samos, west of the Turkish mainland. The artist or artists are unknown—that is often so until much later art. She is now thought to be not Hera herself but a priestess who held in her right hand the keys to the temple. That we still call her Hera is a custom and a tip of the hat to the archeologists who discovered her in 1875 and, understandably, thought she was a goddess.[3]

Especially when life-size or nearly so, sculpture of the human figure speaks to our bodies. It is a body, I am a body, and there may well occur an instinctive, empathetic feat as our living bodies directly attune, without asking permission, to the sculpture. We come under its dominion and in this surprisingly intimate way discover its message—not a message expressed in words but instead in attitude, posture, gesture. The message here is surely one of dignity and quiet, more potent at this early stage of Greek art than at many later stages.

I remember standing in front of this sculpture as a very young person. It is almost certainly the first work of art that claimed its place as an icon on the empty shelves inside me. It was a meaning visualized that I could not evade and would not forget. It provoked an unusual state of questioning. Instinctively, I wanted to understand what she had understood, so to speak, eons ago. I didn't understand the basis for her attitude—her dignity, uprightness, and quiet. But she inscribed new marks on my incomplete inner compass. I looked

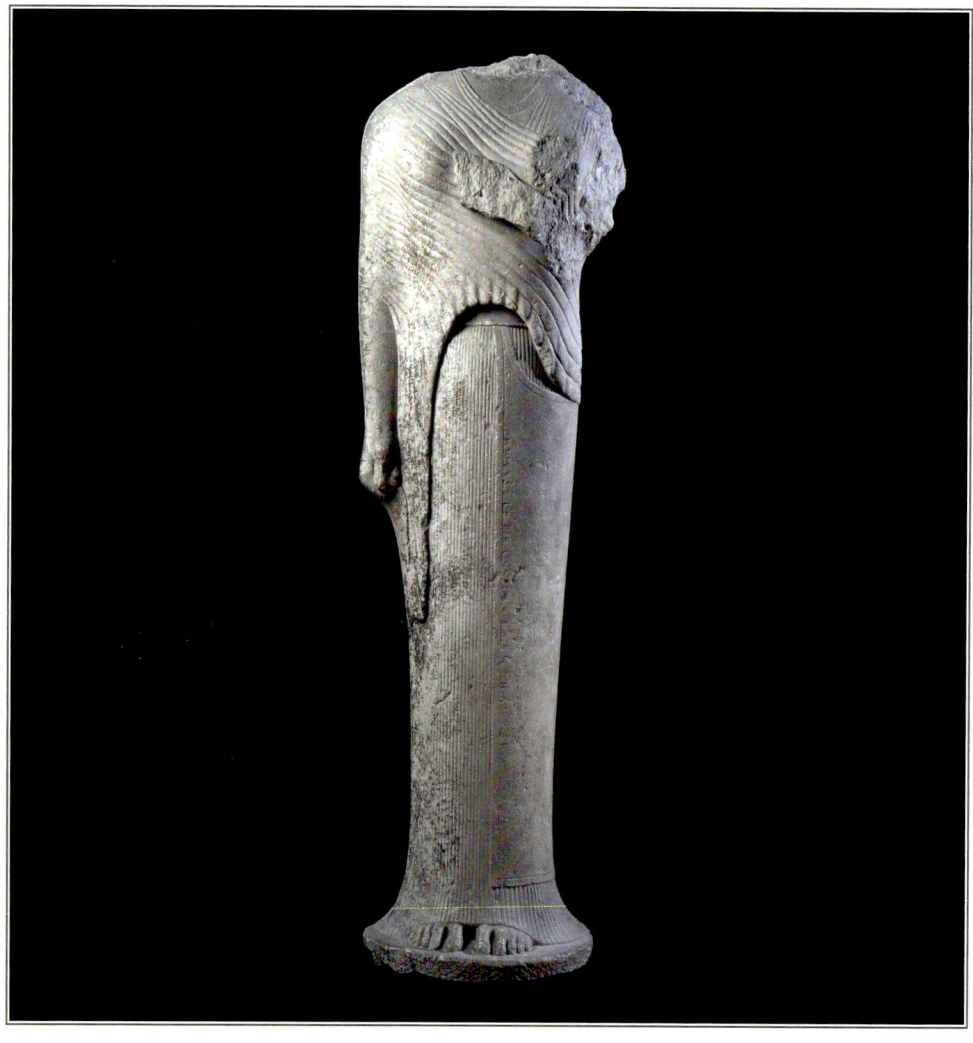

past her to the artists who made her and whose work was accepted, no doubt with gratitude, by the temple patrons. The artists surely knew what I spontaneously found myself wishing to know. It would be some years before I had glimpses, and then it was through dance.

Sculptors in virtually all cultures have been aware of the expressive power of clothing; it is never an afterthought, always part of what we are meant to notice. Here the shallow vertical channels of her gown—as austere as her still posture—contrast with the more freely conceived, flowing pattern of her shawl. The contrast suggests a balance between stillness and motion, between the deep quiet she conveys and yet some readiness for movement, for engagement.

I have long admired her feet. Altogether human, flesh of our flesh, discreetly revealed at the base of what could have been just the completion of the column. The counterpoint between impersonal verticality and the warmth of life is apparent even in this minor sculptural passage.

2. DIGNITY IN MOVEMENT

Bronze figure of the falcon god Horus making an offering
Egypt, Third Intermediate Period, 1069 – 664 BCE
Height: 37.6 inches
The Louvre Museum, Paris
Source: Alamy

Dancers will understand at once, but I suspect that we can all find in ourselves something of the dancer who understands the balanced grace of this figure. Little more than three feet high, it registers nearly as a miniature, not overwhelming despite its intense expressive power. It is easily taken to heart as a sign of dignity in movement, reaching us with authority from long ago.

Horus was the Egyptian sky god; his left eye was the moon, his right eye the sun. He was a key adviser to pharaohs, who themselves were considered gods. Yet grandeur and hierarchy are dissolved here by a figure in which we recognize ourselves. Why does dignity in movement matter? That is nearly to ask why we ourselves matter, because most of the time we are in movement. Many inherited religions and teachings, and some educational forms, have deliberately patterned movements—for example, yoga asanas, tai chi, the Gurdjieff Movements, Zen Buddhism with its rituals of sitting and walking, Christian postures of prayer, communal gestures of prayer in Islam. Such influences don't touch every life, but some people don't need them to discover how to move with dignity at just the right pace with economy and the beauty of "rightness." That is one of their gifts.

Ancient works of art often survive in different forms than they start out. Art historians tell us that this figure was originally covered with gold paste and gold leaf to distinguish the body of a god from ordinary bodies. Further, the falcon mask now somewhat separate from the face would have been fully integrated—it would not appear to be a mask. The figure was part of an ensemble in which Horus makes a water offering to a pharaoh; he would have been subordinate to that more central figure.

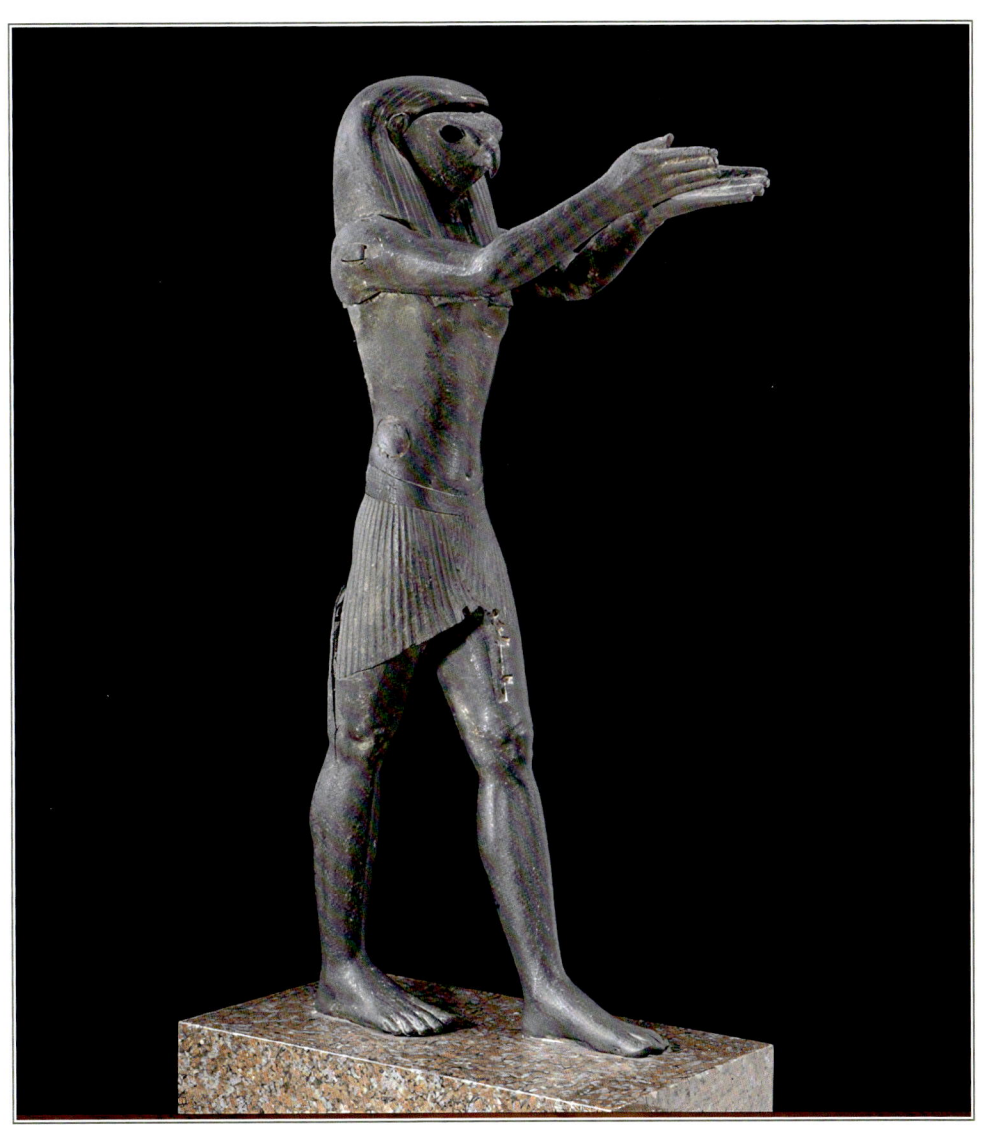

But now we perceive this work differently. He stands alone, an icon of dignity in movement, and because the falcon mask has partially separated from the whole, we can't help but perceive it as a facial covering worn by a human being like ourselves. An implicit question asks to be heard: to whom, to what would we care to make such an offering—fully giving what we can? This eloquent figure invades the space of that question and makes it briefly real.

I have often been impressed by the way Meister Eckhart, the medieval Christian teacher of genius, ends certain sermons with a short prayer. Having spoken of some good thing, some excellent way to be, typically in intricate ways as his mind was intricate, he would sometimes conclude: May the Lord help us to be like this, amen. Something of that impulse of prayer and hope moves toward this majestic yet approachable image. One of the challenges facing the icon collector is to remember. The shock of encounter with a great work of art marks you. You know that what you perceive in the long moment of encounter is important. Then inevitably the impact fades: you are plain again, unmoved again. This raises a question without an easy answer, but it can be a slow question. It doesn't have to be answered right now.

3. RELATION WITH THE DIVINE

Principal image:
Pharaoh Khafre and the falcon god Horus
Egypt, Old Kingdom, Fourth Dynasty, ca. 2570 BCE
Life size, carved in a hard stone (anorthosite gneiss)
The Museum of Egyptian Antiquities, Cairo
Source: agefotostock

Image immediately below:
Source: Terence Waeland / Alamy Stock Photo

On the following page:
Joan Reinach (1431 – 1486)
Saint John the Evangelist
Source: Peter Horree / Alamy Stock Photo

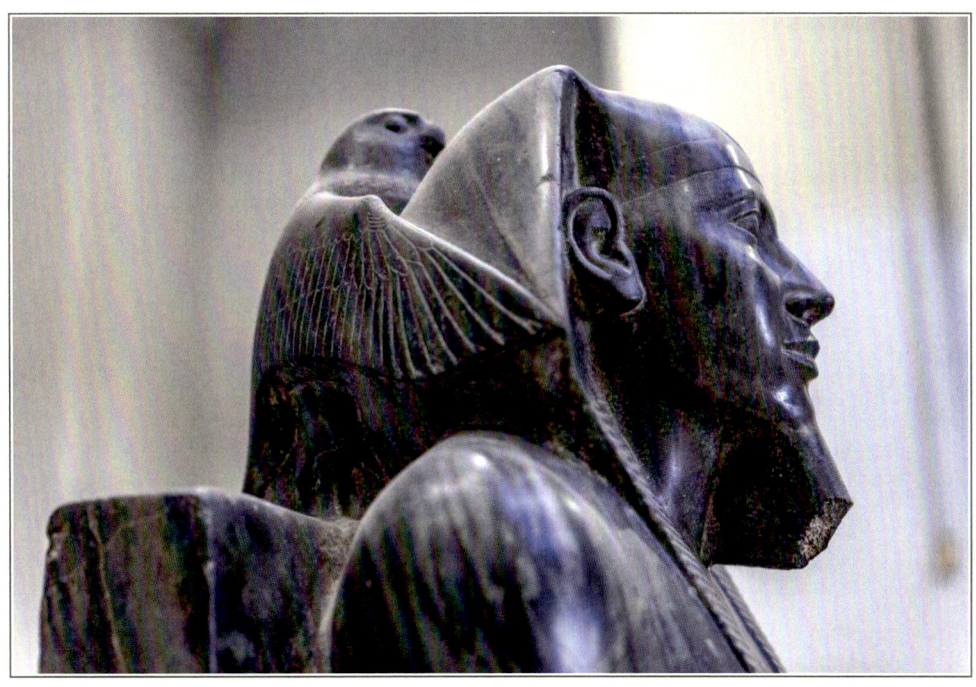

I hesitate to write about this sculpture. Initially we can take refuge in historical knowledge; ultimately we should explore matters closer to home. Khafre was one of the greatest builders of any era. His burial place is the second-largest pyramid at Giza, the "city of the dead" just west of Cairo. The Great Sphinx is likely to have been part of the ensemble, as were other structures including the Valley Temple at some distance from the pyramid, where this sculpture was discovered. It is a *ka* figure, a dwelling place after death for the pharaoh's life force. The immensely hard stone in which it was carved assured its survival nearly intact. Like most images of high-born individuals in that era, Khafre is represented in the prime of life with a strong, gracefully proportioned body. Viewed from the front, the falcon god Horus remains unseen as if Khafre the god-king were wholly independent. Viewed from the side, the larger message of the sculpture is revealed.

Nearly everyone is aware at times of a higher, an other—perhaps I should write Higher and Other, although I don't favor weighty capitalization. It may be understood in terms of a traditional religion and the vertical relations which that religion holds to be true, or it may be a felt moral code, a set of boundaries and encouragements that shape a life. Socrates spoke of his *daimonion*, a "divine something" that stopped him from missteps. Some

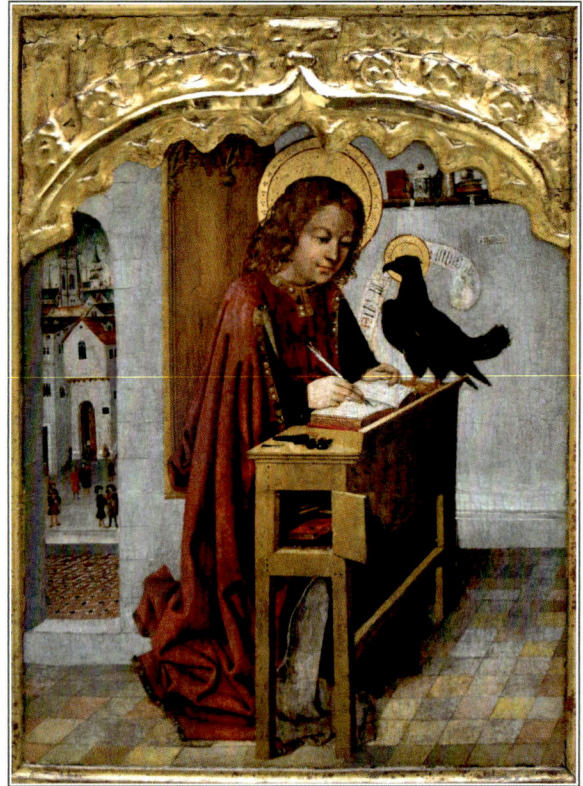

of the truly great human beings of our time who have professed atheism—for example, Albert Camus—were nonetheless and obviously guided in some way from within. Call it intelligence or Intelligence, conscience or Conscience, that hardly matters.

The *ka* sculpture of Khafre conceives relation with the higher and other as movingly as any work of art of any era. It offers encouragement to continue listening for what the Bible calls the "still, small voice." It gives visible form to an invisible relation. And it is reassuring: behind us, within us, there is something more, close yet separate, close because it chooses to be close. The falcon god's wings clasp Khafre's head in a way that suggests what it would be to be helped to think and to know.

This approach to representing relation with the divine persisted in Western culture. Portraits of the evangelists—Matthew, Mark, Luke, and John—often depict them as obedient scribes receiving what is to be written from a source higher and other, for example in this mid-15th-century Spanish image of John listening to his supernatural symbol, the eagle.

There is an odd, quite beautiful connection between a surviving late prayer to Horus and biblical Psalm 20, both apparently rooted in a still more ancient Canaanite liturgy. "May Hor grant to us as is in our heart . . . . May the master not diminish any request of our heart"—so the prayer to Horus. "May he grant you your heart's desire and fulfill all your plans!"—so Psalm 20. The falcon god is not so far from us. He is in our religious genealogy.[4]

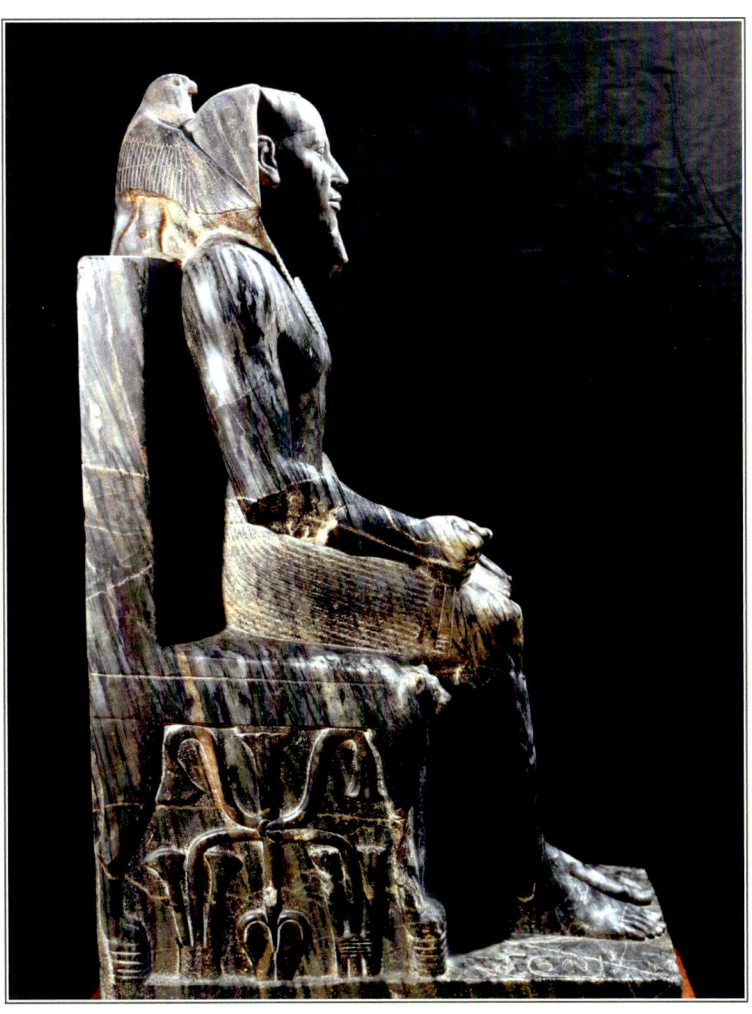

4. THE SWEETNESS OF LIFE: EGYPT

Tomb-Chapel of the Royal Grain Accountant Nebamun
New Kingdom, Eighteenth Dynasty, ca. 1350 BCE
The British Museum, London
Source: Wikimedia Commons / public domain

Looking back to the three preceding icons from the brilliant youth of the human race, you might easily conclude that it was an era of unbroken solemnity. No, there are works so bright with life, joyful and varied, that you nearly hear the music, smell the delicious food, admire the dancers—and wish to join the party. The party is eternal, ever accessible: that is one of the

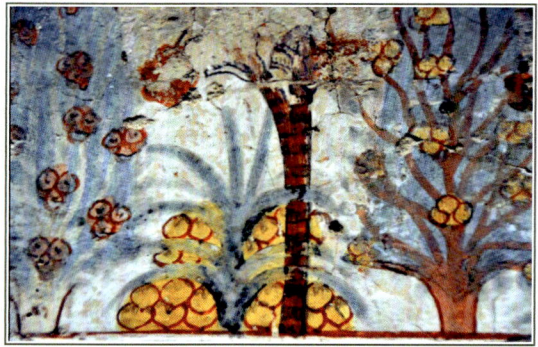

messages of the wall paintings from a chapel or meeting place where the family and friends of the late royal grain accountant, Nebamun, would gather periodically for ceremonies and remembrance. These frescoes, somewhat clumsily broken away in the nineteenth century from their original site, are one of the great treasures of the British Museum. It is strictly impossible to be despondent or indifferent in their presence. The sweetness of life is their theme.

For our purposes I've chosen two of the frescoes: Nebamun—of course represented as a young man—hunts in a jubilant marsh crowded with birds and reeds, a hungry cat and more still, accompanied by his beautiful wife just behind him and their daughter below expressing affection in a memorably tender gesture. This is a perfect world of natural abundance, of beautiful people and love. There must have been irritating insects in the air and watchful crocodiles in the water—it was a marsh, after all—but they have no place in this vision of total well-being.

The other fragment is a banquet scene with musicians, dancers, and a stack of wine jars graced with flowers, one of several banqueting fragments.

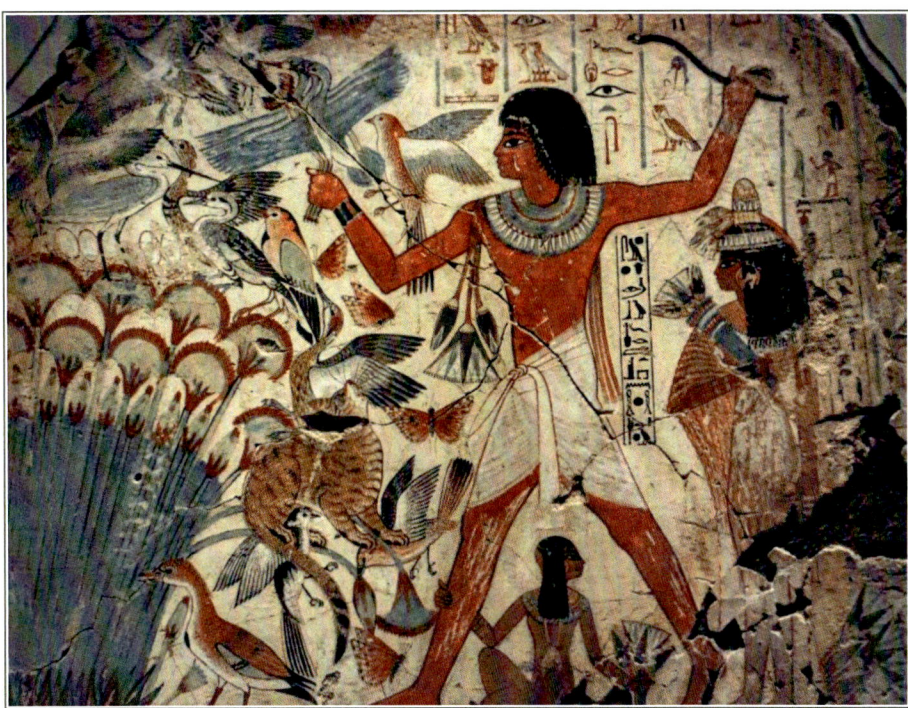

The eyes of the artist or team of artists who created this ensemble were eyes of love and appreciation: in another fragment a flock of geese is closely patterned as if the geese were playing cards laid one upon the other; Nebamun's garden pool surrounded by flowering trees is nearly a flat map of paradise—and so on. This is a masterwork. On the facing page, fruits from the garden are available.

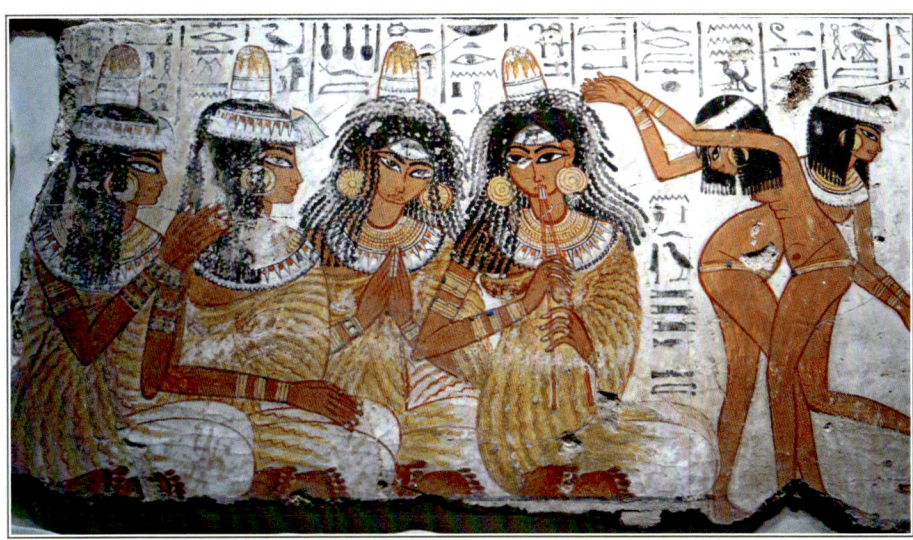

5. THE SWEETNESS OF LIFE: ETRURIA

Tomb of Hunting and Fishing, 530 – 500 BCE
Tarquinia (Italy)
Source: Wikimedia Commons / public domain

Tomb of the Leopards, 480 – 450 BCE
Tarquinia
Source: Wikimedia Commons / public domain

From another region and era we are again looking at tomb art, but the message is one and the same: the sweetness of life. Etruscan culture in central Italy, ultimately crushed by Roman conquest and assimilation, strikes virtually everyone who encounters it as joyous and life-affirming. D. H. Lawrence visited the Tomb of Hunting and Fishing in 1927: "In the dimness we perceive flights of birds flying through the haze, with the draught of life still in their wings. . . . It is all small and gay and quick with life, spontaneous as only young life can be. . . . Profound belief in life, acceptance of life, seems characteristic of the Etruscans. It is still vivid in the painted tombs."[5]

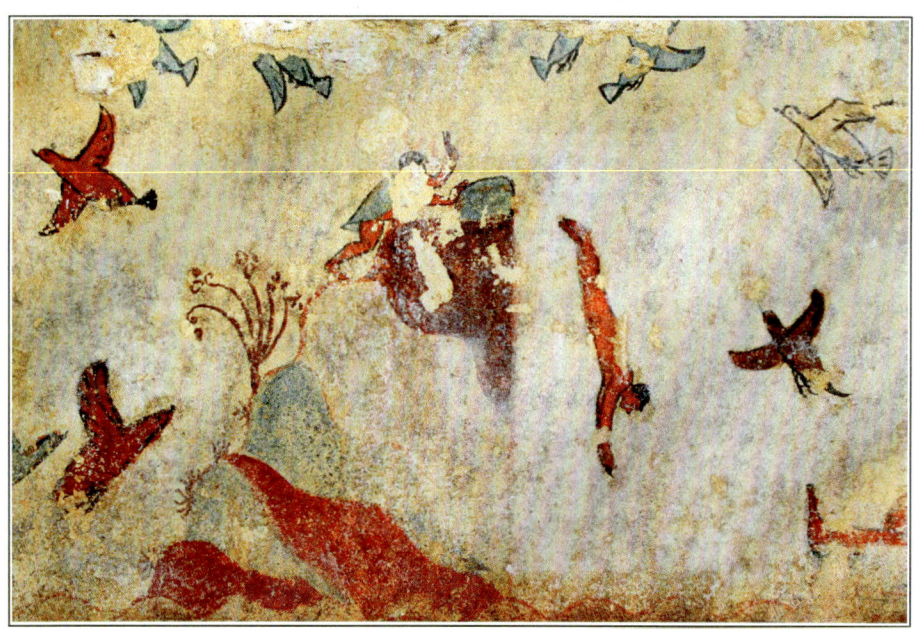

Visiting the nearby Tomb of the Leopards, he found exceptional words to express what his eyes told him—and didn't neglect to include an unfamiliar Etruscan-Latin term for flute player. "The dancers. . . move with a strange, powerful alertness onwards. . . . The *subulo* plays the double flute the Etruscans loved so much, touching the stops with big, exaggerated hands, the man behind

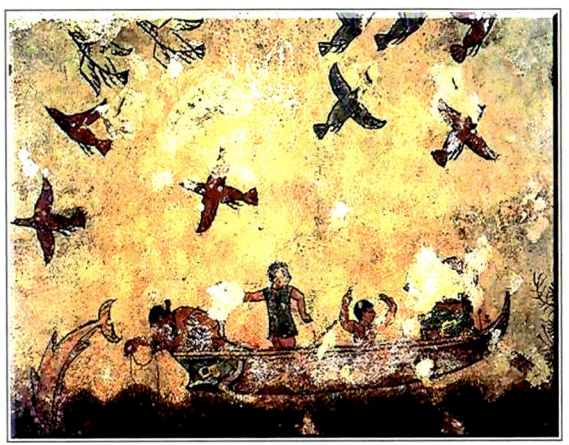

him touches the seven-stringed lyre, the man in front turns round and signals with his left hand, holding a big wine-bowl in his right. And so they move on, . . . with their limbs full of life. . . . This sense of vigorous, strong-bodied liveliness is characteristic of the Etruscans, and is somehow beyond art. You cannot think of art, but only of life itself. . . . There is a mystery and a portentousness in the simple scenes which go deeper than commonplace life. It seems all so gay and light. Yet there is a certain weight, or depth of significance that goes beyond aesthetic beauty."

As at the Tomb-Chapel of Nebamun a full millennium earlier, the scent of eternity is near but not through stillness: rather through enjoyment and celebration as if both can and must go on forever. Our search for icons of the essential human doesn't end here—there is much more. But these images deserve a place close to the center.

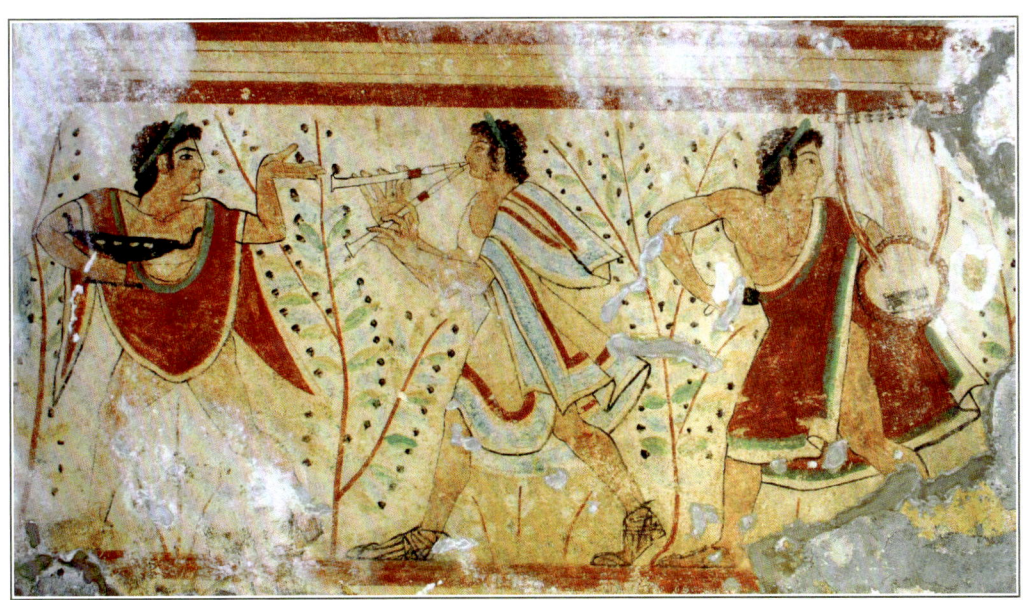

6. DANCE: APULIA

Tomb of the Dancers
Wall painting transferred from the region of Bari, southern Italy
Ca. 500 – 450 BCE
National Archeological Museum, Naples
Source: Wikipedia / public domain

It is a funerary dance of some thirty women and three men circling the burial chamber of a prominent warrior of his time and tribe. We are looking at the art of the Peucetians, a community little known to history, well to the south of Etruria but influenced by Etruscan art and customs. Certain images you never quite forget, and to rediscover them is to be startled back to that first encounter. This is one such in my icon collection.

I have seen certain dances, and even participated years ago, that convey the same sense of inevitability as this women's circle. The women's forward motion and uprightness, their concentration, their bonding gesture from one to the other: it all speaks to what D. H. Lawrence describes as "a certain weight, or depth of significance that goes beyond aesthetic beauty." The early arts we have been exploring reveal norms; they give visual presence to the essential human. Cultures move on, but there are images of dance in virtually

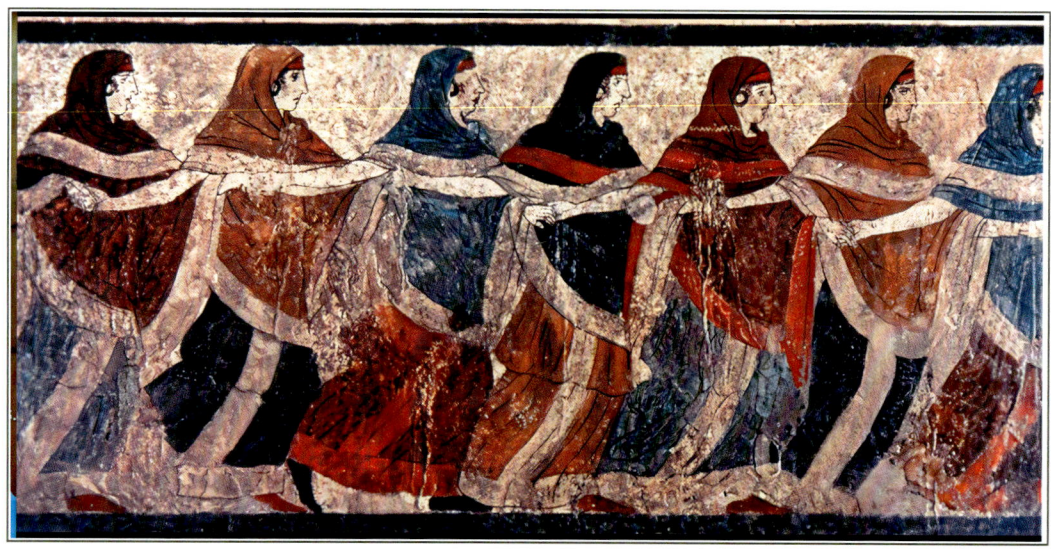

every time and place. One era forgets another or never knew of it, but still there is dance.

The posture and movement of the dancers are uniform—these are practiced dancers—but the deliberate variations of color in gown, shawl, and veil eliminate all trace of dull repetition. There is always something more to see. The dancers' profiles make clear that they are individuals, for the most part women of middle years. This brings to mind a remark by G. I. Gurdjieff, a master choreographer, to a dancer who had expressed to him her fear that age was catching up with her—perhaps soon she could no longer dance. "'Where I come from," he replied, "in the monasteries, there are a great many dancers at all stages of development, all ages. But only older dancers are permitted to dance in the temples. Only those who have gone through years of apprenticeship. Only older women dance the rituals. And they are all fire, all perfection, their movements are beautiful, performed with precision. All these women are old, over sixty. They dance like goddesses."[6] He was referring to regions of Central Asia.

I cannot adequately convey the impression of inevitability, of something like an objective, undeniable flow of time and life that I have noticed in certain dances. It elicits complex emotions of acknowledgment, surrender, and calm, and a still more complex emotion of joy and sorrow together, as if you finally see and feel life for what it is. Dance can set all of that in motion and show a way to live fully rather than fret and resist or go into a picturesque funk. This is the secret of the Peucetian tomb, a time capsule preserving a courageous attitude.

These are difficult things to speak of. That is why we collect icons.

7. PERFECTION OF FORM: THE GREEK ISLANDS

Principal image:
Storage vessel from the Cycladic islands in the Aegean Sea
Marble, ca. 2700 – 2500 BCE
Height and width app. 8 inches
Source: Christie's Images / Bridgman Images

Image below:
Cycladic head
Marble, 2600 – 2500 BCE
Source: Harvard Art Museums / Arthur M. Sackler Museum, Cambridge
Bequest from the Estate of Alice M. Kaplan

I asked a lifelong working potter to look at this vessel before I could write a word about it. What is its beauty? Continuing, I asked a painter with an incomparable understanding of the Golden Section—an ancient key to harmonious design—to indicate whether the vessel reflects that canon. No, the Golden Section isn't present here; there is beauty but not that beauty. The potter, who has surely thrown ten thousand vessels on the wheel, saw "such incredible ripeness balanced on a small but substantial base. The top part tapers in, containing, preserving the contents of that wonderful roundness. The vessel is almost precisely divided into

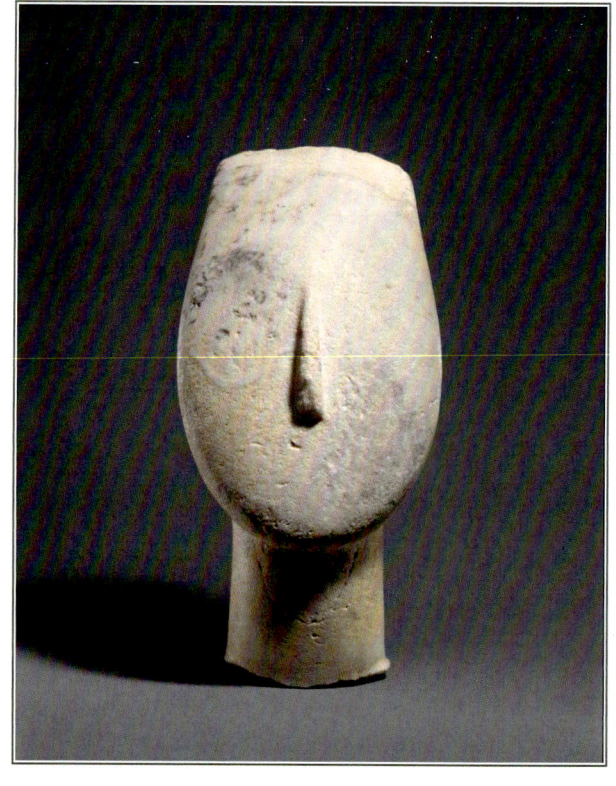

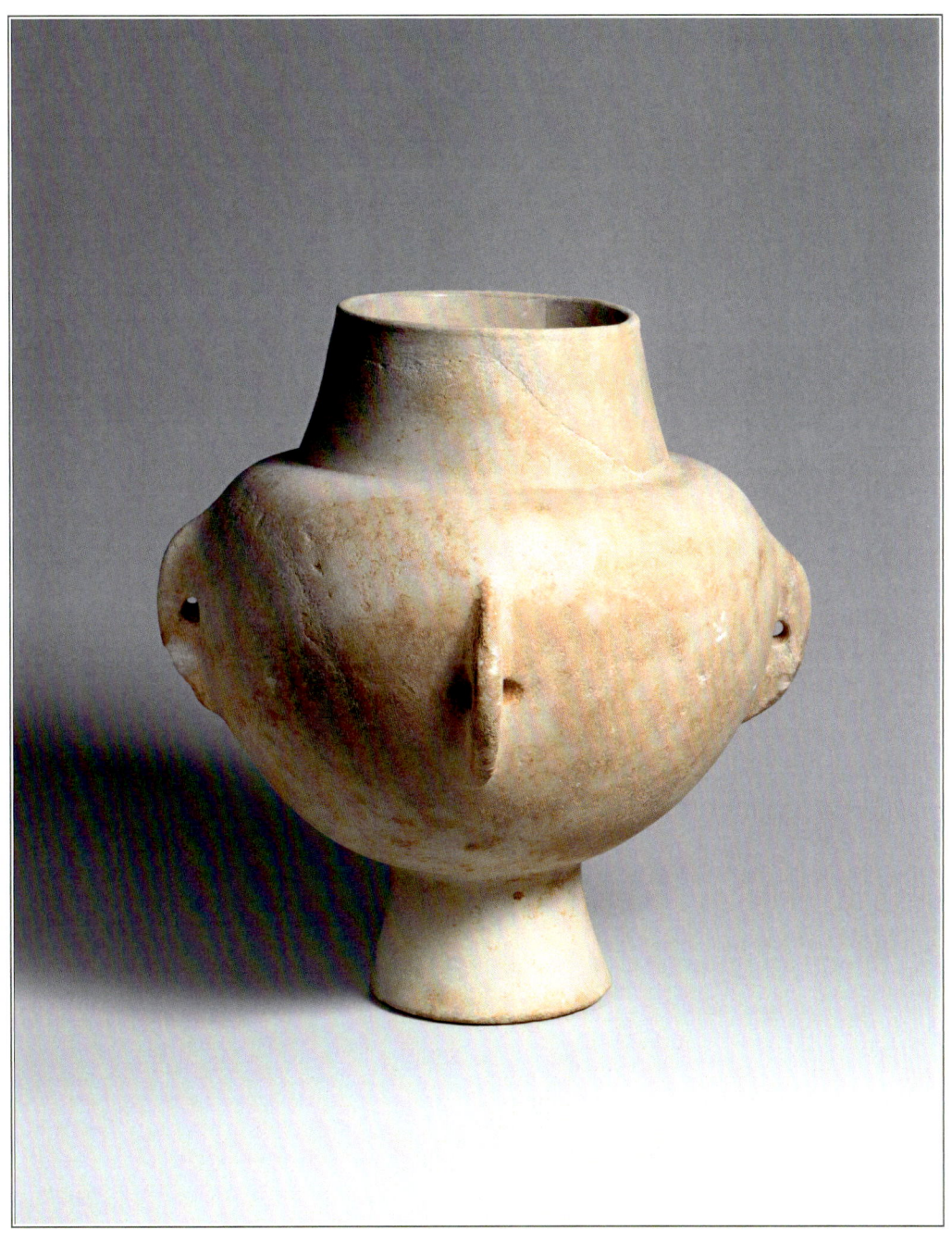

three integrated parts belonging to each other." Her word ripeness leads us toward the perfection of form so evident here.

We need to be all attention, all perception, to appreciate the finesse of this vessel, a common type in its place and era but uncommonly beautiful. Cycladic culture of the third millennium is likely better known for its elegant marble heads and figures, which influenced major sculptors of our time, Brancusi and Noguchi among them. But I have never forgotten the still, sculptural beauty of these marble vessels, thought to have stored olive oil or wine with four pierced lugs serving to suspend the vessel or secure a lid. Who were these persevering artists, carving and polishing the white marble of their islands with hard obsidian chisels and sand or pumice? There is no literature, no sound through which we can hear or know them apart from these vessels and sculpture such as the fragment at the top of this page.

Because vessels stand with a bottom, middle, and top, the convenient custom is to speak of them in terms of the human structure: here we have a conical foot, a middle torso of sorts, a collar or neck. This is more than custom: as noted a few pages earlier, sculpture and sculptural works such as this engage the body. We read our own physicality in the object, sense its parts and connections, weight and lift through ourselves.

The impeccable elegance of this ancient vessel leads toward awed respect for the minds and hands that could conceive and make such a thing. It is an ancient provocation. Perhaps it's a bad habit of mine to experimentally translate iconic works of art into questions. All the same, there is a question here. It fills the space between us and the object. For me—but you will have your own question—it has to do with becoming silent enough to see this vessel without a stray thought.

8. WE TWO: EGYPT

Pharaoh Menkaure and his queen (possibly Khamerernebty II)
Old Kingdom, Fourth Dynasty, 2490 – 2472 BCE
Nearly life-size, carved in a hard sandstone (greywacke)
The Museum of Fine Arts, Boston
Source: The Museum of Fine Arts, Boston

When Herodotus visited Egypt fully two thousand years after the reign of Pharaoh Menkaure, there were still priests with tales of their great ancestor. The son of Khafre, and like his father a pyramid builder at Giza, Menkaure was remembered as generally kind to his fellow citizens. We can't possibly know Menkaure or his wife, but this shard of memory is reassuring.

A theme of importance to this icon collection is "we two": the loving, determined couple who make their way in life together. By today's standards, the notion of "we two" needn't be restricted to heterosexual couples. The point isn't gender; the point is the stubborn vitality of partners who do many things together, who sit down day after day, year after year if they are

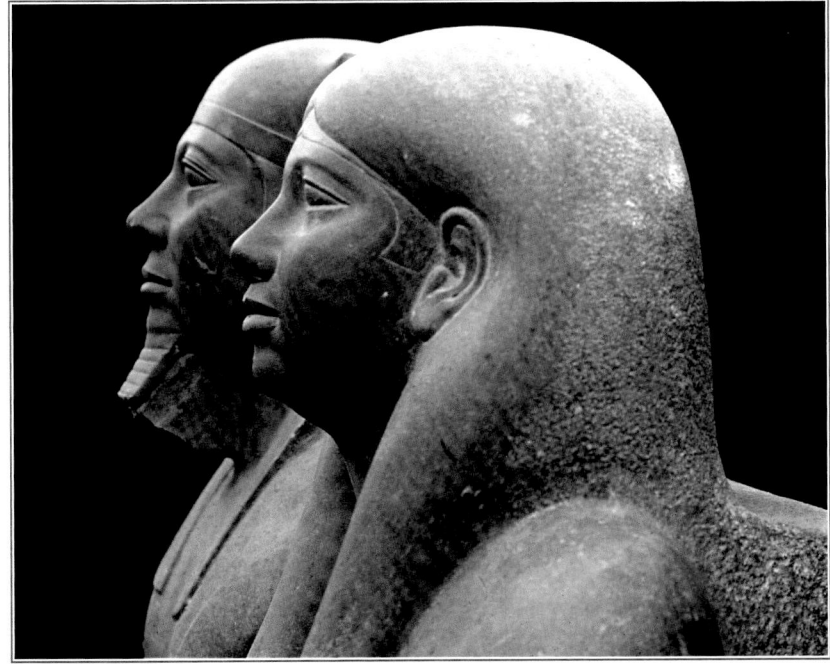

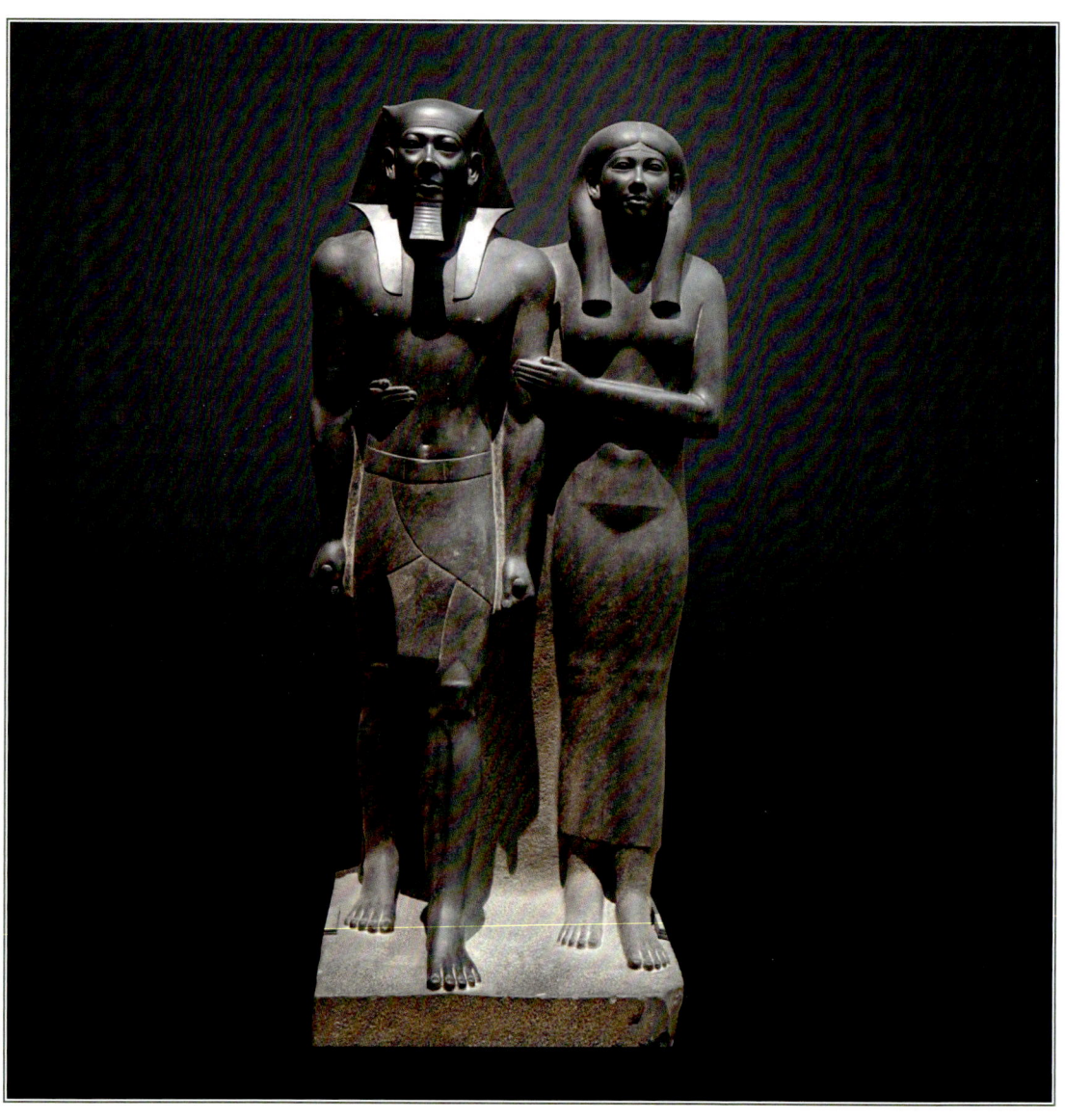

fortunate, to enjoy their food, to discuss events, to plan, to hear one another's voice, the most familiar sound in their world. While the body ages, mind and heart typically age much more slowly or not at all—consequently couples old by calendrical reckoning scarcely know that they are old. Laughter has no age. Eternal youth willingly lives in the body that no longer struts its stuff so well.

All of which comes to mind in the encounter with this justly famed sculpture of the pharaoh Menkaure and his queen. They step forward together and confidently, united by her tender gestures, one hand embracing his middle, the other reassuringly placed on his arm. They are equally vertical in posture, their facial expressions equally even, quietly glowing. There are suggestions of their sexual bond—his strength, her clinging gown and accented pubic triangle. They are youth itself, the prime of life, no matter to what age they lived. Whatever the Egyptian sculptor and his royal patrons had in mind, what flows through to us is an unforgettable vision of "we two." We are not kings and queens, most of us are plain, but at some level this sculpture is our portrait, too, if we willingly embrace it as such—if not always, then sometimes. In photos we don't look like Menkaure and his queen, but photos are deceptive.

8. WE TWO: ETRURIA

Sarcophagus of Larth Tetnies and Thanchvil Tarnai
350 – 300 BCE, travertine limestone
The Museum of Fine Arts, Boston
Source: Flickr / Sebastià Giralt

Ancient Egyptian and Etruscan cultures are proving to be touchstones in this first set of icons. Egypt denied time and made its home in eternity; on the walls of tombs even their festive banquets and scenes of the good life are forever. Etruria embraced the sweetness of life and made its home there until the moment came to part, although they too had their eyes on eternity. Both cultures bore witness to the essential human. What we have from them is an inexhaustible treasury of painting, sculpture, craftwork, and (predominantly for Egypt) architecture. There is no need to be a scholar of these things—that is a calling to which only a few in each generation will be dedicated. But how good to know of them, to know where to look for refreshment of our concept of the human and our feeling for ourselves. Pharaonic Egypt and ancient Etruria are distant—and not distant at all when you encounter their art with the sense of kinship that naturally appears.

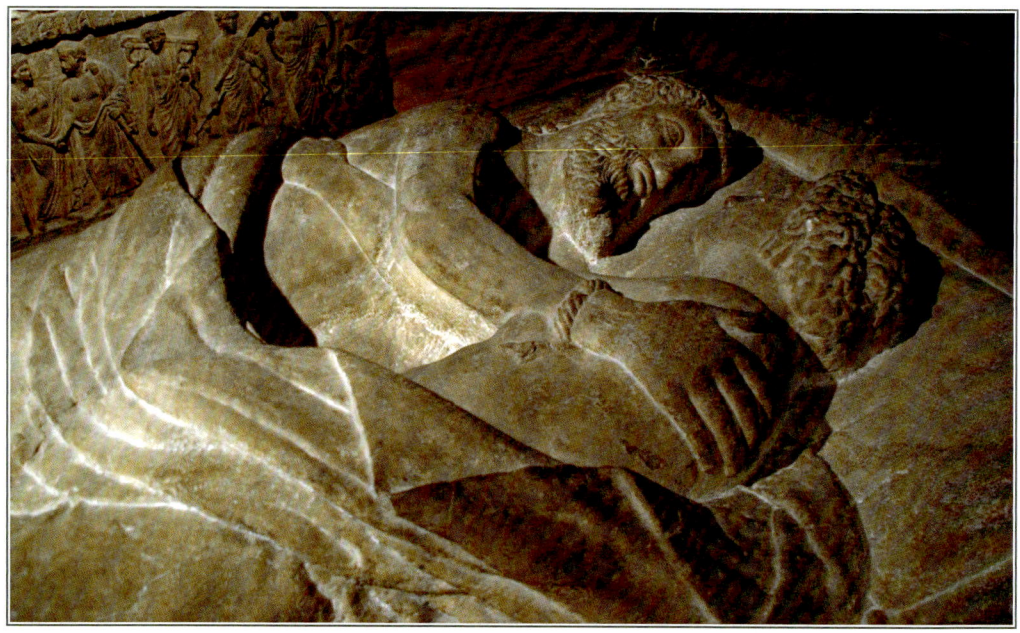

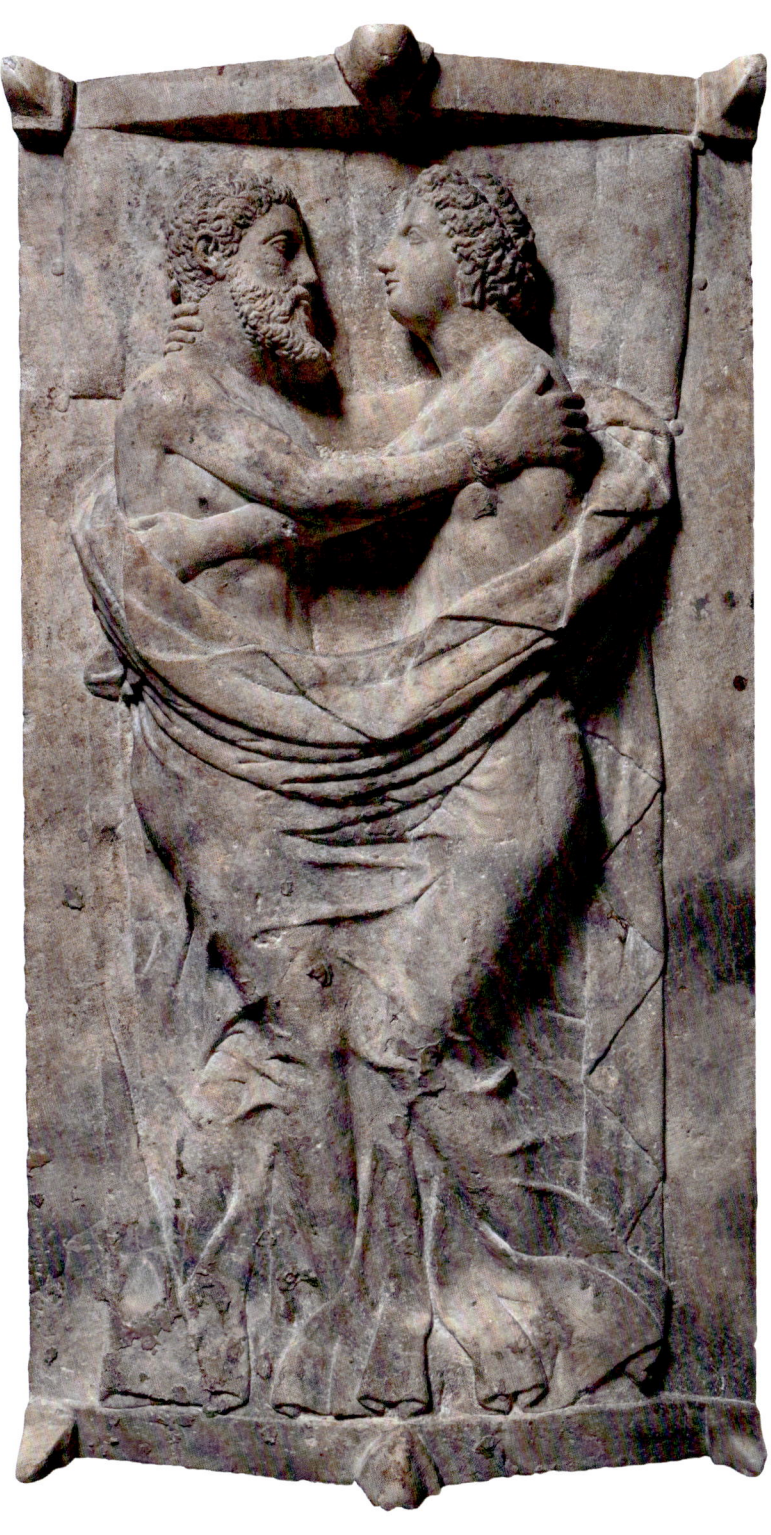

High-born Etruscans never figured out that women are, oh definitely, to be subordinated to men. Their art reflects an easy sense of equality, of shared responsibility for family, religion, pleasurable gatherings, and surely much more. Adjacent cultures—Rome, Greece, the strong Greek presence on the Italian peninsula—apparently didn't approve.

We don't have lengthy Etruscan texts or inscriptions; we can scarcely decipher their language. Bad luck, a twenty-volume study of Etruscan culture by the first-century Roman Emperor Claudius, a scholar at heart, is long since lost. However, we have their art.

And so this exquisitely carved and felt tribute to a married couple. The museum that has the privilege of owning and exhibiting it writes of their "eternal embrace." Who would disagree? This relief sculpture of the later fourth century BCE speaks the common visual language of much of the Mediterranean Basin at the time: fundamentally Greek, though absorbed here with local sensibility and purpose. We are encountering a poetry of contact—of arms, of eyes, of identities. This is, as well, our first encounter with a trait that flickers into and out of art at different periods and in different artists' hands: psychological presence. With their individual inner lives gently apparent, this couple journeys together. Imagine looking at this double portrait for the first time, I suppose at a funeral or subsequent rite ever so long ago, and remembering Larth Tetnies and Thanchvil Tarnai.

10. COMPANIONS ON THE WAY: EARLY EGYPT

Bust of Prince Ankhhaf
Old Kingdom, Fourth Dynasty, 2520 – 2494 BCE
Height: nearly 20 inches
The Museum of Fine Arts, Boston
Source: Wikipedia / Keith Schengili-Roberts

I have long thought of Ankhhaf as a friend with whom there would have been much to discuss and similarities of perspective. The abyss of time between us notwithstanding, something about this face says "friend." But reading summaries of recent archeological literature, I have developed doubts. Consider his status: half-brother to the pharaoh Khufu, who was the builder of the Great Pyramid at Giza; vizier or chief executive responsible for that construction and possibly the Sphinx; uncle to Pharaoh Khafre, whom we have already encountered; honored at his passing with a large ceremo-

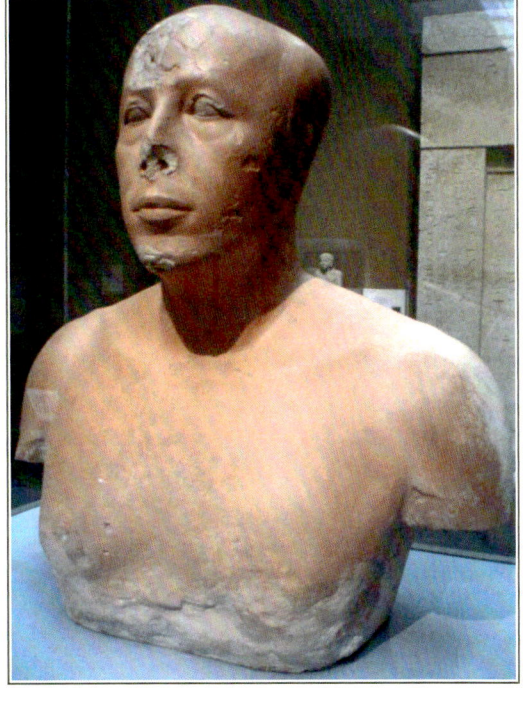

nial tomb where this exceptional portrait sculpture was discovered. Prince Ankhhaf moves a little past the solemnities of history in the newly discovered papyrus journal of a shipping executive, Merer, who mentions "the noble Ankhhaf" as present at deliveries of sheathing stone (long since removed) for what was once the smooth outer skin of the Great Pyramid.[7]

Yet I would have wanted to speak with him. To the collector of icons, many kinds of ties are possible: awe before great works of art, delight in works of charm and insouciance, sorrow and pity, the sudden return

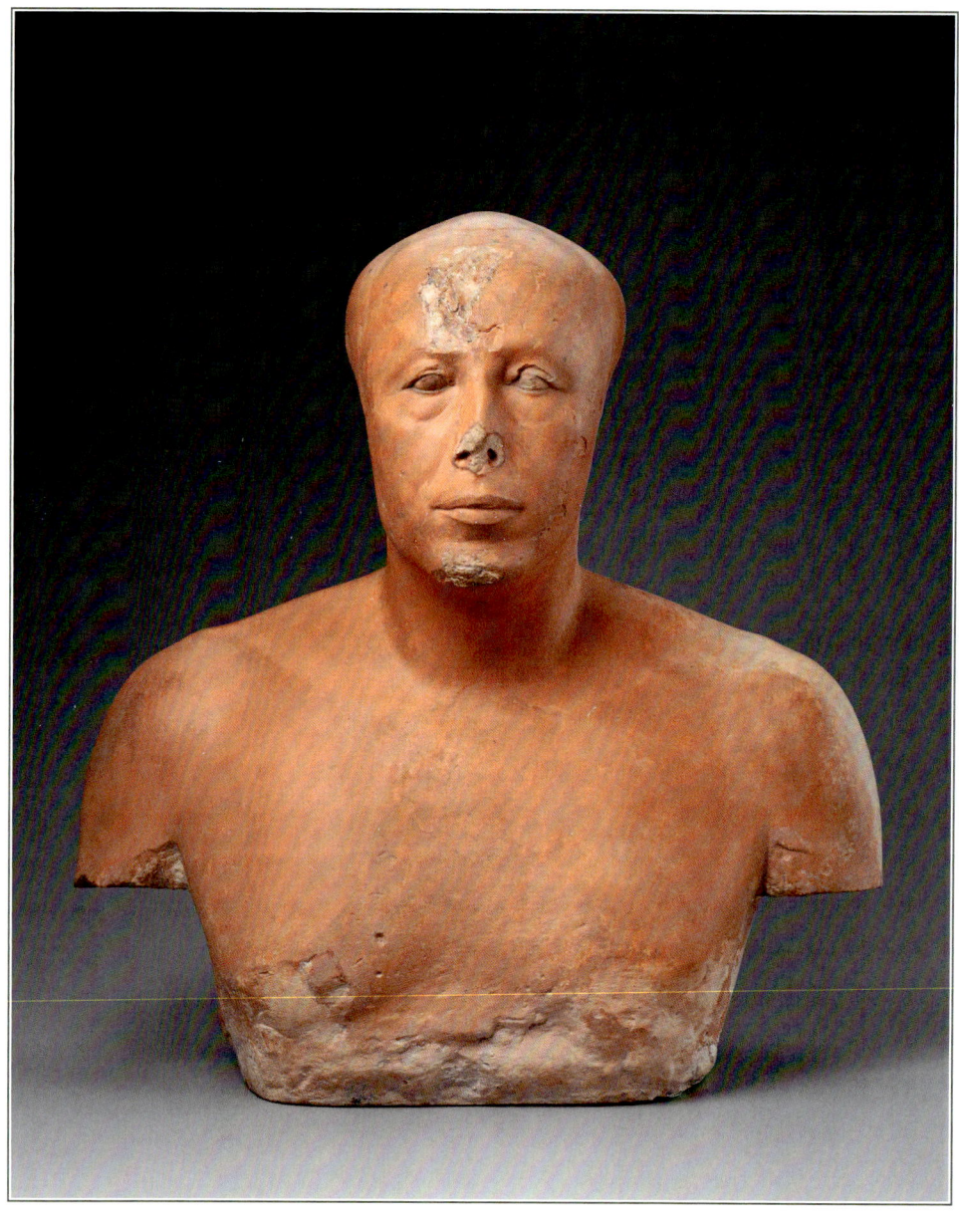

to oneself and to intimate questions of meaning and identity—and on occasion an inexplicable sense of kinship. So it is here. I am glad that the prince's right eye is for the most part undamaged; he still can see.

As scholars have long indicated, the artistry here is superb and highly unusual. This is not an idealized image but a true portrait of a thoughtful, resolute man of middle years. A limestone core is covered with a thin layer of plaster modeled and painted by a master sculptor to capture the actuality of the man. This impressive fragment would have been joined to a complete representation of Ankhhaf seated for eternity in the shelter of his tomb.

I mentioned in the introduction to this book that art history is, among other things, an argument with time. It marshals against the unyielding passage of time and the glaring fact of impermanence our capacities for memory and kinship. And when we, in turn, are no longer here, others may remember what we cared to remember. For example, they will remember Prince Ankhhaf and converse with him across time.

11. COMPANIONS ON THE WAY: ROMAN EGYPT

Portrait of a Young Woman
Egypt, ca. 130 CE
Encaustic (pigmented wax) on cedar panel, with added gilding
Height: 16.5 inches
The Louvre Museum, Paris
Source: Wikipedia / public domain

The notion of mummies and of mummy portraits positioned over the face of the deceased seems remote from the stunning beauty of this young woman. Such is nonetheless the source of this remarkable portrait, discovered in a burial in Antinoöpolis, a city founded by the emperor Hadrian. Portrait panels of this kind, none more beautiful and moving than this, are nearly all that remains of the Greek panel painting tradition, vastly admired in its era but too fragile to survive elsewhere than in Egypt, where it was put to a new use: memorializing the departed. The use of encaustic—a palette of warm tinted wax—for many of the hundreds of surviving panels ensured their freshness, as if painted yesterday. Many depict younger men and women; scholars tell us that this reflects the short life expectancy of the era rather than the ancient custom of representing the deceased as forever young and strong.

Those are our facts. What more, then? It does feel as if the young woman's family and the unknown artist refused to let go, or refused without a final exquisite gesture toward her. This is a record of specific beauty—oval face and large eyes, long nose, mouth both prim and sensual, meticulous grooming, elegant jewelry and clothing, the lively look in her eyes that conveys demure consciousness. She doesn't stare us down; she is still looking into the world where she once lived. It comes to mind that she is an ancient Mona Lisa.

I cannot claim her as a companion. I wouldn't dare. She belongs with her own people, whoever they were. But her portrait evokes a society—cosmopolitan, Romanized Egypt—that must have had merit. Where one could walk the streets and from time to time respectfully notice a person of this kind.

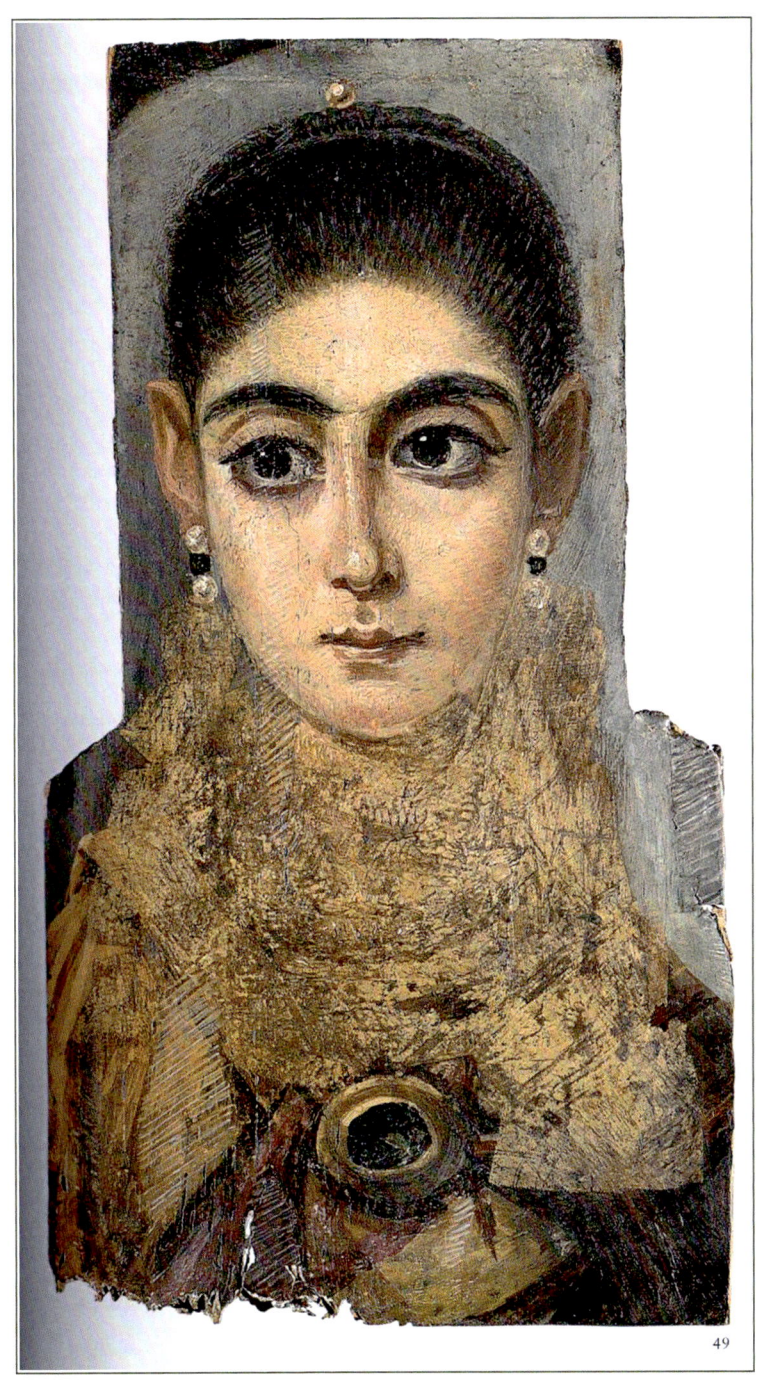

49

PARENTHESIS: INFLUENCES

In the introduction to this book I noted in passing that I came early under the influence of people who could "read" works of art as if they were texts. A friend has asked who they were and how I learned from them.

In my late teenage years I had been in effect adopted by, and adopted, a French family whom I visited typically in summer. Like many thoughtful French families, after World War II they had become passionately interested in their own long culture, especially the art and architecture of the medieval period. For them, and increasingly for me, the map of France wasn't a thing that lies flat on the table; it was a minutely detailed relief map of churches, monasteries, chapels, castles, and associated sculpture, painting, and other treasures—encompassing hundreds of monuments in varied landscapes and regions. This cultural interest was nourished by the remarkable publishing program of a Benedictine monastery, La Pierre-Qui-Vire, whose beautifully produced, historically well-founded books under the Zodiaque imprint offered regional studies of Romanesque art and architecture of the eleventh and twelfth centuries. With that guidance, the entire country could be understood as an open-air museum—not a confined museum with fixed captions but a realm of visions, lessons, mysteries, memories. There was so much to explore.

As a family, we did so rather silently. No one stepped forward as the tour guide; typically on our way elsewhere, we knew what detours to make from the national highway to visit, for example, a wayside chapel, perhaps with twelfth-century frescoes or notable sculpture. There was respect and love in these quiet visits, which didn't prevent any of us later from reading explanatory texts by good authors.

The national renewal of interest in cultural treasures was one influence, reflecting pride and restored freedom of movement after the devastation of the European war. But there was another influence, a hidden stream that I understand better now than when it first reached me. I've written briefly elsewhere about a remarkable individual whom I came to know quite well. Before

I met Henri Tracol, his influence reached me through the parents of my adoptive family, who were members of his circle. Tracol had a profound and, I'm sure, lifelong interest in art, owed initially to his uncle, the celebrated art historian Élie Faure, author of a multi-volume general history of art and many other studies. Alongside the familial influence of Élie Faure was a second influence, the writings of Ananda K. Coomaraswamy, which Tracol recognized and valued at a time when Coomaraswamy was little known in France. On pp. xvi–xvii we encountered a glimpse of Coomaraswamy's approach to sacred art. As few of his essays had been translated and published in French in those years, the 1960s through the 1980s, Tracol founded a translation team that worked for many years with admirable diligence to translate key essays. My own eventual interest in Coomaraswamy and my doctoral work on his life and writings created a bond, one of several, with Henri Tracol.

Coomaraswamy and to some degree Élie Faure were the undisclosed guides of my adoptive family's explorations of medieval art. In this rather complex texture of ideas, there was a third influence, G. I. Gurdjieff, with whom Tracol had worked throughout the last decade of Gurdjieff's life (1866? – 1949). Gurdjieff's concepts of what he called objective and subjective art had a dry rigor but also deep appeal: they sent you forth, so to speak, to find in your environment—be it an entire nation or a local museum—works that met his demanding criteria. In P. D. Ouspensky's account of meetings with Gurdjieff in Moscow and St. Petersburg before the Russian Revolution, Gurdjieff once evoked an encounter with art of a special kind. Ouspensky had asked him, "Do . . . works of objective art exist at the present day?" "Of course they exist," answered Gurdjieff.

> The great Sphinx in Egypt is such a work of art, as well as some historically known works of architecture, certain statues of gods, and many other things. There are figures of gods and of various mythological beings that can be read like books, only not with the mind but with the emotions, provided they are sufficiently developed. In the course of our travels in Central Asia we found, in the desert at the foot of the Hindu Kush, a strange figure which we thought at first was some ancient god or devil. At first it produced upon us simply the impression of being a curiosity. But after a while we began to feel that this figure contained many things, a big, complete, and complex system of cosmology. And slowly, step by step, we began to decipher this system. It was in the body

of the figure, in its legs, in its arms, in its head, in its eyes, in its ears; everywhere. In the whole statue there was nothing accidental, nothing without meaning. And gradually we understood the aim of the people who built this statue. We began to feel their thoughts, their feelings. Some of us thought that we saw their faces, heard their voices. At all events, we grasped the meaning of what they wanted to convey to us across thousands of years, and not only the meaning, but all the feelings and the emotions connected with it as well. That indeed was art![8]

In our modest family travel in parts of France, and later my independent travel in many parts of the world, there was nothing so dramatic as hearing voices, seeing faces. But there was a distinct sense of receding in time to other eras, to whole atmospheres that we felt and valued, to meanings displayed and preserved in sculpture, painting, and architectural environments. It was time travel.

That we had something like "eyes to see", however little, however much, we owed to others: to Faure, to Coomaraswamy, to Gurdjieff, to Tracol who had sent their influences on. For Tracol it wasn't only an intellectual or spiritual matter. In later years he developed relations with the *Compagnons du Devoir*, the Companions of Duty, a surviving guild of highly trained artisans and craftspeople with roots in the medieval past, who built a community hall for him at a retreat house in the south of France.

At some point I was moved to visit the Benedictine monastery in Burgundy that was responsible for Zodiaque books. Those books are still beautiful—try to find one. Dom José Surchamp, the moving force behind the publishing program, received me kindly, and we spoke of many things; by then I was a graduate student in art history. He invited me to lunch in the refectory with his fellow monks: a new experience. At the end of the meal everyone meticulously gathered even the smallest crumbs that had fallen on the table. I remember their hands.

12. DRAWING: ANCIENT GREEK POTTERY

Hermes, satyr, and fawn
Amphora (storage vessel), ca. 500 – 490 BCE
The Berlin Painter
Height: 27 inches
Staatliche Museen, Berlin
Source: Wikipedia / public domain

The composition of this famed amphora recalls a balletic *pas de deux*, as if it were the photograph of dancers caught mid-motion—or a *pas de trois* if we acknowledge the exquisitely posed fawn. Among any number of possibilities I have chosen this work as the icon of the entire tradition of painted pottery in the ancient Greek world. Every major museum today offers what can easily seem more than enough of this art: from mid-second-millennium Crete to seventh- through fifth-century Athens and other creative centers for centuries more, there are innumerable fascinating survivals owing to a commercial activity—the making and decoration of clay vessels for all the uses of daily life and special occasions—that was capable of the highest artistic standards.

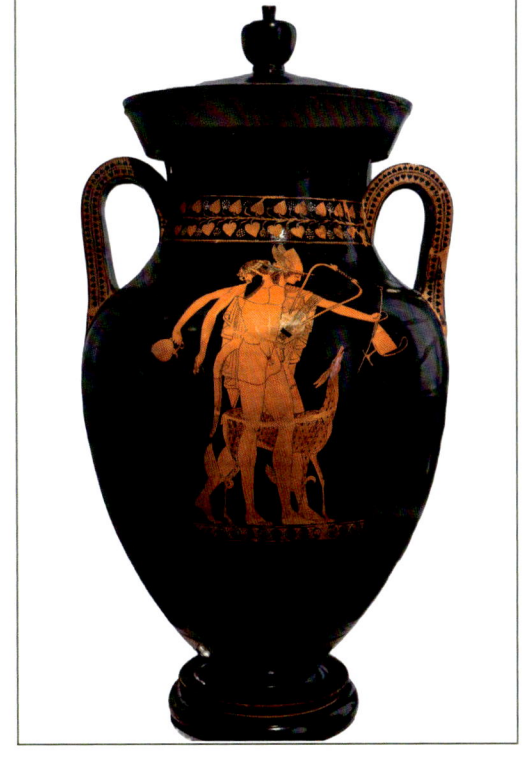

The quality of drawing here, in every detail large and small, conveys to perfection what we do well to recognize at this point: the power of drawing. But something first needs to be noticed about the figures from Greek myth joined here in a visually

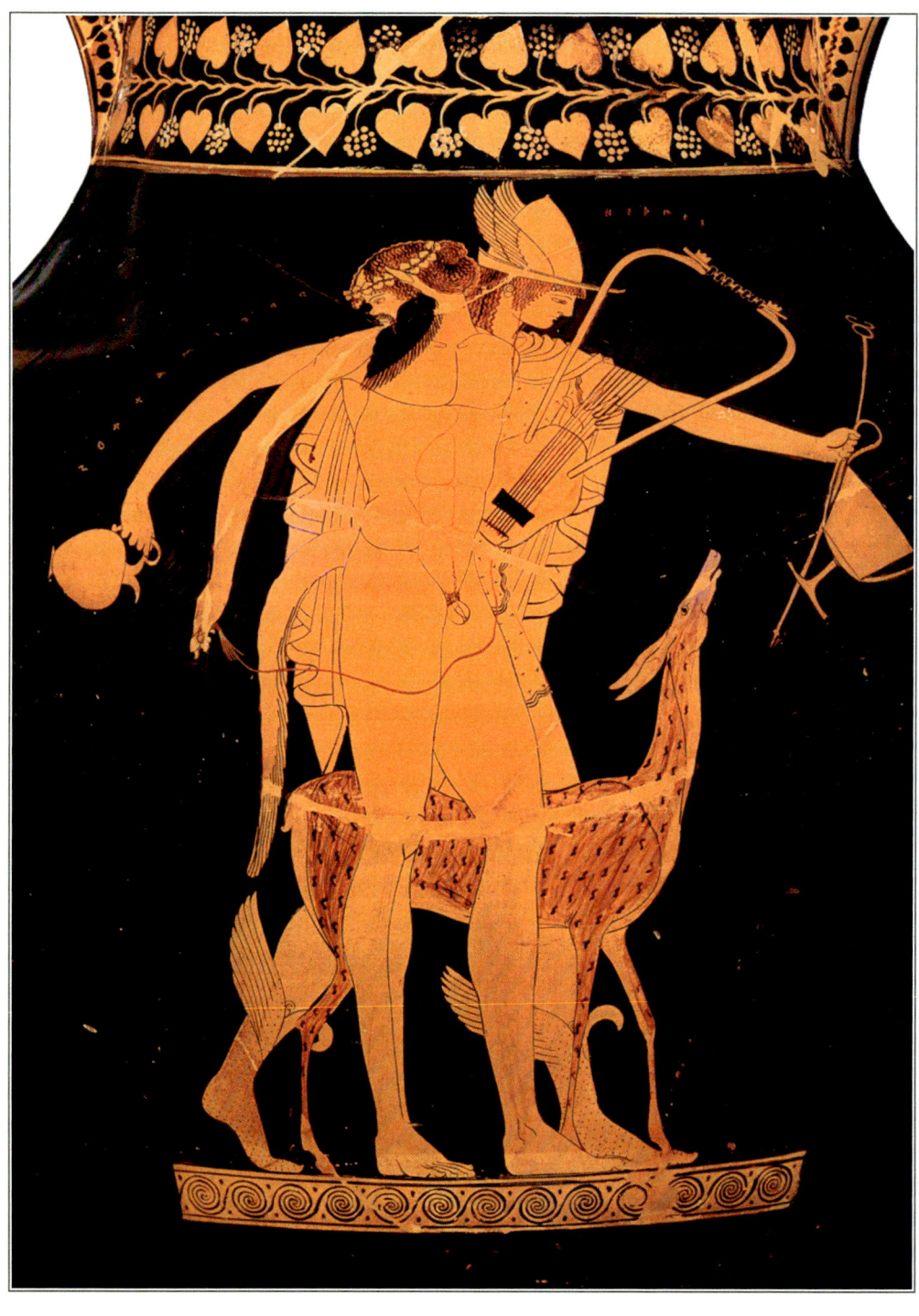

puzzling choreography. Much of what I can share on that topic builds on a brilliant interpretive article published not long ago.⁹ Satyrs, half-animal, half-human, were part of the entourage of Dionysus, fond like him of drink and celebration, rarely dangerous but sometimes a nuisance. Some satyrs, more civilized sorts, were musicians; that is so here, where our satyr cradles in his left arm a lyre-like instrument called the barbiton. The red cord passing in front of him secures the pluck in his other hand. Hermes, in winged cap and boots, is the messenger of the gods who travels far and wide and, according to some antique texts, fathered the race of satyrs. Now a question: why is the satyr looking back, and at what? Is this only elegant choreography or something more? A reasonable guess: he is a musical satyr, yes, but not without regret for the life he lived as a carousing, fun-loving satyr. He looks back at the pitcher, likely of wine, which Hermes is emptying. If this reading has any merit, then we are being shown "the education of a satyr" at a milestone moment when, guided by Hermes, the satyr must choose between inclinations. Looking up with what seems longing, the fawn emphasizes the peaceful sweetness of the overall scene and moment. It, too, wants something from Hermes, if only affection.

Consider the quality of line throughout this image: simple, descriptive, precise, unerring. Drawing of such finesse and sensitivity had a long future: in our time, Picasso and Matisse gave it new life, as if they rejoined the Berlin Painter and his peers.

13. THE RISK OF GREAT ACCOMPLISHMENT

Three goddesses, Dionysus
East pediment, the Parthenon, Athens
Phidias, master of the works
447 – 432 BCE
British Museum, London
Source: Wikipedia / Marie-Lan Nguyen

"There are mighty monuments of our power which will make us the wonder of this and of succeeding ages. . . . I would have you day by day fix your eyes upon the greatness of Athens, until you become filled with the love of her." As recreated by Thucydides, these are words from Pericles's funeral oration of the year 431—and an injunction heeded to this day by much of the world. Every introductory course in art history includes the Parthenon and its sculpture, virtually all visitors to Athens climb the Acropolis to the great temple complex, and many visitors to London make a point of seeing the Parthenon sculptures at the British Museum. These works represent the apex of a certain vision of humanity. They are also the culmination of a powerful inquiry among artists and their patrons, focused on the physicality of human being and the expressive power of posture, gesture, clothing, and narrative. Even within the confines of this book we can look back at the Hera of Samos, a masterpiece created some 130 years before the Parthenon sculptures, and measure how much has changed.

The theme of the east pediment sculptural ensemble, much of which has been lost, was the birth of Athena. Gods and goddesses have gathered as witnesses. The works illustrated here—three goddesses united in a single flow of form and energy, the god Dionysus at ease—are more than enough to show the great accomplishment of the Parthenon sculptors. Generations of scholars and museum goers have admired and surely been awed by the majesty of the three goddesses and the wave-like, intricate patterning of their gowns. The minds that conceived these figures were attuned to two contrapuntal realities in human experience: stillness and weight, dynamism and change. The

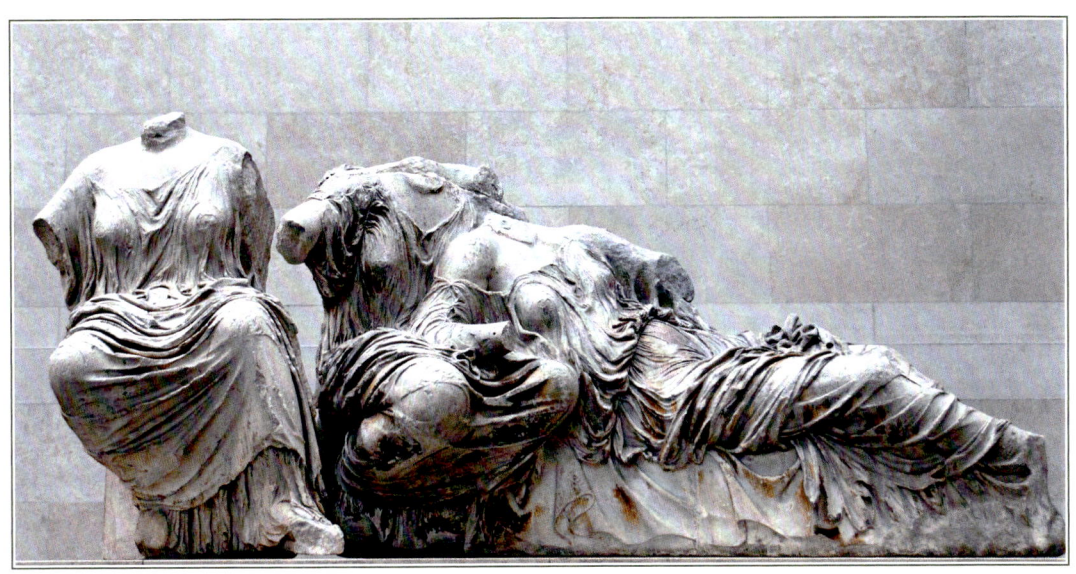

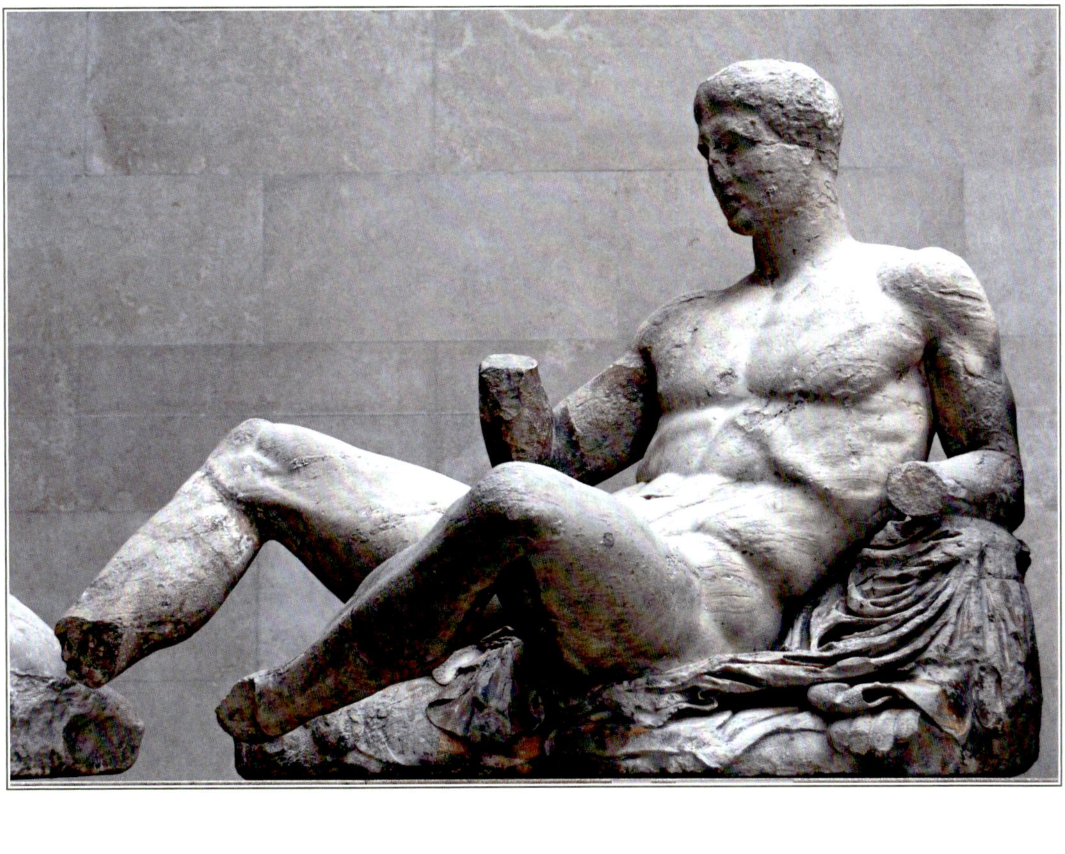

figure of Dionysus reveals the sculptor's understanding of the physical tissues of a perfectly developed male body, with a flow of patterned drapery serving as contrast. Further, the alert tilt of Dionysus's head and his calm expression convey something more than bodily perfection. Pericles, the leader of Athens in its golden age, had been a student of the philosopher Anaxagoras, and Phidias—both sculptor and master of the works—was a close friend. Something of that intellectual heritage feels present here. However that may be, the level of culture—of conversation, of inquiry and careful decision—that must lie behind these works is truly remarkable.

Revisiting these familiar works, why am I anxious? Why do I have thoughts about the risk of great accomplishment? The history of Athens in the years just following the completion of the Parthenon was in part tragic: the death of Pericles in 429 in an epidemic that took many Athenian lives, the intensification of war with Sparta that would cost Athens its empire by the end of the century. That was then, as people say. But it echoes now, in the year 2025, when we face our own pandemic, political turmoil, wars and the reality of climate change and its devastations. We are capable today of such great achievement; no doubt on that score. We are also terribly at risk. Dionysus looks out and sees—what? One of the greatest icons of human accomplishment in the arts is not just "a mighty monument of power," it is a call for vigilance.

14. EMPATHY

Villa of the Mysteries, Pompeii
Wall painting (fresco), mid first century BCE
Life-size
Sources: (principal image) Hemis / Alamy Stock Photo; (overall view) Classic
Image / Alamy Stock Photo

The recurrent and necessary conversation about this masterwork of Roman wall painting concerns its meaning. A women's ritual progressing in stages around the walls of a room of modest dimensions, the initiation of a young woman into a cult of the god Dionysus—so much has been clear since the discovery of the villa in 1909. Beyond that, much difficulty. My favorite classicist, Mary Beard, wrote in 2010 that "no amount of modern scholarship has ever managed to unravel the meaning."[10] On the other hand, a fearless and learned scholar of Western esotericism, Peter Mark Adams, recently published a study that probably comes as close as one can to unraveling the meaning.[11]

However that may be, we should speak again of empathy, of the ways in which our bodies, here and alive, respond to images of bodies painted or sculpted. Often without knowing it, most of us attune to what we perceive of other bodies and psychological attitudes. Posture, weight, density, texture, movement, gesture, facial expression, eyes, attraction or aversion, respect or disquiet: instinctively we read these things. This capacity must have helped in

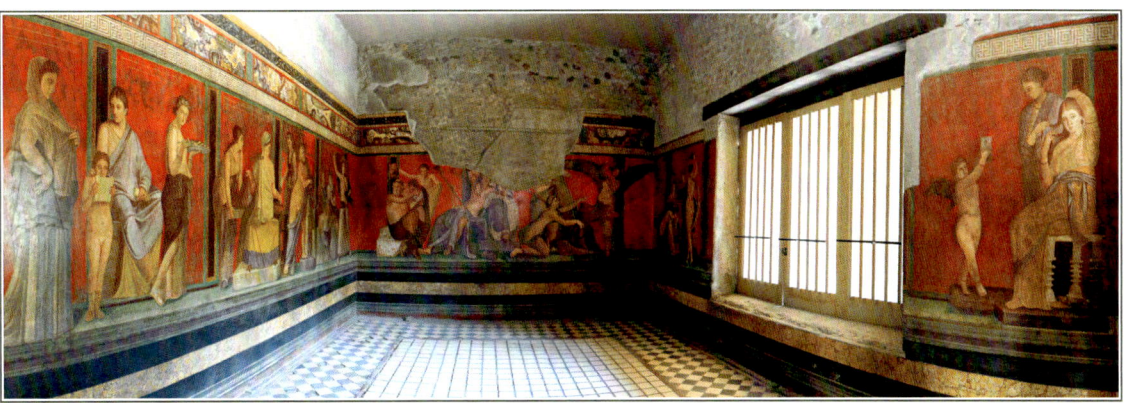

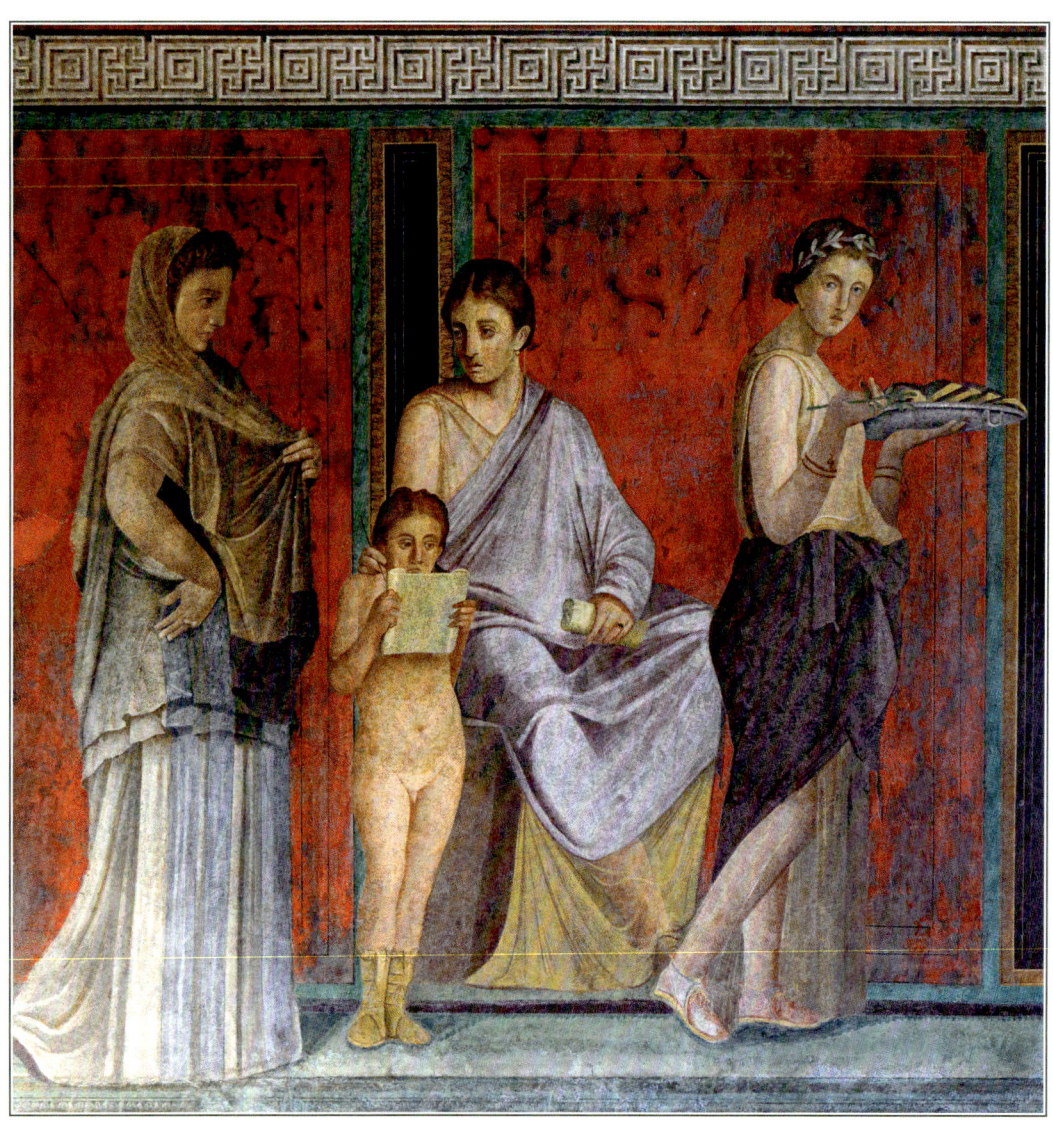

pre-history—and still does. We read one another. There is captivating work by medical scientists on the role of mirror neurons in our makeup; they are part of the infrastructure of empathy.

The women and boy in this initial narrative panel are represented in such a way that we sense them. The unknown painter understood how to create a sculptural "feel" in figures through skilled use of foreshortening and the suggestion of mass and volume, in part through the movement of light and shadow across bodies and clothing. The figures occupy a shallow shelf of space set against a beautiful cinnabar-red wall, a color favored by Roman painters. There is no excess of detail, just enough to persuade us at an instinctive level—the level of empathy—that these figures, like us, are endowed with motion and psychological life. What is that life here? Solemn, inward, focused, shared with one another and by an occasional glance toward us: we are witnesses in this panel to the first stage of a ritual in which all participants are deeply invested, as we are also owing to the intimate tie of empathetic response.

The centuries of tradition that precede this work have left little trace. This is the earliest occurrence I know in pictorial art of a certain vision of body and psyche that later found its place repeatedly in Western art. Monumental, utterly serious, calling to our instinctive responsiveness. As we'll see in later pages, the artists of the Italian Renaissance resumed and advanced this vision of the figure—of ourselves—in space. Ever after it has remained latent, at the ready. It represents an extraordinary way to explore experience and address one another.

To visit the Villa of the Mysteries is to encounter a hidden current in ancient culture. This feels like a privilege, offered to all and a privilege for all.

15. LOOK BENEATH THE SURFACE

Bronze equestrian statue of Marcus Aurelius
170 – 180 CE
Height: nearly 14 feet
Capitoline Museums, Rome
Sources: (principal image) Stefano Politi Markovina / Alamy Stock Photo;
(detail) Wikipedia / public domain

"Look beneath the surface," the emperor wrote in his journal, "Never let a thing's intrinsic quality or worth escape you." It could be the watchword for this book; certainly its aspiration. I have wanted to end this exploration of ancient art not so much with a monument—though we have one here—as with a person: the emperor Marcus Aurelius. He was necessarily a warrior; this rare surviving equestrian bronze tells us so. It is captured in the indoor space of a museum; it wants to be outdoors, as it was for

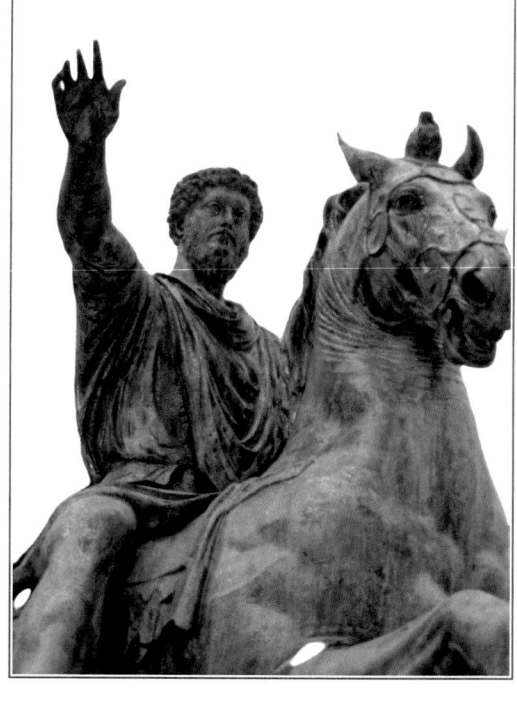

centuries. Marcus's armies defended the northern and eastern borders of the Roman Empire as they came under pressure throughout much of his reign (161 – 180 CE); to this day in Pannonia, a region of Austria, people recall his long sojourn and archeologists have restored his military camp, its halls and baths. But, as you know, Marcus was more than a warrior and sagacious leader in the civic affairs of Rome; he was the author of a private journal now known as the *Meditations*.

Marcus's mind was a work of art. Shaped by his spirit of inquiry, his self-discipline, his immersion in Greek philosophy from Socrates forward to

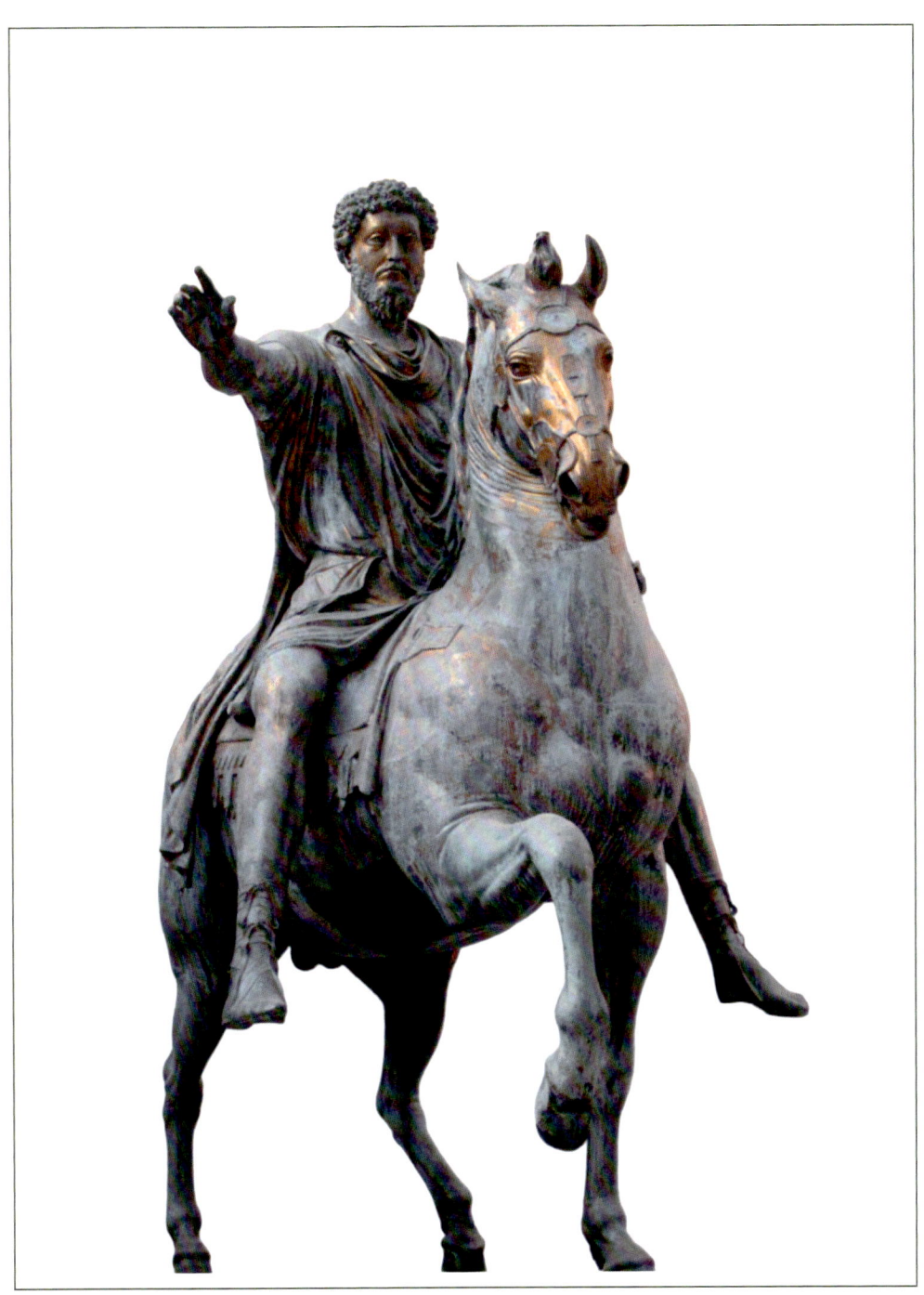

his own Stoic teachers, and not least his meticulous training in the uses of language, which could have made a pedant of him but instead freed him to know and to speak what he knew. He wrote the *Meditations* in Greek; there could be no more vivid sign of continuity between Greece and Rome.

I hesitate to quote further from the *Meditations*. It is vast in its approach to living, to leadership, to care of the self, to relation with the divine. An entire way of life unfolds in its pages through direct, day-to-day observation and reflection. For a taste, look at the first entry in Book Two.

There is much ahead in the pages of this book, many icons to be collected and understood in worlds of art subsequent to the ancient West and wholly unrelated to the West. Working with this material from Egypt around the Mediterranean to Italy, I trust that we have grasped together what an icon can be, where it fits in a life as "a reminder and support of contemplation," to return to Coomaraswamy's insight. As for Marcus Aurelius, what comes to mind are words with which he often closed letters to his teacher Fronto:

Vale mi magister optime: Farewell, my best of masters.

16. IN THE VERY BEGINNING

> Decorated passage tomb
> Gavrinis Island (Gulf of Morbihan, Brittany)
> Ca. 3500 BCE
> Sources: (principal image) Ian Shaw / Alamy Stock Photo;
> (general view) Wikimedia Commons / Myrabella

It isn't easy, or even settled, where and when to locate the very beginning. The choice may depend on where one is born. For the peoples of Central America, the very beginning might be Olmec civilization. For North Americans, it could be the work of the indigenous Mound Builders in the upper Midwest. For Australians, it might be the rock art in the northwestern Kimberley Range—astonishingly beautiful images of an early, vigorous culture. For many of us, without regard to place of birth, it is the cave paintings in central France: Lascaux. The word alone evokes greatness, elegance, sure hands and minds at work in the very beginning. I haven't dared reach back to Lascaux for this icon collection. Many of us know those images by heart; they belong to a global heritage. But apart from Lascaux, there is a beginning I recognize instinctively: the passage tomb with massive engraved stones on an island, Gavrinis, just off the coast of Brittany.

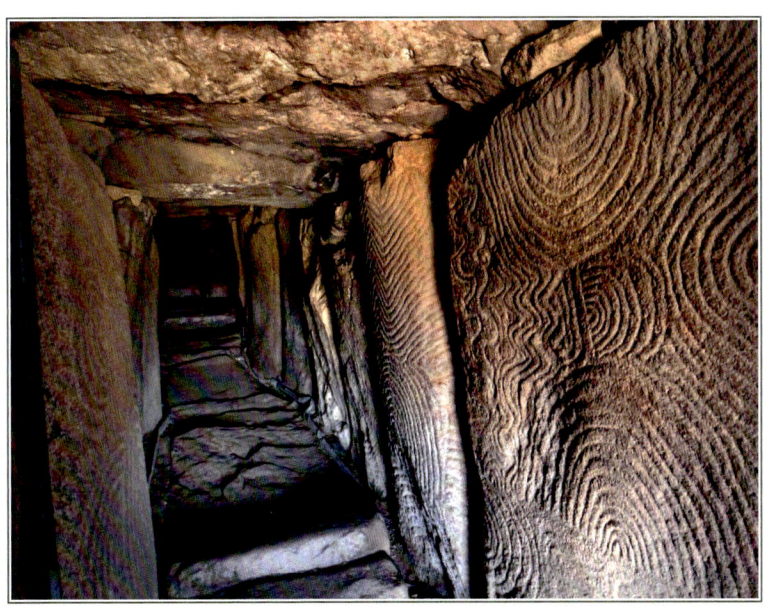

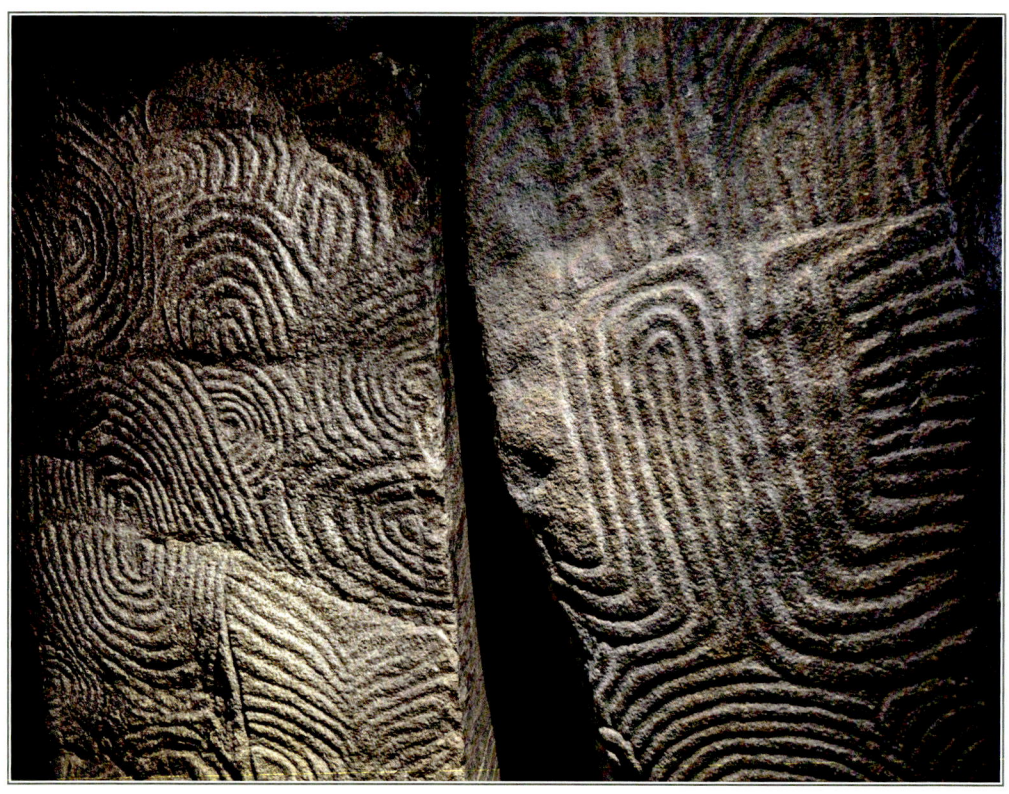

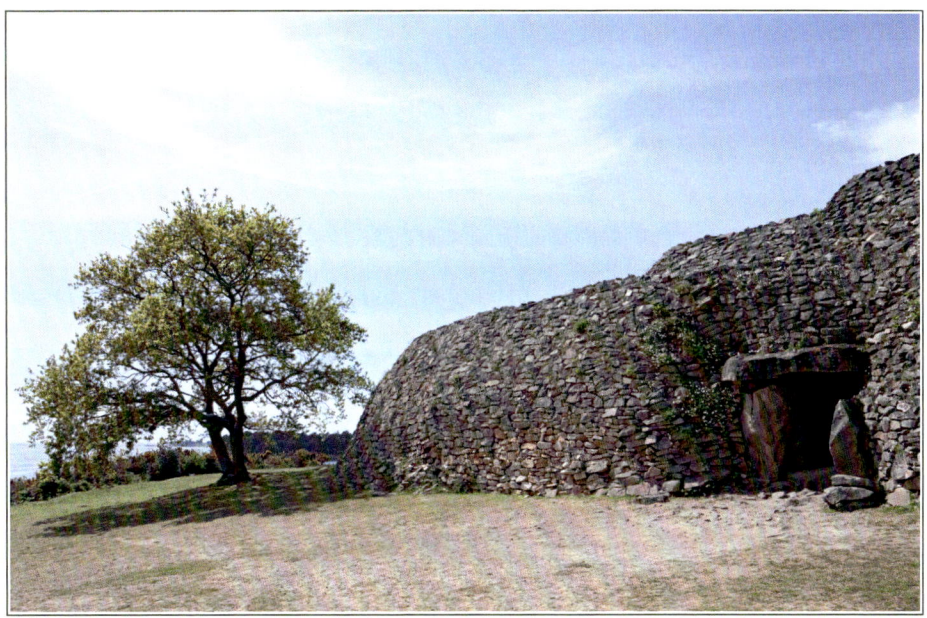

The trip out to the island by small boat is an expedition in space and time, full of anticipation. Engineers need have no concern: at the time of construction the island was still part of the mainland. First you see a placid, well cared-for burial mound, then you enter a narrow passage toward a larger space at the end, and then you enter into the mystery of this fabulous site. I have never seriously tried to understand it intellectually, though there is excellent scholarly material on the Neolithic period—the New Stone Age. I have no idea why the community responsible for raising these massive stones and engraving them with repetitive flowing patterns actually did so. I am unable to "read" them; I don't know what they convey. Whatever it is, I agree. This is tangibly a sacred place, as if human being has stirred here in a most unforgettable way. There are such places around the world, you detect them not just with the mind but with sudden conviction.

Gavrinis Island is remote, though not far from the famed massive stone alignments at Carnac on the mainland. The recipient at Gavrinis of such honor and effort must have been very powerful, very excellent, or both. There is a similar, equally memorable passage tomb less than an hour north of Dublin, Ireland: Newgrange. In the end, this book of icons can't help but lead to travel plans.

17. SPIRALING ON: A CELTIC CLASP

Spectacle fibula
Hallstatt (Austria), bronze
Width: nearly 6 inches
ca. 750 – 400 BCE
Hallstatt Museum, Austria
Source: Hallstatt Museum

Head of a man, Mšecké Žehrovice
Ca. 150 – 50 BCE
Source: Azoor Photo / Alamy Stock Photo

To be certain that we are now entering a different realm, consider the marvelous Mšecké Žehrovice Head, dating to 150 – 50 BCE, from an archeological site northwest of Prague. Not Roman, not Greek, this is a different creature: a Celt. In the first millennium BCE, Celtic migrants settled across Europe, reaching from

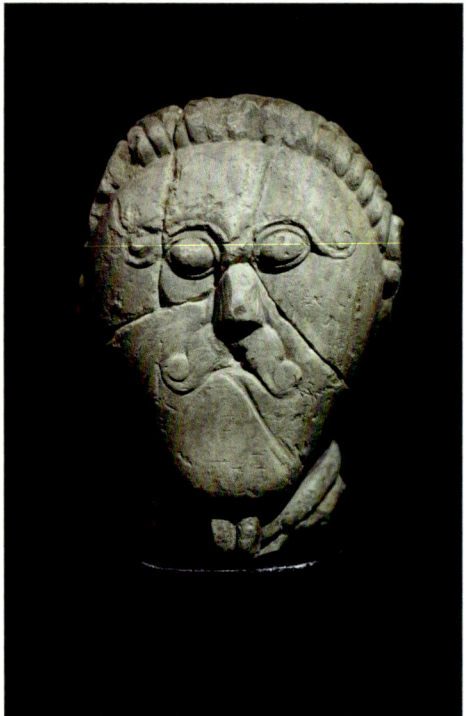

Ireland and France, where they eventually tangled with Julius Caesar, to the Balkans, Central Europe, and Greece. They were the bearers of a different art, destined to influence early medieval art in the West as far as Ireland, and to lay some part of the foundation for extraordinary, intricate visions to come.

I have never liked the term "spectacle fibula," though it's descriptive, for this remarkable element of women's wear: typically a sizable pin or clasp (Latin: *fibula*) with a safety pin-like fastener at the back, used to secure clothing at the shoulder or where needed. Widely distributed

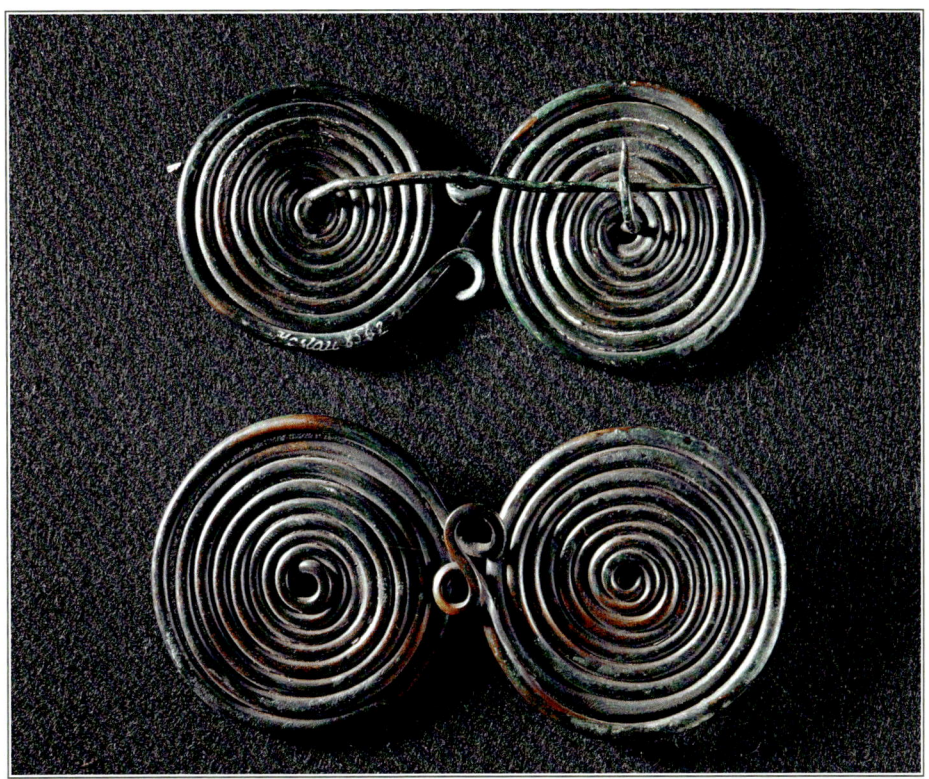

in time and across geographies, the double-spiral design was appreciated by metalworkers and their clientele for something like a thousand years; there were many variations featuring additional spirals. Scholars have made serious effort to understand the possible symbolic meaning of the double spiral, but it's difficult to be certain of meanings in pre-literate cultures and about objects of daily use. Spirals are a fundamental form in nature, from the organization of galaxies to the patterning of sunflower seeds and mollusk shells. We know that they are rooted, so to speak, in nature. They are also rooted in our minds. It is this affinity that endows the spectacle fibula with deep appeal.

The spiral is an object of keen interest in fields ranging from Jungian psychology to occult and New Age speculation. Here I don't wish to make high-flown claims—the beautifully crafted double spiral from Hallstatt speaks for itself and asks to be remembered, as if it were in some way important. How is that so? I can say that the spiral is the long way around from a start to a finish, and in that respect mirrors our lives. I can say that the spiral repeatedly offers the same vistas from a sequence of different locations, implying something about continuity and change. I can say that the double spiral reflects the fundamental duality of experience—contented/sad, friend/foe, heaven and earth,

I and thou—and that our awareness of duality is a third factor that immeasurably enriches experience. I hesitate to say more. But this much I'll add: if you were to place even a photograph of an object of this kind in a special place—in a home or a public space where issues are debated and decided—it would, I think, steadily send a message of calm, of order, and for some souls it might give rise to a fugitive sense that we are designed just as it is designed, and the point is to be at the center while the rest spirals on.

18. A CELTIC COSMOS?

Bronze box lid
Somerset Hoard (County Galway, Ireland)
1ˢᵗ century CE, diameter: 3.2 inches
National Museum of Ireland, Dublin
Source: National Museum of Ireland

This is one of the most remarkable objects I have encountered, and I am not alone in that conviction. The immensely gifted and thorough art historian, Françoise Henry (1902 – 1982), on whom many have relied to understand Irish art, held much the same view. The design of this lid, she has written, "is infinitely pleasing, partly because of its puzzling enigma which cannot be resolved at a glance." Elsewhere she evoked the early Irish "use of geometrical instruments perversely turned to the construction of asymmetrical or irregular patterns." In this design "the outcome is the most incredible sleight of hand where all symmetry is eluded."[12] I don't know that she's right about perverse intentions, but the rest cannot be better expressed.

It's an engrossing exploration to take up the tool used by the master designer here, a simple compass, to trace the eccentricities of the pattern. The standard language for describing design elements of this kind is likely to be unfamiliar—the nearly central boss, the trumpet spiraling around, the mouth of the trumpet or "lentoid boss" vertically aligned above its starting point—but that language helps us see the dynamic. The energy or force of the thick raised spiral gives the impression that it pulls the pattern of concentric punch-marked circles down and to the right. Looking again, do we see something like two firmaments, the first and smaller one defined by the regular concentric circles framed by the trumpet, the second lying beneath and outside the trumpet—a starry night? What is the significance of the nearly central boss, the hemisphere, which seems to set the spiral in motion? What is the meaning of the vertical alignment? All of this occurring on a circular surface scarcely more than three inches in diameter.

I have no idea how to read this object, though at first glance years ago it became an icon. It seems to announce cosmos—to announce a dynamic order in which parts fit exquisitely without being captured in predictable symmetry. It unquestionably announces that our bronze-working ancestors looked into the night sky and—why not?—looked into themselves to discover the nature of things. They were inquirers, intellectuals. Our only way to speak with and learn from them is through objects such as this. In art-historical perspective, here in the Late Bronze and Early Iron eras we are looking at the origin of a brilliant Christian art to come, realized in part with the compass and an intensity of attention rare in the history of art.

Some works send one back to the beginning.

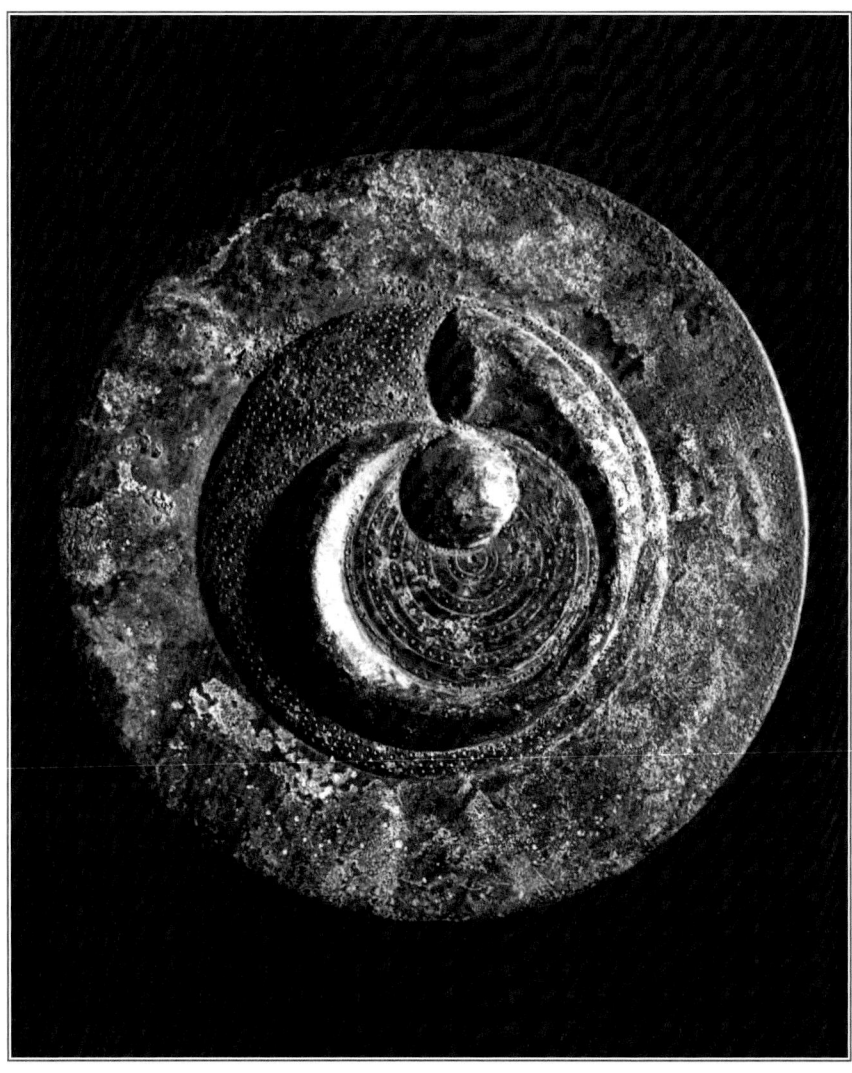

19. THE SUNBIRD

Eagle fibula
Visigothic (the Migrations period), sixth century CE
Gold over bronze with gemstones and glass
Height: app. 5.5 inches
Walters Art Museum, Baltimore
Source: Walters Art Museum

Inset: The Gelasian Sacramentary, detail, 701 – 725 CE
The Vatican Library
Source: Wikimedia Commons / public domain

Found at a site in southwestern Spain, this elaborate clothing fastener, one of a pair, could have been found nearly anywhere in Europe at a time when the Roman Empire in the West had faded and whole peoples were resettling. It was the era of the Migrations. Newcomers and former Roman client states were competing by war and alliance for land and dominance: the Dark Ages, nonetheless with zones of light. It was, as well, the long moment of transition to Christianity. The delightful bird-and-fish lettering just below appears in the Gelasian Sacramentary, a liturgical book from Paris, mid-eighth century, reflecting the wit and playfulness of monastic scribes of that era. They were heirs to the art exemplified by the eagle fibula of several centuries earlier.

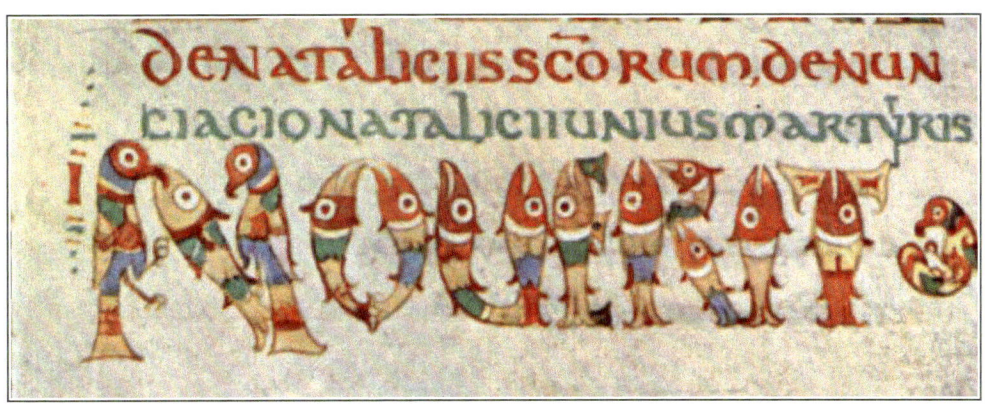

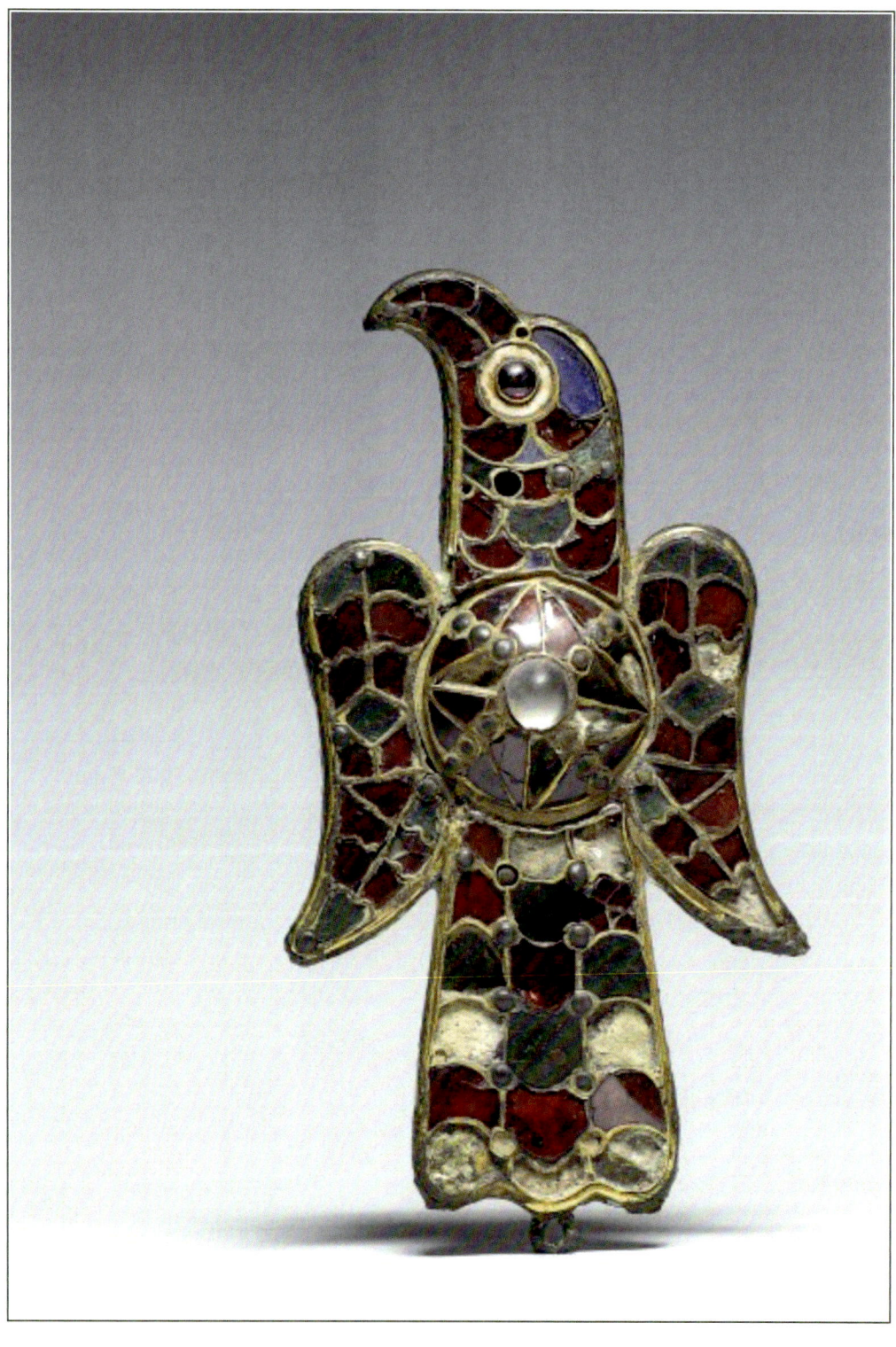

The Visigoths were one of the migrating peoples, among the most successful in establishing not just a kingdom in southern France and Spain but also a culture that left lasting monuments. Their artisans were not alone in their mastery of cloisonné technique (cells defined by bronze strips, filled with colored glass, gems, or enamel). In museums from St-Germain-en-Laye, near Paris, to public collections up and down the Rhine there are countless examples of this craft which was an art. The pair of eagle fibulae in Baltimore stands out.

The eagle is the sunbird. Ancient peoples observed its flight high in the sky, they recognized its power and majestic appearance, they imagined that it alone could look directly at the sun as like to like. Our eagle here carries the sun within it, at the central place we still call the solar plexus. With its innocent round eye, unthreatening upturned beak, and slender wings, this is a pacific, self-possessed eagle, a convert from its wild ways. Again I must say that I have no idea of its maker's intentions. What I see is a certain ideal: strength and obedience brought together, as if the sun has been earned. The combination of noble eagle and solar emblem signals a state of being.

In the effort to express something more about this icon, what comes to mind is a passage in Dag Hammarskjöld's journal *Markings*. He in turn was quoting his medieval teacher Meister Eckhart: "You must have an exalted mind and a burning heart in which, nevertheless, reigns silent stillness." The Walters eagle fibula is one possible representation of that condition, which may in the end defy representation. How unexpected: a somewhat battered piece of ancient jewelry preserves a noble symbol that tells us a tale of ourselves—of what is and what could be in an interior place to which symbols can do little more than point.

The Christian world and its arts are complete in themselves. Here is everything: great meanings; visions of God, Nature, and humanity; tales sacred and profane of heroes, sufferers, and villains; awesome skill and expressiveness; successive levels of artistry from grand achievement to the work of local artisans who also had a thing or two to say. We should immerse in every world of art as if it were the only one; that is the way to perceive it clearly, passionately. But, after all, it is not the only one; there are worlds adjacent to Christendom—Islamic, Buddhist, Hindu, and others—which are no less endowed and brilliant. We belong here; we belong elsewhere also. An icon collection is a meeting place.

Errata

1. p. 59, line 7: "facing page" should be "next page."
2. p. 103, lines 9-10: The *luohan* in the British Museum is not illustrated in this edition.
3. p. 112, line 5: The portrait of Rikyu appears on p. 110.
4. p. 122, line 3: The image of a scholarly gathering appears on p. 120.
5. p. 125, lines 7-8: The detail of arabesque patterning in the ivory panels is reproduced here.

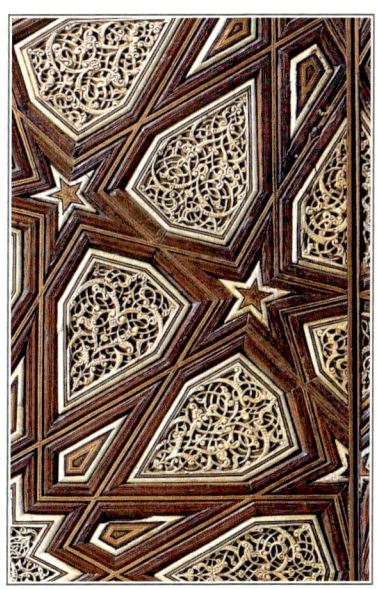

20. THE MONK HAS SEEN BETTER DAYS

Symbols of the Evangelists Matthew and Mark
Echternach Gospels (probably produced at Lindisfarne Abbey in modern Scotland)
ca. 690 CE
Bibliothèque nationale, Paris
Source: The Yorck Project (2002) / Wikimedia Commons / public domain

I suppose that the symbol of the Evangelist Matthew—the *imago hominis* or image of a man—should be solemn, and it often is in medieval book art. The extraordinarily beautiful *imago leonis* on this page, symbol of the Evangelist Mark, leaves no doubt that the monastic artist who shared responsibility for this early medieval manuscript is capable of solemnity, grandeur, and a kind of tensile vitality as the lion leaps across a satisfyingly intricate maze. What, then, to think of what I take to be a monk on the facing page, something of a self-portrait or generic portrait of the monastic artist and his fellows? It is deeply, permanently witty and kind, a self-reflection that invites us to know the constraints of monastic discipline at the time, and even now as the life hasn't changed that much.

The characteristic gift of monastic artists in early medieval Ireland and Scotland is complex, immaculately ordered decoration, be it the woven interlace of the border or the abstract treatment and decoration of the monk's robes. The Celtic and Migrations repertories underlie what we see here, but more than that: illuminated books, textiles, or richly decorated objects for use in church

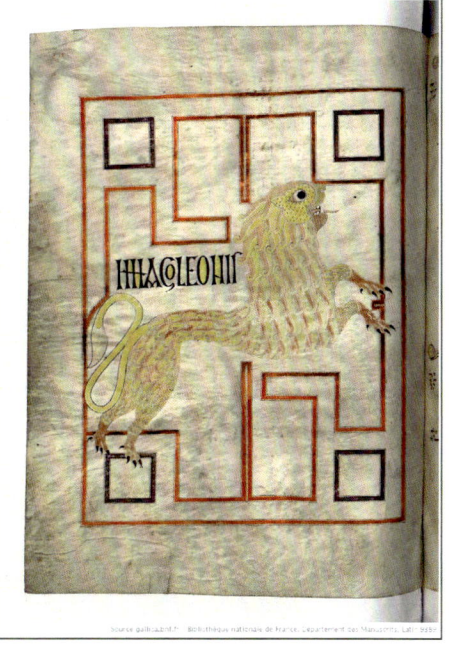

would have found their way west from the Christian East—Egypt, Byzantium, Armenia—in traveling monks' backpacks.

We are being told something, not through an elite creature but through an ordinary monk who seems hard-pressed, literally. The image is full of humor and good will but leaves no doubt about the rigors of the life. Sitting in what looks to be a choir stall, his head immobilized, eyes straining as if under pressure from above, delicate feet poking out from beneath the habit, he is a most dutiful monk. Everyone today who has some sense of following a path, of passionately engaging with a personal, professional, or artistic discipline, will recognize him as a brother. How did the abbot at Lindisfarne react to this page when first shown it? After all, he was the guardian of the life. He too must have had a sense of humor alongside a strong sense of purpose.

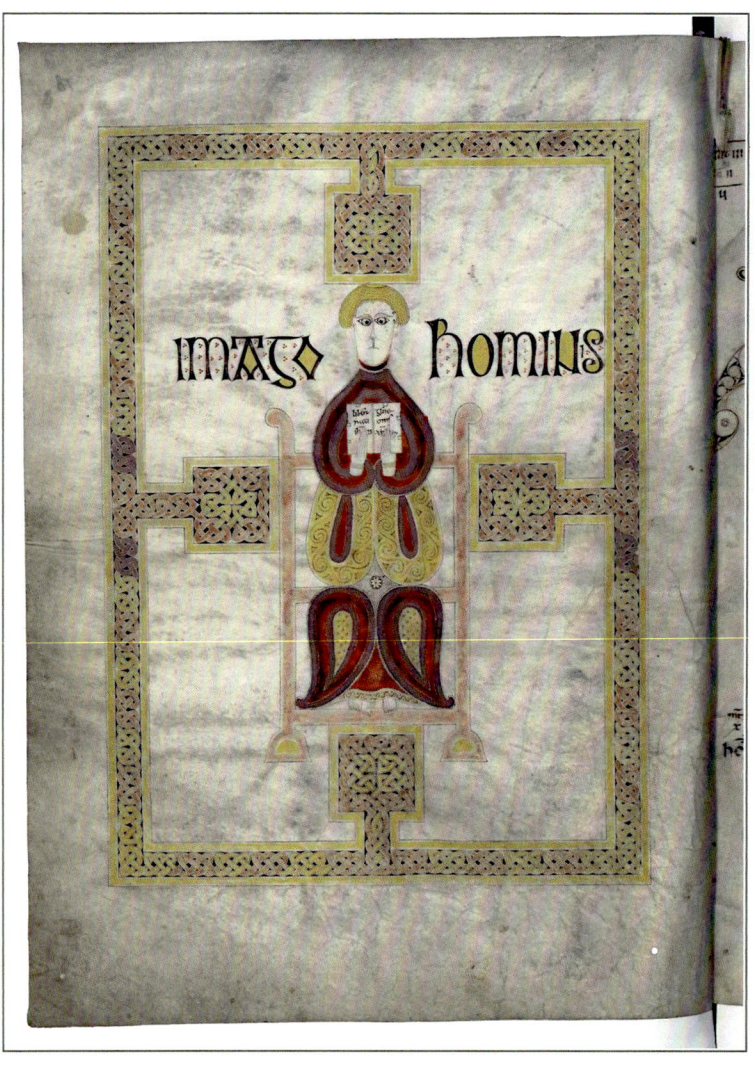

21. INTRICACY

The Book of Kells (produced in Ireland, Scotland, or England)
Chi Rho Page
ca. 800 CE
Trinity College Library, Dublin
Source: Wikipedia / public domain

Imagine a network of small monasteries founded by a courageous missionary monk, now known as St. Columba. They are not well defended—Viking raids from further north are a recurrent, mortal danger—but the communities persist in their multiple roles as preservers of text and knowledge, houses of prayer, and missionary teachers. In such modest, threatened circumstances, how could it be that artists and scribes conceived and executed illuminated gospels of overwhelming intricacy and beauty? What minds were at work; what will? These are questions that can scarcely be answered, but to ask them pays homage to the unique creativity of the Columban communities.

I have chosen the Chi Rho page from among quite a few possibilities in the 680 pages of the Gospels associated with the Columban monastery at Kells, not far from Dublin. Showing principally the opening letters of the word Christ in Greek, it comes just before Matthew 1.18, where the Nativity narrative begins. One can think about this page from any number of perspectives—for example, it's interesting to explore likely sources in prior Celtic and Migrations art, in illuminated books, textiles, and metalwork from the Christian East that must have found their way to the Columban monasteries. But the issue that strikes me as most important is the practice—intellectual, manual, and heartfelt—of the

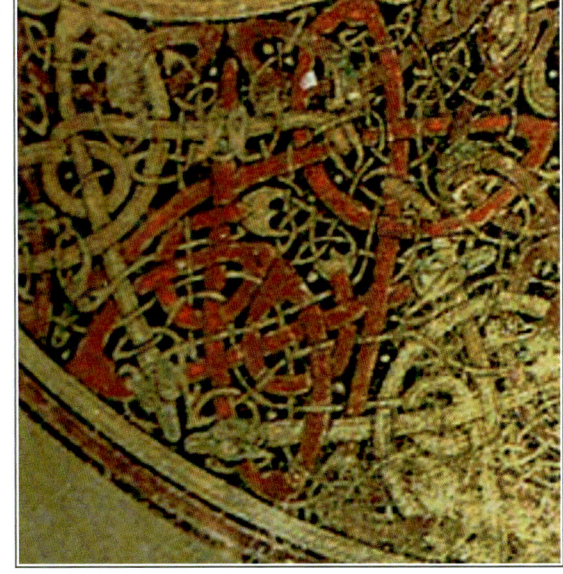

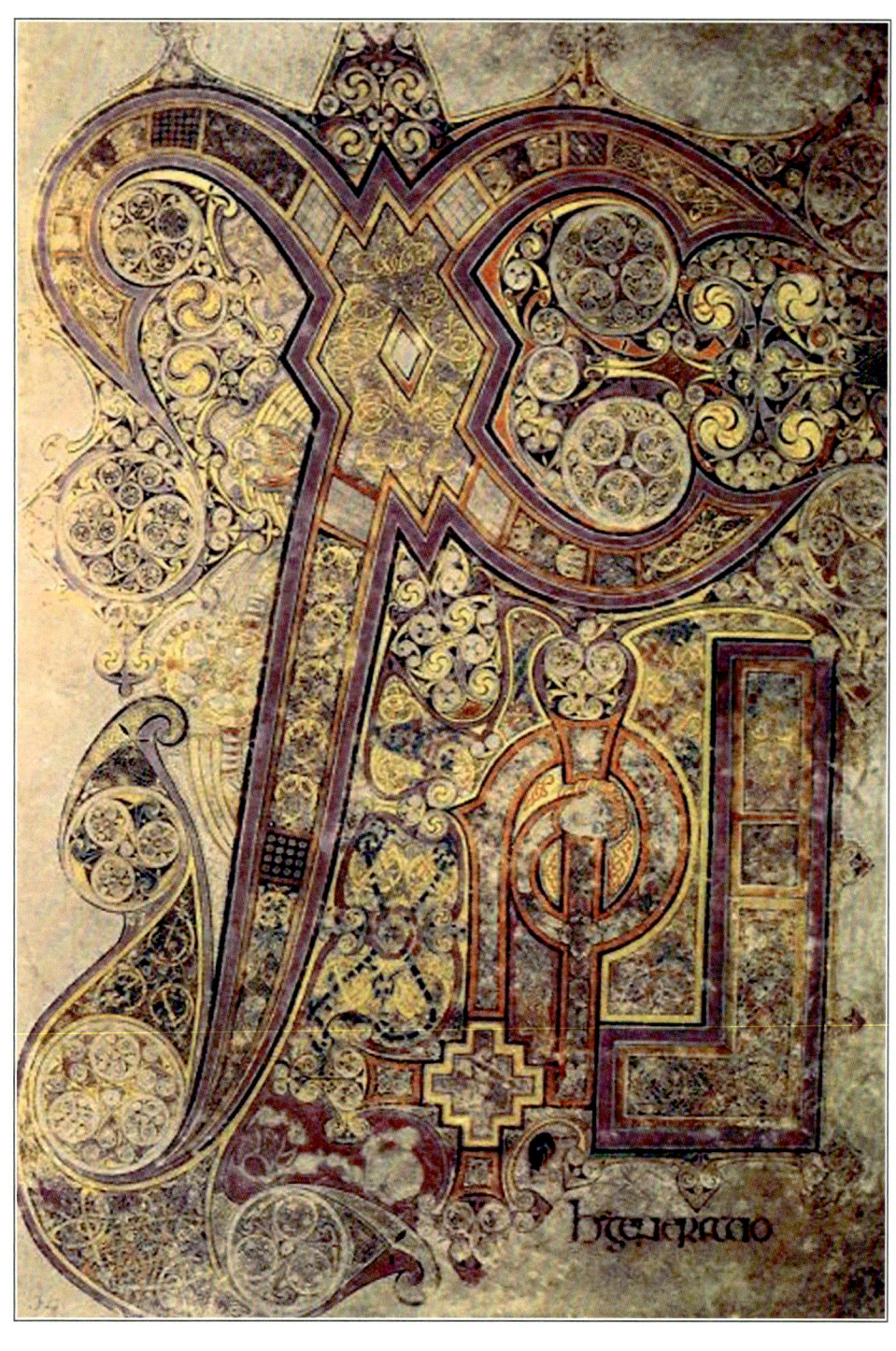

artist-monk who designed and executed this page and others like it in the book. It is a consummate work of attention.

I can't read that artist's mind, but what I see are minutely swirling worlds within worlds dominated, magnetized, and, so to speak, called to order by Chi Rho, by the presence of Christ. Everywhere complexity, worlds entangled in themselves and with other worlds, yet above them all and easily distinguished from them all, the presence of Christ. How remarkable.

The Book of Kells, and comparable books such as the Lindisfarne and Echternach Gospels, are acknowledged miracles. A twelfth-century author who encountered one or another of these books agreed: "You might say that all this was the work of an angel, and not of a man." They are icons of the reach of attention. Sometimes even now, though in other fields of research, we achieve no less. Why not design a tiny helicopter, transport it to the planet Mars, and set it flying? A secular achievement, no doubt of that, but a splendid feat by men and women living in the small monastery called Earth.

22. SIMPLICITY

Abbey of Saint-Philibert at Tournus (Burgundy)
Early 11th century CE, with later building campaigns
Source: Michael Hawkridge / Alamy Stock Photo

No photograph can convey the direct experience offered by the interior of the abbey church at Tournus or, I'm quite sure, any work of architecture. Nonetheless, if a photograph is a pale reminder, the memory of a visit to Tournus is an icon—Christian of course, but universal and fundamental because great architecture isn't about religious tenets, it is about sensations. In style this is the First Romanesque, an early period in the elaboration of the skills of building and sculpture that would fire one of

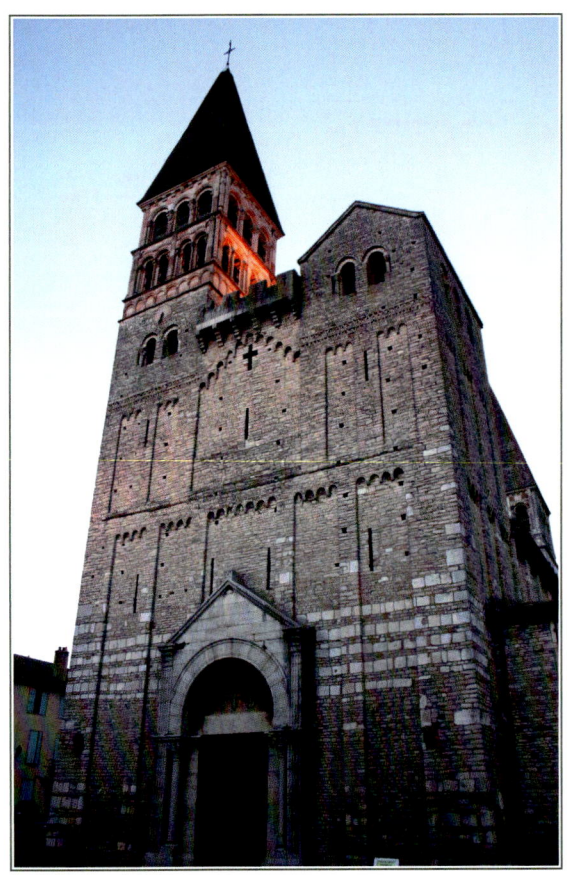

the great periods of Christian art in Western Europe in the 11th and 12th centuries. The builders' material here, a pink or rose-colored stone quarried into bricks of modest size, would fall out of use as a major component. The church represents a brave beginning.

How to speak of two linked experiences provoked by this space? Bathed in light from windows high and low, massive cylindrical columns define the central nave and flanking aisles. Their simplicity and quiet majesty prompt an internal change: in your own way, you become a little like them—simpler, freer from inner commotion, more spacious and sunny. Architecture has the potential to shape our experience intimately. Indifferent architecture may be just a "machine for living," but great architecture is an enveloping experience. So it is at Tournus.

There is a second experience on offer there, based again on response to a visible feature: the warm color of the stone. One feels unexpectedly at home in the space, as if one has entered a living organism: Jonah in a whale that means no harm. I could as well say: as if our flesh recognizes the flesh of the sanctuary. But these words are approximate. At times experience laughs at words.

The elaborate, dark pulpit of much later date, winding its way around a column, is an offense to the eye, so out of keeping, but it can help us better see the grand simplicity and warmth of this sanctuary. The sermon is the church itself.

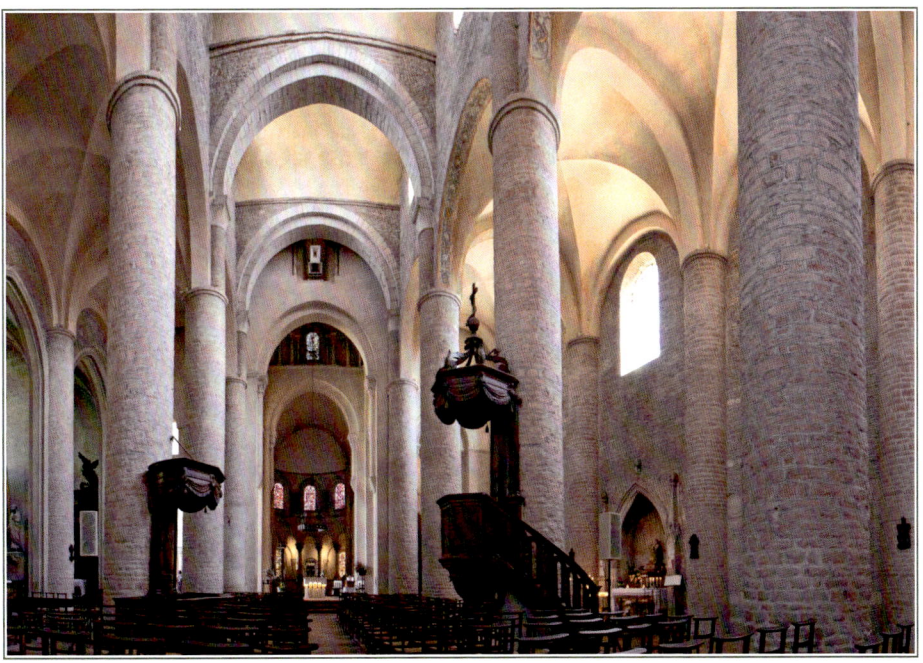

PARENTHESIS: UNIVERSITY AND SPIRITUALITY

This book could not have been written without academic training in the history of art, but not all art historians will recognize in its pages our shared passion for knowledge. There is more than one knowledge. The standards and methods of historical research are a precious acquisition, exemplified by the difference between early nineteenth-century treasure hunters in the sandy sites of Ancient Egypt and archeologists today willing to brush away particles of sand to uncover what a site reveals through fine detail. The disciplines of art history, archeology, and conservation have preserved worlds for us, restored worlds to us.

There is another way of knowing and another need to know, situated in knowledge of the heart and the responsive body in dialogue with works of art. I am certain that virtually all art historians experience these orders of knowledge; it figures strongly in what draws us to one period of art or another, to lifelong specialties that never lose their savor. One could as well speak of love. The great catalogues raisonnés that set the boundaries of a field of inquiry, the seemingly dry surveys, the meticulous explorations of style, patronage and social conditions, of provenance and masters' workshops, are ultimately gestures of love. Where this book and its icons differ from proper art history is its shift toward love of the objects, expressed, and acknowledgment of their teaching power. This is a pilgrim's chronicle for pilgrims. I have studied *about* these objects, as one must; I have also studied *with* them. To that I invite you. Read a dozen books concerning any era of art we touch on in these pages, but bring some of the objects inside as "reminders and supports of contemplation," as a communion with meanings and with men and women even of very distant times and places. Preserve instinct even while learning in depth. Saint-Exupéry, whom I never forget for long: *"Ce qui est dur c'est de sauver l'instinct quand on raisonne"*—what is hard is to preserve instinct when one is reasoning.

Coming as I did from a familial, amateur exploration of art history to a truly great graduate school staffed for the most part by German-Jewish refugees to

America who were among the founders of modern study in their fields, there were bound to be awkward moments and unexpected reconciliations. I have in mind to recount two incidents, but my first duty, gladly discharged, is to thank the faculty members with whom it was such a privilege to work at the Institute of Fine Arts (New York University). The spirit of the place, the *genius loci*, resided in its director Craig Smyth. A "monuments man" during World War II, he completed his education at Princeton University in the post-war years and dedicated himself to Renaissance studies. Other professors who deeply moved me included Richard Krautheimer, an architectural historian endowed with a ferocious love of exact knowledge; Peter von Blanckenhagen, short in stature with a dry voice, who generously opened for me—and for all of his students—the history and character of Greco-Roman sculpture; Günter Kopcke, of the next generation, specialized in early Greek and Mediterranean arts, a man of learning and kindness who became a friend; Colin Eisler, also of the next generation, a true humanist for whom the history of art is a history of human concerns; Richard Ettinghausen, yet another German-Jewish refugee, foremost expert on Islamic art, a field that I perceived as a measurelessly large, magic carpet of figurations and meanings; Erwin Panofsky, the undisputed master of art history and iconography, with whom I studied for only a few months in what sadly proved to be his last seminar; and Stella Kramrisch, the outstanding historian of Indian art of her generation, elderly when I studied with her but retaining the grace of a dancer, nearly floating at the lectern as she introduced us to the notion of *prana*, of breath as a key element in the aesthetic of classical Indian sculpture. There were still others: I operated the slide projector for Alexander Soper, a leading scholar of Chinese art, simply to have the privilege of hearing him on a field I wouldn't be formally studying. It was a golden age, and a golden school for art-historical study. All my thanks. I was not your best student, but I was devoted.

Prior to acceptance as a student, my interview with an Institute faculty member was something of a shot across the bow. Opposite me sat the redoubtable Professor Willibald Sauerländer, German of the next generation and already famed, as he would remain, for work in fields reaching well past our topic that afternoon, Western medieval art. He struck me at the time as a physically imposing man with cool eyes; no paternal welcome there. I told him that I planned to major in medieval art and evoked my summers of travel to the main monuments and hidden treasures of France. I must have expressed regard for sculpture encountered in rural chapels, small churches, and such. Now, he was a world-renowned historian and interpreter of great works; he apparently wasn't one to search the map for out-of-the-way places with decorations by itinerant guilds of craftsmen. "You aren't going to tell me," he said, "that because it's primitive it's better?" I had no such notion, but he must have detected in me an inclination already toward knowledge of the heart and sensation. That would have little place in the Institute curriculum. Anyway, I was admitted.

I was as ferocious in my efforts to learn as every Institute student, and we were all greatly dedicated. We were working with masters of our fields; there was no time to lose. Two years later, studying that summer for oral exams—a rite of passage—at a rented home near Yale Divinity School, I would wander up the hill to the Divinity School library and spend time in the stacks where students had their carrels lined with books on what I took to be high topics, God and man and such. It dawned on me that I had reached a turning point. Would I continue studying to become an academic medievalist—the direction I had been following. Or, more difficult and full of unknowns, could I turn my doctoral dissertation toward the writings and fascinating multi-cultural life of Ananda K. Coomaraswamy. It would be an exploration of a modern scholar—his dates were 1877 - 1947—who had plunged into what he called traditional studies encompassing Asian and Western art, scripture and commentary, and an underlying polemical point of view that rejected what he viewed as the superficiality of modern values. Coomaraswamy had steadily occupied the background as I pursued graduate study. There were united in him and in his scholarly work the primacy of exact knowledge and deepest respect for the metaphysic—the scripture and commentary, attitudes and rituals of making—which gives birth to the best of religious art. I was hungry for another sort of art history than I had been gratefully learning. Could background become foreground?

Formally securing faculty permission to research and write such a dissertation was a difficult process. The faculty seems to have divided evenly. I wasn't made aware of its internal discussions, but three advocates emerged: Professors Kramrisch and Ettinghausen, who had known and admired Coomaraswamy in his lifetime, and of all people the Institute's director, Craig Smyth, who must have thought that it would be interesting to have under his roof a dissertation that used the tools of biography and the history of ideas. It fell to him to inform me that my proposal had been accepted and that I was to work under the guidance of Professor Kramrisch, naturally, and Robert Goldwater, the scholar of Modern art with whom, as it happens, I had little prior acquaintance. That would do. I have never forgotten the gentle smile with which Craig Smyth gave me that news. All my thanks. Dr. Goldwater told me soon after that he regarded Coomaraswamy as a "second-class mind." He must have been conscripted into the role of thesis adviser; Dr. Kramrisch needed no conscripting. No matter, over time he was most helpful.

The challenge, a gift from the Institute, was to learn everything I could from and about Coomaraswamy and to shape that knowledge into a dissertation fully in keeping with the values of the school. Late in life, in an article that it was my privilege to publish for the first time, Coomaraswamy asked a question that captures the dual path, which is one, that I had started down.[13] "Can we imagine," he asked, "a perfected ardor apart from understanding, or a perfected understanding without ardor?"

It is a distant goal. But I can imagine.

23. ULTREIA!

Reliquary: Christ Crucified
Late 10th – 11th century CE, polychrome on olive wood
St.-Michel d'Aiguilhe (Le Puy-en-Velay, southern France)
Length of the cross: slightly more than 10 inches
Sources: (principal image) Peter Willi / Bridgeman Images; (general view)
Wikipedia / Daniel Giffard

The full expression, from a 12th-century book, would be "Ultre ia Et Sus teia, Deus adjuva nos!"—Go further and go higher, God help us! Le Puy was one of four points of departure in France for pilgrims making the 500-mile journey on foot to Santiago de Compostela, burial place of the patron saint of Spain, the apostle James, brother of John. In a beautiful Romanesque chapel in Le Puy, perched on a volcanic core, masons restoring its medieval altar in 1955 discovered a previously unknown circular cavity con-

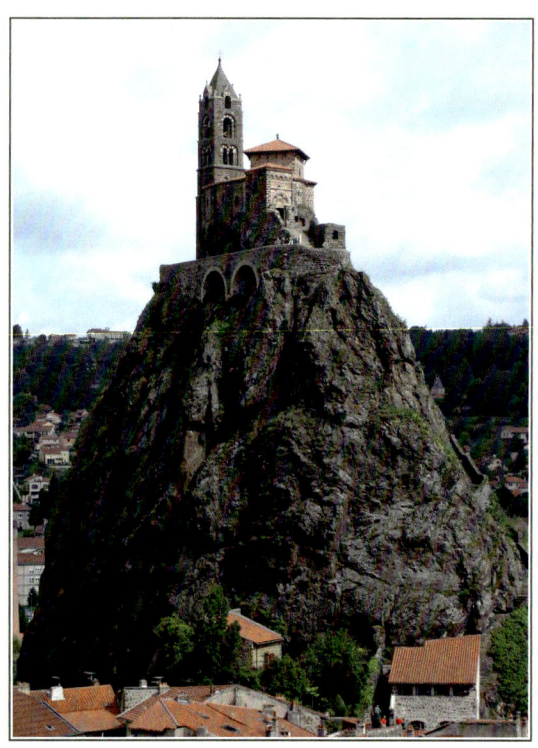

taining reliquaries and other holy survivals from centuries earlier. It was normal, and remains so in many Roman Catholic and Orthodox churches, to place relics of saints within or below altars. Among the finds at St.-Michel d'Aiguilhe (aptly named St. Michael of the Needle) was an exquisite polychrome carving of Christ Crucified, a reliquary with an opening at the back for whatever the priests of that day wished to associate with the altar.

When I visited the chapel decades ago, I recall gazing raptly at this small sculpture. It has permanently fixed the image of the crucifixion in my mind: not the suffering,

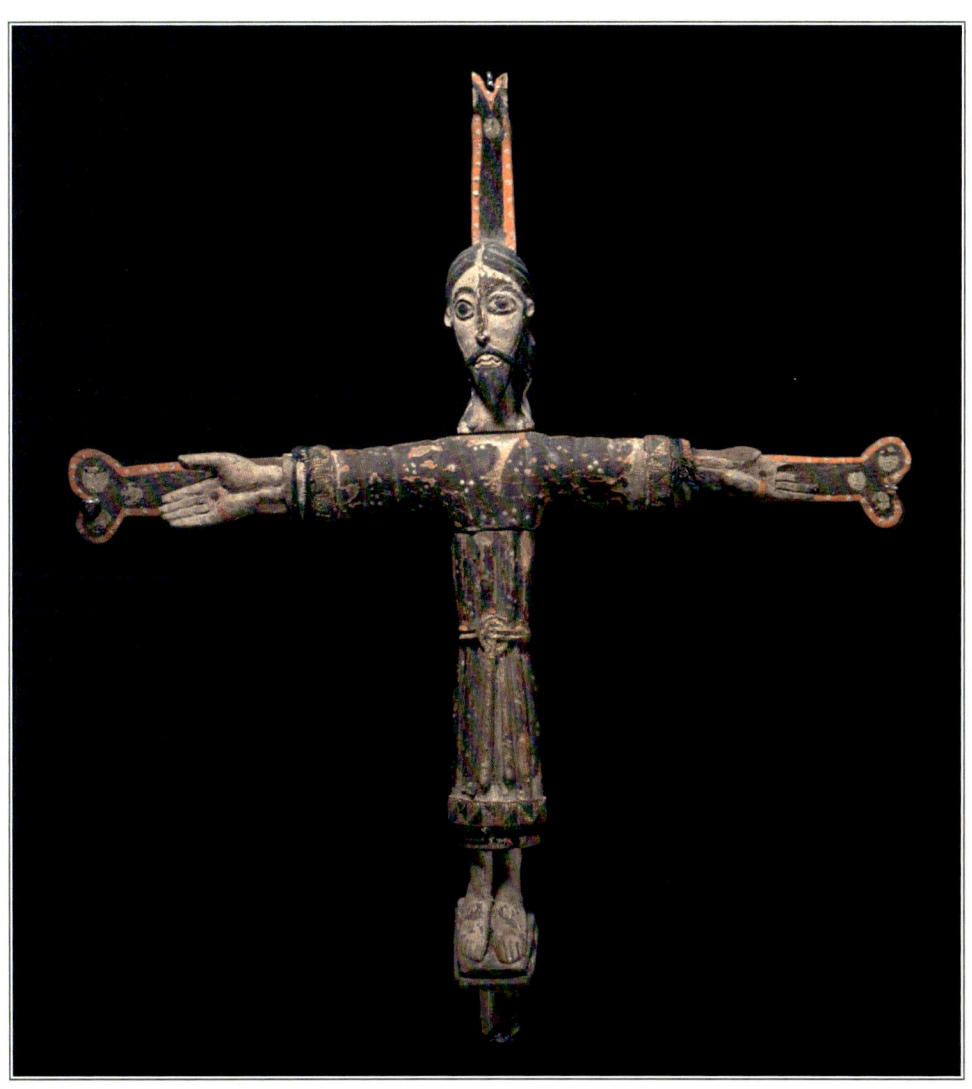

tormented Jesus; not the nearly naked Jesus of later periods of art, which call attention to flesh; not Jesus dead, no. None of that drama. Instead, a serene, saddened, quietly conscious image of the incarnate God on whom pain and death have been imposed by society that knows not what it does.

Christ here looks out at us, as if to say: see what you have done, see who I am. The figure is nearly doll-like and elicits our natural compassion for small living things. Yet knowing choices have been made by the anonymous artist and his clerical patrons. The long gown, sash, and details of the sleeves and hem reflect a representational tradition rooted in Christian Syria, likely flowing up the pilgrimage route from Spain.

It must have been a moment of emotion when this touching image, charged with who knows what relics, was deposited in the darkness of the altar interior, presumably never to be seen again. Just one eloquent icon from a great religious tradition can imply very much about the tradition as a whole. There is a visual poem here about submission to what must be accepted and vast awareness of the order of things divine and human. Ultreia.

24. SACRED NARRATIVE

The Magi Awakened
Artist: Gislebertus
ca. 1130 CE
Cathedral of Saint-Lazare, Autun (Burgundy)
Source: (principal image) Wikimedia Commons / Cancre; (secondary image)
Wikipedia / Zairon

We have so few names of medieval artists, and perhaps it doesn't need to matter to us as it didn't matter to them. Local acknowledgment must have been quite enough. But at Autun we have a name, Gislebertus, to associate with the sculpture and storytelling genius throughout the cathedral. Old theory: this is the artist's name. New theory: it is the donor's name. For simplicity, I'm content with the old theory. We are now in the High Romanesque period, the 12th century, when France

became dressed in works of art and architecture that survive to this day, making much of the nation a landscape of story. Some parts of that story are biblical or based on familiar legend, as here the immense Last Judgment at the main west portal and the much smaller carving in the interior of the Magi or Three Kings, delicately awakened by an angel who indicates the star they must follow to Bethlehem.

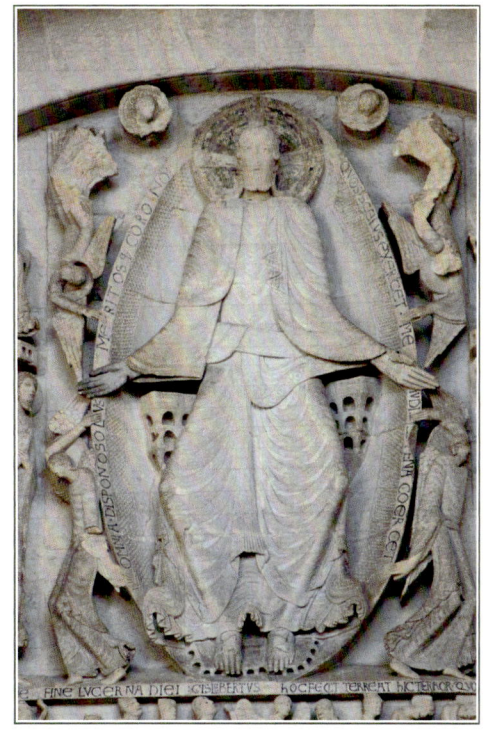

Romanesque art was a magnet for all things interesting, and it all appears in carved portals and capitals, in paintings on walls and vaults: biblical narratives and visions, riddling symbolic images borrowed

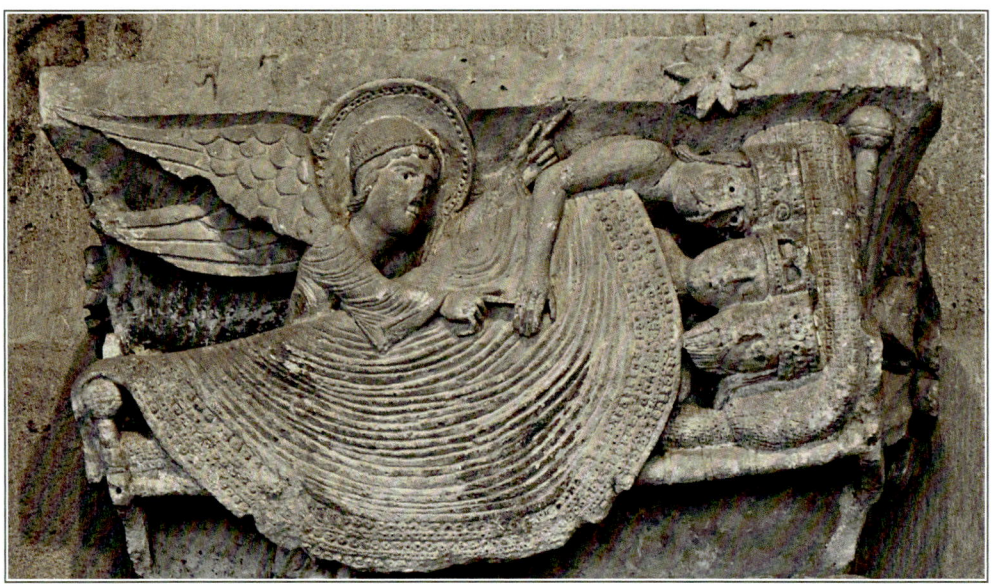

from the East, animals of every kind real and imagined, astrologic symbols, creatures lovely and loathsome that stirred the medieval imagination. The energy for representation in that era was remarkable, supported by sufficient wealth, willing donors, and skilled workers. Few people other than clergy and aristocrats could read books, but everyone could read the visual encyclopedia of the Romanesque church.

Even had we no name, Gislebertus would stand out. His ability to reimagine familiar scenes and personages, and to endow them with warmth, humanity and charm, is instantly recognizable. Though they are kings (and could afford separate beds), for dramatic purpose Gislebertus has economically bunked them together under a superb quilt. The angel's delicate touch, elegant finger to hand, awakens just one king: his eyes open, while the others still sleep. This is the beginning of the story, so well told, and a classic image of awakening in the larger sense of the word.

Gislebertus is more than a warm-hearted storyteller in stone. His image of Christ in Majesty at the Last Judgment, surrounded by souls blessed and damned, is, as it should be, awe-inspiring. These two icons, of Christ at the end of time and the awakening Magi, can only suggest the further riches of Autun Cathedral. We encounter an immensely gifted artist. *Gislebertus hoc fecit*, he wrote into the stone: Gislebertus made this.

25. THE SINAI ICON: CHRIST PANTOCRATOR

Encaustic on wood panel, 33 vertical inches
Mid-6th century CE
St. Catherine Monastery, Mount Sinai
Produced in Constantinople during the reign of Justinian
Source: Wikipedia / public domain

The Divine Ladder of Ascent (manuscript illumination)
12th century CE
Source: Wikipedia / public domain

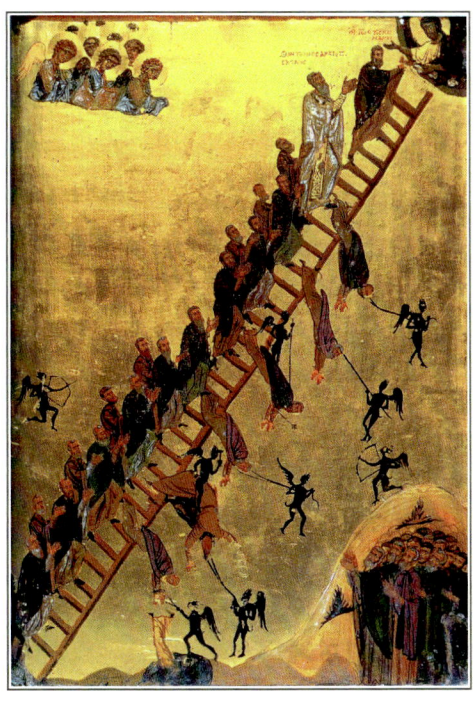

St. Catherine's Monastery, a fortified, high-walled compound of the mid-6th century, sits at the foot of Mt. Sinai in the unforgiving desert of the Sinai Peninsula. It is a treasure house of ancient Greek Orthodox liturgy, monastic custom, and unique art and literature, with the oldest continually functioning library in the world and a storehouse of two thousand icons. Not least, St. Catherine's shelters the spot traditionally believed to be where Moses encountered the Burning Bush—and a living bush, said to be progeny of the ancient one, serves as a focus of prayer and wonder. The life of the monastery over its 1500 years is vividly illustrated by a well-known icon in its collection, The Ladder of Divine Ascent (late 13th century), dramatizing the thirty ascending steps of religious practice and the danger of falling from grace into the hellish realm of demons. The basis for this

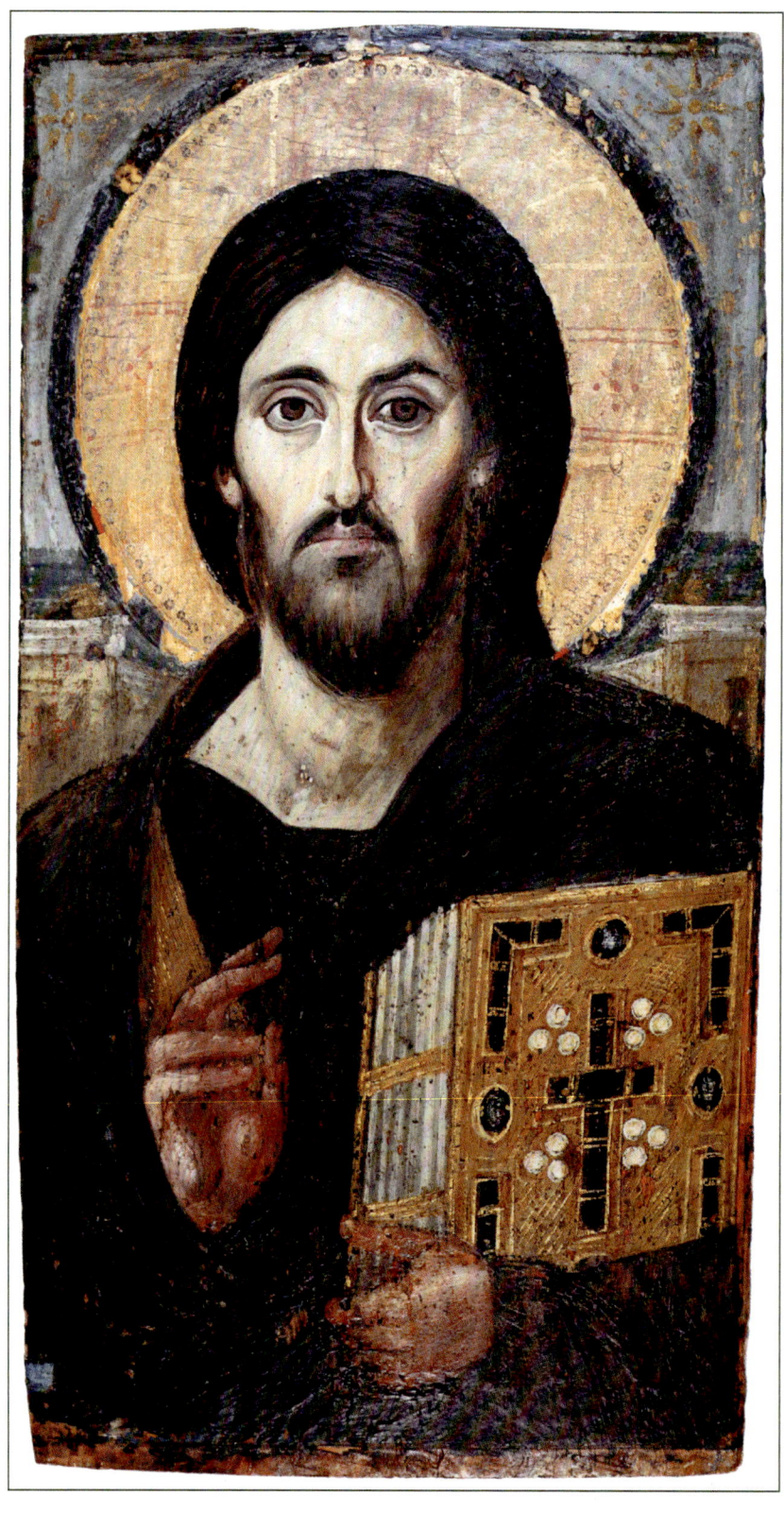

unforgettable image is a book of ca. 600 CE, written by the abbot of that time, known as John Climacus, John of the Ladder. "Take up your seat on a high place and watch," he wrote, "if only you know how, and then you will see in what manner, when, whence, how many and what kind of thieves come to enter and steal your clusters of grapes."

In this intensely rich world of religion, the icon of Christ the All-Ruler occupies a unique place. Protected from harm by the geographic remoteness of St. Catherine's, it is thought to reflect a lost icon of Constantinople, the center of Roman power in the East, an icon that once surmounted the entrance to the imperial palace. This vision of Christ, in its original Constantinopolitan version, became the model for innumerable paintings, sculpture, and even coinage throughout the medieval world: a noble, kingly figure; both distant, heavenly judge and "one of us," involved in our fate as human beings and caring that we find our way. You won't miss the deliberate difference between the right and left eyes. Scholars speak of the right eye, on the side where Christ extends a blessing, as gazing into our world with compassion. Of the left eye, associated with the Gospels cradled in his left arm, they offer the view that it reflects Christ's distance from us, his role as judge, his belonging to another world than ours. Of this interpretation I have never been certain, though I grasp its logic. The right eye strikes me as unyielding, the left as more open, appalled, and approachable: our link to his greatness. See what you think, what you feel. However that may be, it is a privilege to come into the presence of this icon.

26. RUBLEV: CHRIST THE SAVIOR

Artist: Andrei Rublev
Egg tempera on wood
ca. 1410 CE, vertical dimension 62 inches
Tretyakov Gallery, Moscow
Source: Album / Alamy Stock Photo

"Arise now before me, you iconographers. . . . Let me be conquered by your pictures!" The speaker is St. Basil the Great, fourth-century bishop in Asia Minor, famed preacher and theologian, founder of Eastern monasticism. The worship environment of Orthodox Christianity is saturated with icons. They are windows open on another world, and their painted images of the Savior and holy family, sacred narrative, saints, and martyrs are understood to be endowed with some part of the presence of those personages. Properly composed and painted, Orthodox icons aren't flat, passive visions; they are active sources of blessing and reminder. "Properly composed" means in keeping with the traditions governing any particular image: there is powerful consistency from region to region, century to century. St. George always looks like St. George precisely, the dragon he conquers always curls just so beneath his horse.

Yet within these constraints, there are shifts in sensibility and style. Great artists can appear, make their signs, find acceptance, and move on without upsetting the continuity. One such, the greatest of Russian icon painters, was the monk Andrei Rublev (ca. 1360s – ca. 1430 CE). This icon of the Savior from his hand was originally one element in a "Deesis," a horizontal range of sacred images mounted on the high screen that separates the holiest part of a church from the larger space where the congregation gathers. It is fortunately preserved in a museum, like many icons no longer in the settings for which they were created. That is not an indifferent fact: once, at the Tretyakov Gallery in Moscow, I was unable to approach a venerated icon because two men of middle years were praying before it. They refused, so to speak, to release it to secular circumstance. I couldn't help but recall Coomaraswamy's

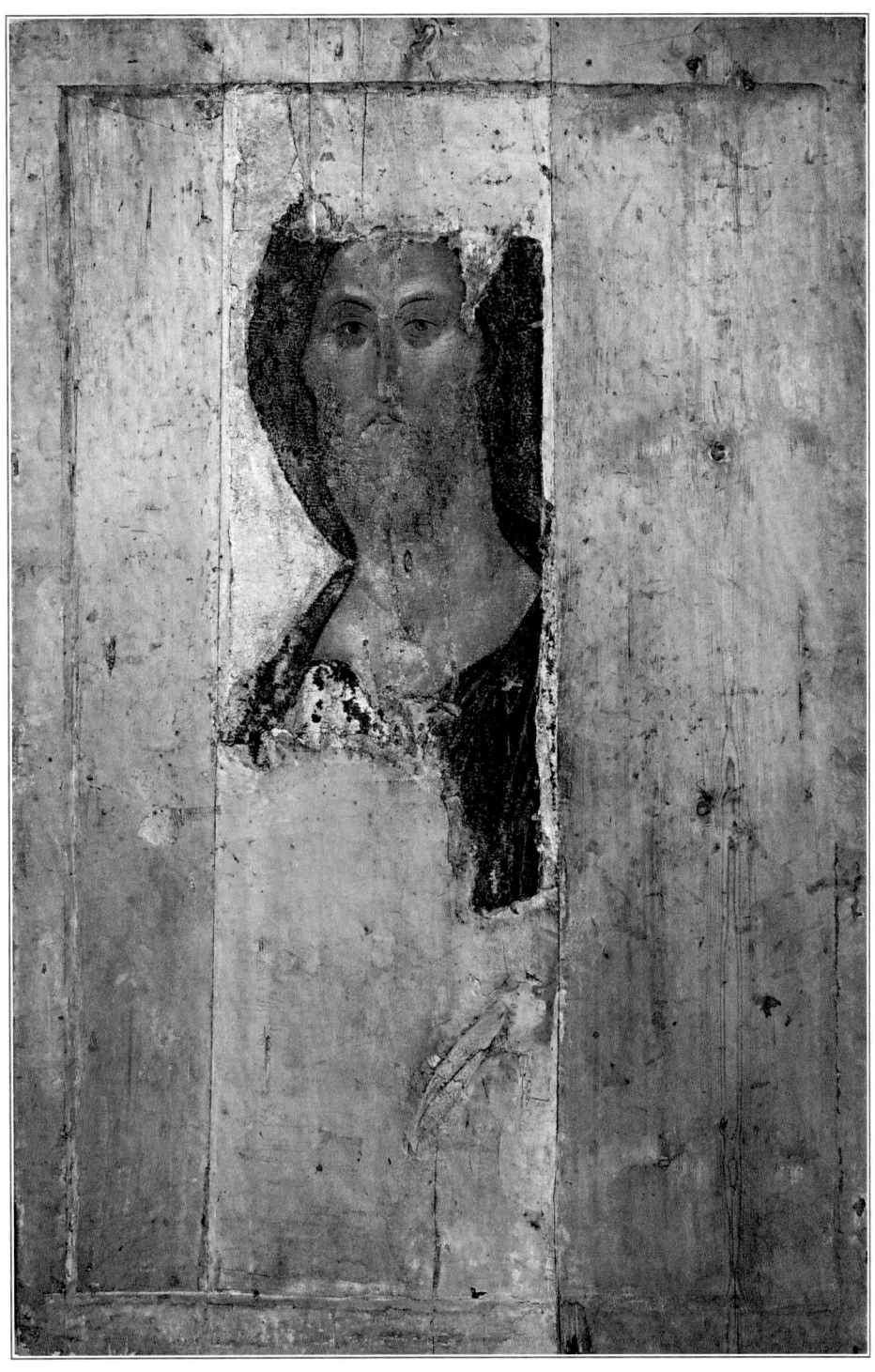

melancholy reflection that museums represent something like the moraine left by a receding glacier, a deposit of displaced objects no longer serving their original purpose.

I have seen this icon. To affirm this has some flavor of accepting an obligation. St. Basil had a point: to come before a truly great icon in Orthodox tradition is to be conquered—not necessarily to adopt particular religious beliefs but to adopt anew and again the shared burdens of what we are, where we are. The conversion is to humanity. In historical perspective, and despite its fragmented condition, you can see that Rublev's vision of the Savior is in the tradition of the Sinai Christ, which in turn reflects the lost Constantinopolitan icon; the lineage is intact. But who can miss what is new here? Majestic seriousness, unwavering concentration, eyes searching us, uncompromising yet reassuring in the sense that there *is* a link between high and low, between the Savior and ourselves, however great the distance and the implicit challenge to be all that we can be and to serve.

At times an icon collection, seemingly a civilized and quiet thing, catches fire.

27. AGHT'AMAR: THE OLD MAN WHO . . .

Detail of low-relief frieze
Cathedral of the Holy Cross
Aght'amar (situated on an island in Lake Van, eastern Turkey)
Mid-10th century CE
Source: Sirarpie Der Nersessian, *Aght'amar: Church of the Holy Cross*
Harvard University Press, Cambridge MA, 1965

View of the church
Source: Wikimedia Commons / Flickr, Ioez Deniel

I want to start by acknowledging a friend, the late Paul Koralek, who with a team of fellow English architects, young in 1956, made the first comprehensive photo survey of this remarkable monument.[14] Their work remains invaluable. This is a cathedral on an island, once the center of a monastic complex and royal residence that has left few other traces. We are in the Armenian

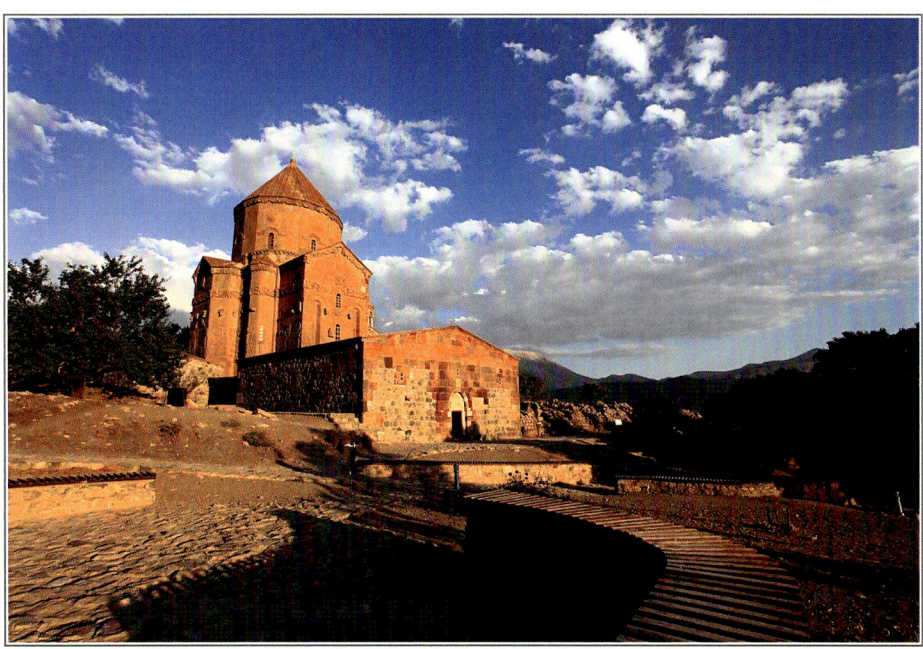

kingdom of Vaspurakan in the time of King Gagik I Artsruni. Every name here is more than likely to be unfamiliar, but when you look at the low-relief sculpture populating the cathedral's outer walls, you will know at once that we are in a devout, brilliantly creative and energized Christian world. An Internet inquiry will show you much more than can be illustrated here.

I have chosen from the narrow horizontal band toward the top of the wall a figure I can only call "The old man who . . .". Or it may be that he chose me years ago. Looking at this image in the context of our growing icon collection, I realize that the central icon of my youth was the Visigothic eagle, the Sunbird (p. 56); it captured much of my aspiration and, though I didn't know it, also reflected something of my naiveté. It is a raptor who will do no harm. But now, and for many years, "the old man who . . ." speaks to me, asks me

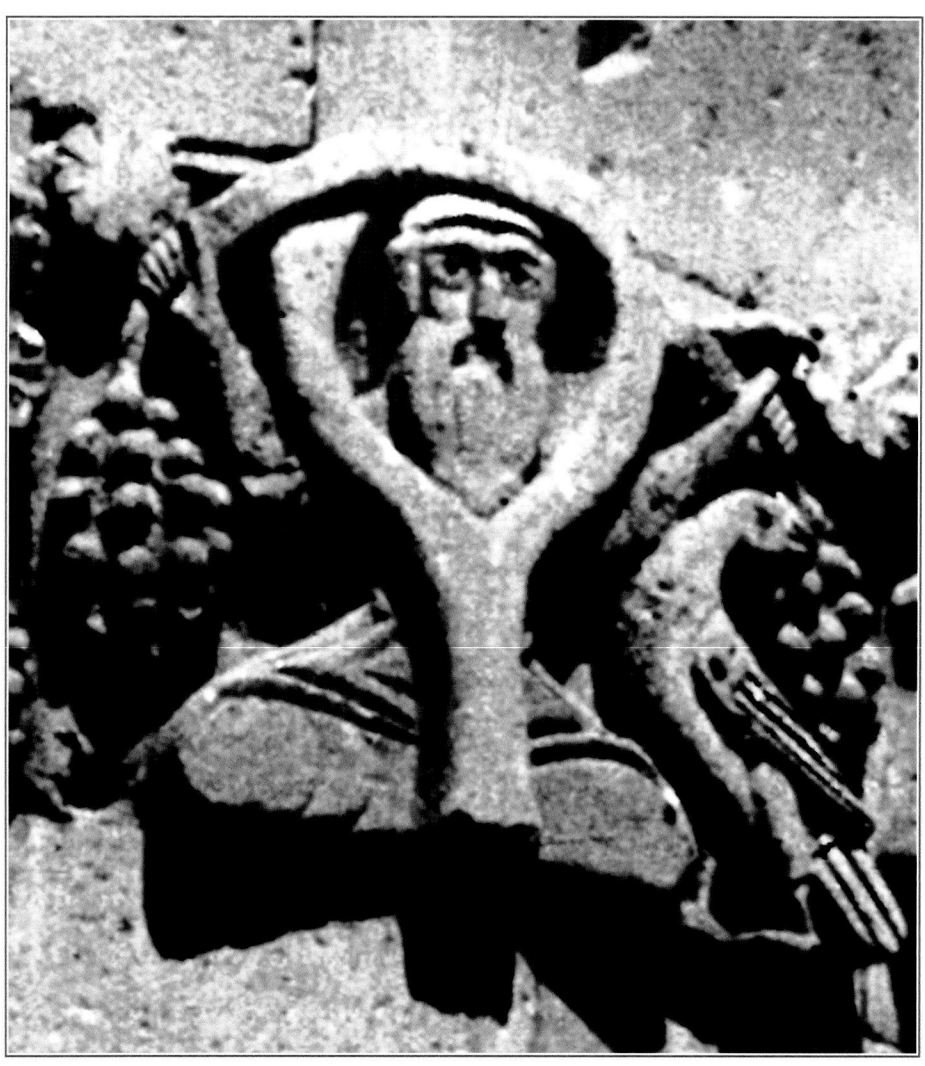

to see things straight and to be willing to strive without going any place in particular.

Some pages ago I mentioned that French and Spanish Romanesque sculpture—the art of the 11th and 12th centuries—was a magnet for imagery from many different sources. A figured textile from the Muslim world, a Coptic Christian gospel from Egypt, patterned jewelry or an ivory carving from Byzantium—it all found new places in new versions in Romanesque art. There were often mysterious images to which we no longer have the key—and perhaps there never was a key other than pleasure in mystery. "The old man who . . ." is of that kind.

His pose and expression bring to mind the teaching of the Law of Three in Gurdjieff's vision of the world: always affirmation and denial, always yes and no contesting, and always at hand the possibility of a third force of reconciliation which understands the other two and brings harmony. "The old man who. . ." strikes me as a demonstration, a vivid QED, that the third force remains always a work in progress: we have to be there for it and care for it. Like the old man.

PARENTHESIS: THE GLOBAL TRINITY

We should speak of the global trinity: Christ on the Cross, Buddha seated in meditation, Shiva Lord of the Dance. While other living religions preserve compelling signs of their beliefs and traditions, Christianity, Buddhism, and Hinduism have cast into the world, and into minds and hearts, three images based on the human figure which belong together without a trace of uneasiness—at least now this can be so, if not in earlier centuries. They have comparable spiritual and moral weight; they have been given material form innumerable times by gifted artists; they are lifelong "reminders and supports of contemplation" for whoever looks toward them for inspiration, solace, and direction. The next three entries in this book of icons pay homage to each member of the global trinity and give voice, however little, to the endless dialogue between them.

But first there is an issue to explore: crossing with confidence the boundaries between great religious traditions and their arts. I often remember Diogenes the Cynic, the fourth-century BCE Greek philosopher; he is a touchstone of courage, truth-telling, and wild freedom of mind. Something of a vagrant among the Greek city-states, Diogenes acknowledged no citizenship but one: citizen of the world, *cosmopolitan*. We owe him that word. "Asked where he came from, he said, 'I am a citizen of the world'"— so it is recorded in the brief, fascinating biography of the philosopher by a much later author, Diogenes Laertius. That word, that condition of mind and heart, is inviting— but it needn't mean rootless and without allegiance. Each of us is rooted in a home culture; it can't be otherwise and needn't be. But a sound home culture in our time is also a passport: it is open to other cultures, touched by what one learns of them through dialogue, study, or travel. A sound home culture teaches openness, not as a designated morality but through warmth, welcome, curiosity, respect for "the other," and today there are many others across the globe. We are "the other" to others. No home culture is complete; they are all sketches toward humanity. To be cosmopolitan means to feel at home wherever common decency is respected. It means unreserved acknowledgment of the ideas and constellation of images important to others and willingness to enter into their world-views as if they were one's own. Yet they are not quite one's own—not in the way that one's home culture is. I am pointing to a lively place, the place of dialogue.

Deeper and wider vision can't help but grow through the encounter with the central icons of other cultures. For example: I am immersed in Judeo-Christian and Greco-Roman culture, my mind and heart are filled with the words and imagery of the circle around Socrates and his heirs (among them, Diogenes); with the passionate dispassion of the Stoic authors of later Antiquity; with the teachings, moods, and lyrical language of the two bibles "old" and "new"; with music from the warm austerity of plainchant through Bach and Italy and Vienna to our own time; with world literature; and, as you can imagine, with the art of the West from the Hera of Samos (p. 4) forward and back. This is my home culture, a world unto itself, grand and inexhaustible.

But there are other meanings and imperatives right alongside in other cultural worlds; other fundamental persons and stories and the images that make them visible. Think of Buddha, the Awakened One. Like the image of Christ Crucified, the image of Buddha seated in meditation has a permanent place in the sensibility not only of Buddhist practitioners but of nearly everyone with the good fortune and freedom to encounter it thoughtfully. The foundational tale of young Prince Siddhartha, to whom all pleasant things are available, yet who realizes that ours is a world of suffering and sets a rigorous course toward awakening, is a perfect parallel to the tale of Jesus of Nazareth, of his firmness, healing presence, teachings, and self-sacrifice. Both Christ and the Buddha show the Way for any and all who are hungry to set out on a Way. They fill out a shared cosmos of meanings, offer two versions of the search for essential knowledge, fulfilled being, and what Buddhist scripture calls "right action" in the world. I wouldn't want a world without these two icons, Christ Crucified and Buddha seated in meditation; through them we are told the tale of ourselves with astonishing depth and force. And each of these icons points toward the large and long tradition it represents, the nearly infinite elaboration of each tradition over time. The Ladder of Ascent, both Christian and Buddhist, is richly populated with teachers, teachings, and tales, with shared liturgies and private meditations.

What, then, of Shiva Nataraja, Lord of the Dance, the third element of the global trinity? What perfect, missing note is added by the image of Shiva dancing? Shiva is divine energy itself, patterned as a dance. Every object in his hands, every gesture, every feature of the traditional composition is a coded meaning that knowledgeable Hindus can read. He is the maker of Creation and the will behind Destruction, thus the master of cycles of time—yet free and beyond this or any other defining world. One sees that freedom in his posture and complex balance, in his expression. His is an image that can be read as if it were a text, but it is not just text: it is a force, modeling, if we dare, the dance of our own lives. Just as Christ invites us to accept and transcend suffering, and as the Buddha invites us to sit in deepest quiet to understand all things about our world and ourselves, Lord Shiva invites us to dance, however awkwardly.

Thomas Merton, a cosmopolitan Christian of our time who crossed cultural borders without fear and with love, turned at the end of his book *New Seeds of Contemplation* to the image of divine dance. I'm sure he was remembering biblical Proverbs 8, but what else was he drawing on? "The Lord plays and diverts Himself in the garden of His creation," he wrote, "and if we could let go of our own obsession with what we think is the meaning of it all, we might be able to hear His call and follow Him in His mysterious, cosmic dance. . . . The world and time are the dance of the Lord in emptiness. . . . No despair of ours can alter the reality of things, or stain the joy of the cosmic dance which is always there. . . . We are invited to . . . join in the general dance."[15] There is as much or more of Lord Shiva in these lovely words as there is of Merton's home culture in monastic Christianity.

One further thought is needed: about the beauty or aesthetic power of images of the global trinity from the hands and minds of great artists, whether or not tradition has preserved their names. Coomaraswamy once wrote that "beauty is the attractive power of perfection." The artists who have given us the three images now following in this book undoubtedly meditated at length, envisioned at length, and fashioned their materials at length to endow their work with the greatest possible beauty as they understood beauty. Not for purposes of seduction in any sense, but to show God and sacredness within the human figure—within us. The aesthetic power of images from across the world, expressing many different cultures, makes it more possible for us, whatever our home culture may be, to open a dialogue that need never end.

I have had the sad occasion to attend two Hindu funerals in recent years. They were perfect in all respects: the Sanskrit chants and available translations, the priests' clothing, customs honoring the departed, the homage of young people singing and playing Indian stringed instruments, the arrangement of all things from flowers to much else. So very rich. And what struck me after a time is that there was no mention of Jesus or of Moses, no text from

St. Paul or psalms, no Lord's Prayer or Kaddish. This tradition was entirely independent and entirely suited to purpose.

Similarly, it has been a joy and an education from time to time to attend Sunday liturgy and meditation in a Zen Buddhist temple. The rhythmic chants, the instrumentation of drum and bell, the prolonged silence of sittings, the sermon often focused on the meaning of explosive eighth-century conversations between teachers and students, the sole image on the altar of Lord Buddha: entirely independent, entirely suited to purpose.

Neither setting had much to do with my home culture. Each was and is entirely sufficient. Each can help a man or woman awaken to what we are and what we must.

28. THE GLOBAL TRINITY: CHRIST CRUCIFIED

The Batlló Majesty
Mid-12ᵗʰ century, polychrome wood
61 inches vertical
Museu Nacional d'Art de Catalunya, Barcelona
Source : Wikipedia / Roger Ferrer Ibáñez

With reverence for this touching work of art, I must write that it strikes me as a celebration. Some elements are now familiar: as in the little reliquary crucifixion at Le Puy (p. 71), we encounter again the dignified, saddened, awakened face of Jesus; this work is not about physical pain, it is about the immeasurable, heartfelt pain remembered in the words of Luke 23:34: "Father, forgive them for they know not what they do." Yet the beautiful red, blue, and yellow painted fabric of the Lord's tunic—in part based on cinnebar and lapis lazuli, rare pigments—and the extension of those uplifting colors to the Cross itself signals that we are invited to a party beyond all imaginable parties, celebration of the fulfillment of an earthly mission that would change the world. A crucifixion of this type in Catalonia and southern France is called a Majesty with good reason. This is the outstanding example, likely from the region of Girona (northeast of Barcelona), contributed to the museum by a generous donor, Enric Battló, whose name accompanies it.

There is a charming legend surrounding images of this type, which carry forward a model originating in the ancient city of Lucca, just west of Florence: the Volto Santo or Holy Face, late eighth or ninth century, again a life-size crucifixion, comparable in some respects to the Batlló Majesty although by far darker in mood. The Volto Santo attracted pilgrims from far and wide because it was said to have been carved soon after the crucifixion by Nicodemus, the appealing elderly companion of Jesus who helped lay him to rest (John 19). Not only that, but one evening Nicodemus had in mind to carve the head the next day—and when he awoke it had been miraculously finished to perfection. We encounter here the notion of the True Portrait—reason enough to make

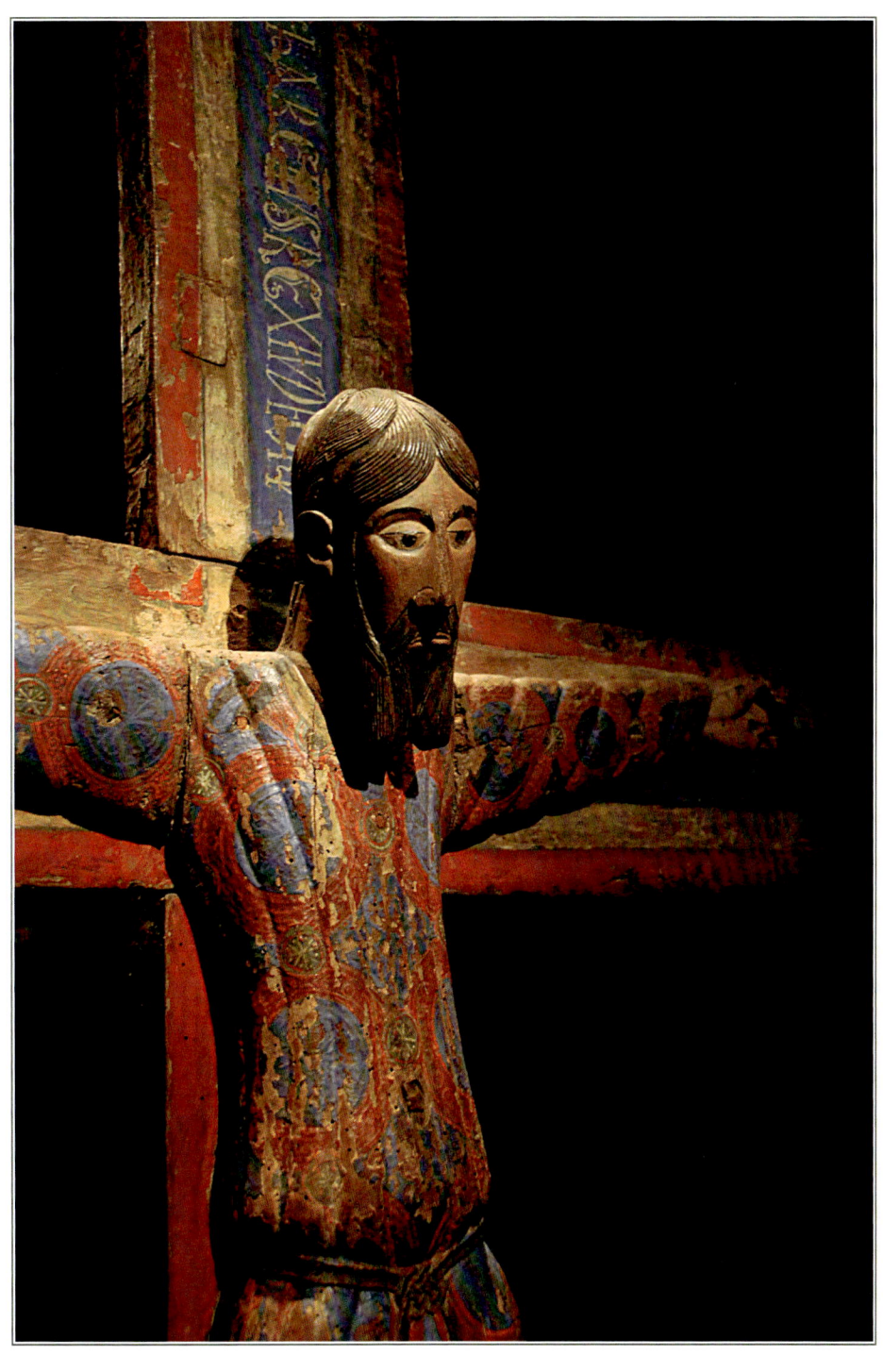

the pilgrimage to Lucca. There is a similar current of legend and conviction, especially in Eastern Orthodoxy, concerning images thought to be "not made by human hands," *acheiropoieta*. The characterization of the holy figure, be it Jesus, Mary the Mother of God, or another, is shifted upward from human to miraculous authorship. In the West, the Shroud of Turin bearing the image of the entombed Christ is the most familiar example. There is something quite arresting in this drive to authenticate key images by placing their origin beyond ken—as if we humans can't be trusted to get things right.

In an example notable for its quiet beauty and compelling message, this is the first member of the global trinity.

29. The global trinity: Buddha in meditation

> Samadhi Buddha
> 4th – 6th century CE
> Height: slightly more than 7 feet, dolomite marble
> Later 19th-century photograph
> The sculpture is now in Mahamevnawa Park, Anuradhapura, Sri Lanka
> Source: W. L. H. Skeen, 1870

There are much more elaborate images of the Buddha preserved in Buddhist lands from India and the Himalayas to Southeast Asia, China, Japan, and Indonesia. The most memorable of those carvings, bronze castings, and paintings are majestic, altogether beautiful, and often endowed with symbolic detail conveying a firmament of meanings. I have stood, stilled and awed, before some of these images. Yet when I search my memory for the single image that embodies, at least by implication, the entire Buddhist tradition, it is this one.

I have deliberately chosen a photograph dating to the rediscovery of this sculpture. It was overturned in the forest, forgotten for centuries, and somewhat damaged. In the photograph it has been summarily set upright; the seated boy gives the scale. Today this sculpture is sheltered in an elegant open-air pavilion, damage repaired, revered by Buddhists fortunate to find their way to Anuradhapura. Scholars believe that it was one of four comparable images set around a bodhi tree—the tree (in far-away North India) under which the Buddha in meditation attained Enlightenment. It may once have been sheathed in gold with gemstone eyes. So many differences from its time of origin, and yet a masterwork just as it is.

Meditation, for which Buddhism has provided a model and teachings throughout well more than two millennia, strikes me as the barest thing there is. However structured or unstructured by traditional guidelines, it is an encounter of oneself with oneself. It asks for courage and humility; it asks the question "Who am I?" without presuming to answer in advance or once and for all; it asks the meditator to appreciate the process of turning toward

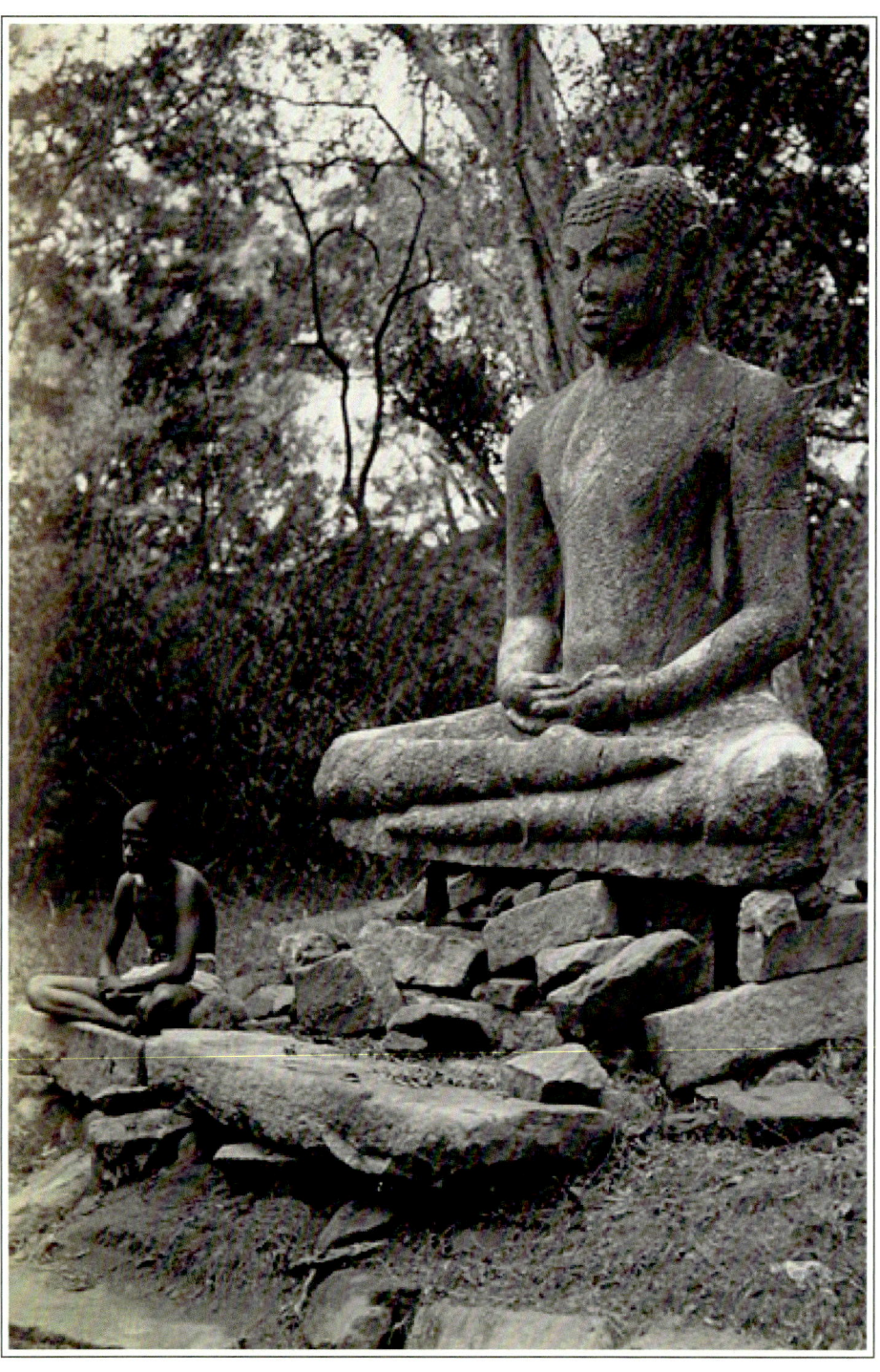

oneself and to recognize as self-serving any thought of where the process should lead. It is an unassisted leap, a request for nothing but the truth. It doesn't acknowledge superficial differences between people—skin color, sexual orientation, wealth or class or accent, none of that. It is an invitation to rejoin the essential human, to rejoin who and what we were before we became what Coomaraswamy often called "this man so-and-so." And the "picture" of all this is something like the Samadhi Buddha. It is scarcely a picture at all; the events are internal.

I have long been fascinated by the language of the Pali Canon, the set of three "baskets" of early Buddhist writings codified at about the time this sculpture was carved. The great commentator on these writings was Buddhagosa, also of that period. He was an incredibly exacting intellectual and religious seeker, one of whose main works is entitled *The Path of Purification*. The language of the Canon, which claims relation with how the Buddha taught in his lifetime (6th – 5th century BCE), has a great love of repetition, through which a thought is focused, insisted upon, and more easily remembered in an oral tradition only later consigned to writing. For example, this passage from Buddhagosa (where the Buddha is referred to as Gotama):

> While the Blessed One was living at Sávatthì,
> it seems, a certain deity came to him in the night,
> and in order to do away with his
> doubts, he asked this question:
> "The inner tangle and the outer tangle—
> This generation is entangled in a tangle.
> And so I ask of Gotama this question:
> Who succeeds in disentangling this tangle?"

That is the question, and this second element of the Global Trinity suggests a strong response.

30. THE GLOBAL TRINITY: SHIVA, LORD OF THE DANCE

Tamil Nadu (southeast India), Chola period, ca. 950 – 1000 CE
Height: 30 inches; copper alloy
Los Angeles County Museum of Art
Source: Art Resource NY

The choice here is a taste or a plunge. It is reasonable to learn just enough to set a light structure around the natural response of admiration and wonder elicited by this icon. That is a taste, and all we can hope for on this page. The plunge, more than worthwhile, is to explore scholarship that begins with a groundbreaking essay by Coomaraswamy (1918),[16] who first brought this icon to wide attention, and goes on from there in recent decades to reexamine the history, meanings, links with myth and text, and transformations of the image. The result has been a rich new understanding, a careful homage to Lord Shiva.

An eighth-century text, cited by Stella Kramrisch in her book *The Presence of Śiva*, can set the stage for us. Shiva is speaking: "I am the originator, the god abiding in supreme bliss. I, the yogi, dance eternally." Kramrisch continues: "Nataraja, the lord of dancers, dancing, shows . . . his divine totality. . . . [He] dances the cosmos into existence, upholds its existence, and dances it out of existence. . . . There is no end to Shiva's dance, it disperses . . . his fiery energy and glory in his world."[17] Elsewhere Kramrisch refers to "the unfathomable mystery of the image of Shiva Nataraja." So be it. Still, the image is before us and, like all pilgrims whether of great learning or none, we can move closer.

Closer to a sacred figure which is both a beautifully realized sculpture and the bearer of a view of cosmos and human experience encoded in every centimeter. Shiva's dance has a name, *ananda tandava*: bliss and ferocity, translated by some scholars as "ferocious bliss." The ferocious energy relates both to his cosmic role of creator, preserver, destroyer and renewer of worlds, and to his role in some myths as a god who quite liked to dance among the ashes at cremation sites; not squeamish, this one. The bliss is just what you would expect

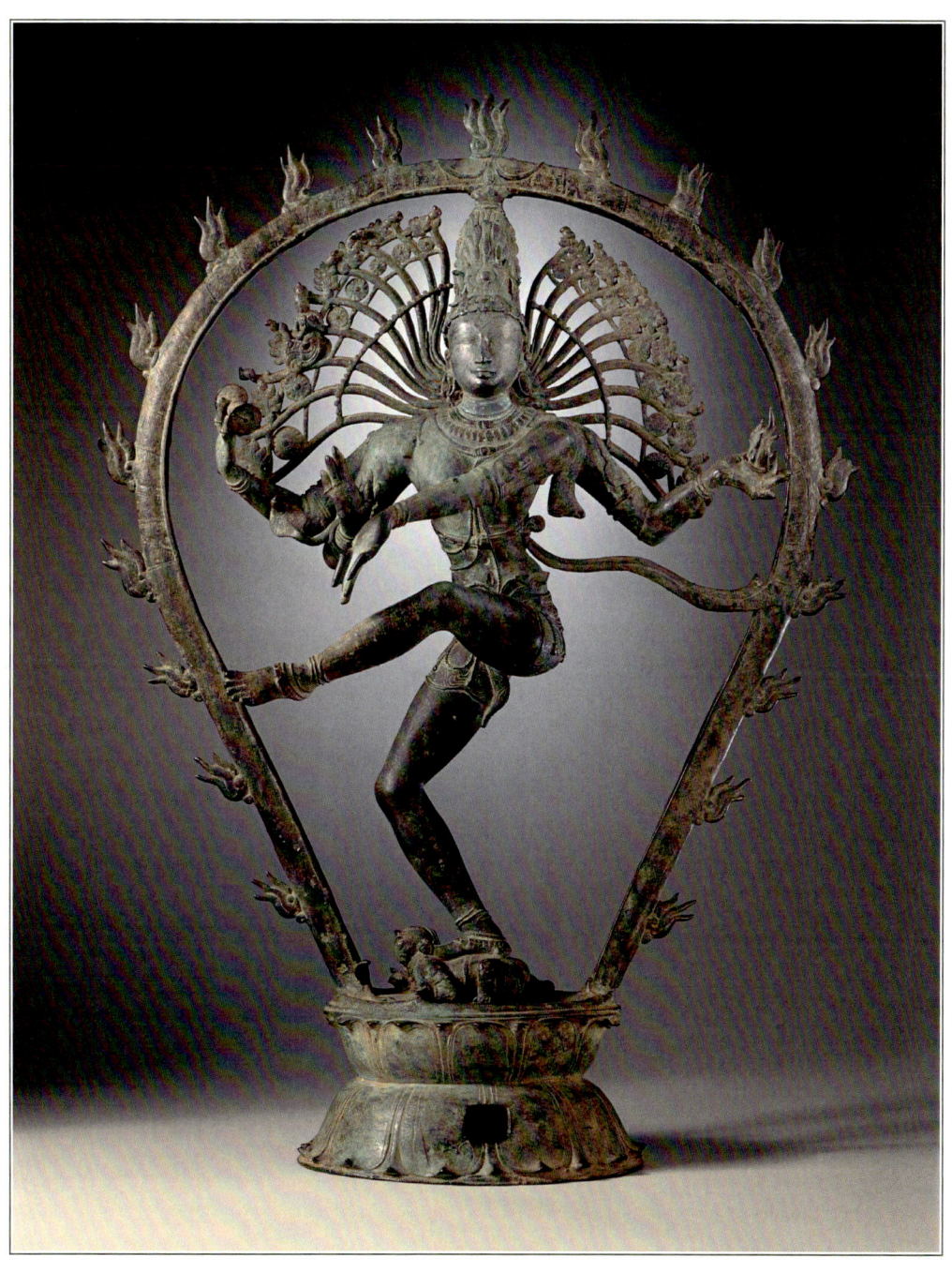

of a god who knows no limit, who presides, grants our chance to live, and to whom we can turn.

In his right upper hand he holds the drum whose vibratory beat sets world creation in motion. In his left upper hand, fire—the consumer of worlds when the time comes to destroy and renew. His right lower hand offers the traditional Indic gesture of reassurance, of peace, while the left lower hand, crossing the body, points toward the freely raised foot, a promise of liberation. Shiva dances upon a dwarf-like figure, the embodiment of ignorance and forgetfulness, and the locks of his hair fan out to express the overwhelming kinetic energy of his dance, which ignites the arch around him. And his face. . . Here there is a parallel to a classic icon of Orthodox Christianity, St. George and the dragon he slays: St. George's face is traditionally calm, untouched by conflict though fulfilling what must be fulfilled. Shiva's face is of that kind. The ferocious bliss of his dance is the engine and fulfillment of what must be.

This third member of the Global Trinity invites us to see divine energy superabundantly at work in the world and to learn—somehow—to be both active and engaged, as Lord Shiva is, yet to find a place in ourselves that is free, again like Shiva, though on our human scale where the dance sometimes stumbles. Then we get up.

In both artistic and religious perspectives, the design of Shiva Dancing is a masterwork. So too is this particular example.

31. THE BUDDHA LAYS DOWN HIS LIFE

Parinirvana of the Buddha
Gal Vihara (Rock Monastery), Polonnaruwa, Sri Lanka
12th century CE, carved into the face of a cliff
The main figure exceeds 46 feet in length
Sources: (principal image) Alamy; the Buddha's head, Merton Legacy Trust

Owing to its great size and intensely spiritual atmosphere, this sculptural ensemble cannot be properly conveyed through photographs, but there is no question in my mind that it must be included here. I have had the good fortune to visit Gal Vihara and, although that visit occurred decades ago, have never forgotten. A technical feat, this massive yet exquisitely sensitive sculptural ensemble is carved "from the living rock," as the expression goes. The dominant figure is the recumbent Buddha at the moment of death, the Parinirvana—a term that doesn't mean "death" at all but rather a return to the infinite from which he came and to which he found the way for others.

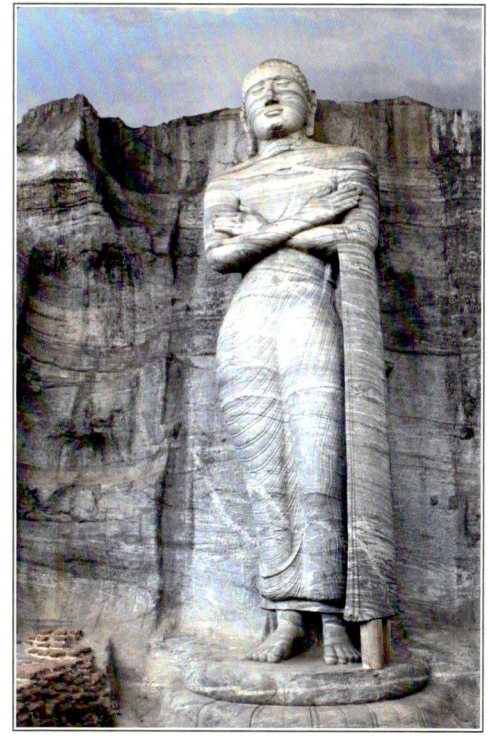

This is surely one of the most peaceful places on Earth, one of the rare places where heaven and earth seem to meet and touch. The photograph on the facing page, made by the monk and author Thomas Merton when he visited in the late fall of 1968, conveys that quality as well as any I know. The full, rounded contours of the head and overall figure find their counterpoint in the regular wave-like patterning of the Buddha's robe.

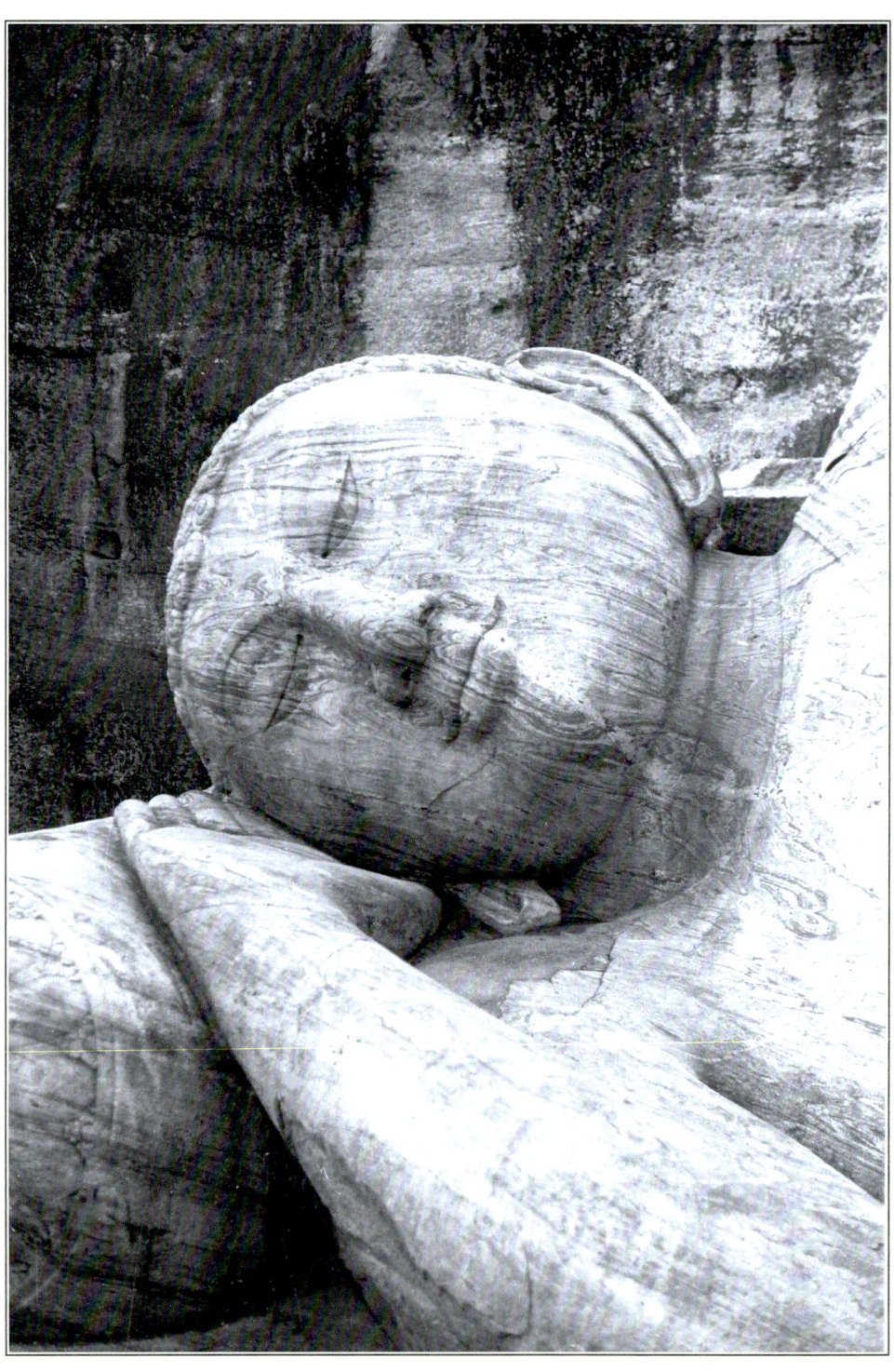

Such quiet. Incomparable—though it may help to recall in Western art the quiet focus and presence of many figures in the art of Piero della Francesca (see p. 150ff). Piero would at once have understood the art and minds of the sculptors at Polonnaruwa. "Those who carved those statues," a Buddhist elder said to Merton, "were not ordinary men."

The figure standing with crossed arms has been taken to be Ananda, although there is no proof that this is so. Ananda was one of the closest disciples of the Buddha, not yet enlightened, so they say, at the time of his master's passing. His dilemma has long interested me. I am grateful for this figure, proof if need be that enlightenment will come, if it is to come, in its own time, and that the point is to participate. Buddhas may even appreciate faithful participation more than they appreciate enlightenment. I don't know, but that wouldn't surprise me.

Thomas Merton's experience at Polonnaruwa has inscribed this monument in the modern history of spirituality, East and West. There isn't space here to quote at length from Merton's journal, but this at least: "Looking at these figures I was suddenly, almost forcibly jerked clean out of the habitual half-tied vision of things, and an inner clearness, clarity, as if exploding from the rocks themselves, became evident and obvious. . . . I don't know when in my life I have ever had such a sense of beauty and spiritual validity running together in one aesthetic illumination."[18]

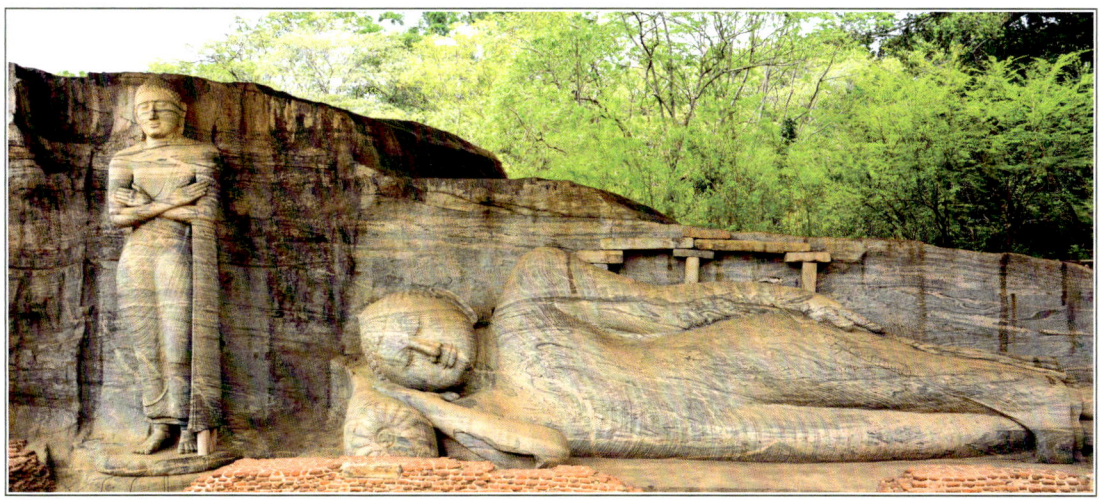

32. THE NEW YORK LUOHANS

Two Arhats (Luohans)
ca. 1000 CE, Liao dynasty China, region of Yixian
Stoneware with three-color glaze
Height with base, 92 inches
The Metropolitan Museum of Art, New York
Source: Art Resource NY

The Penn Museum Luohan
Source: iStock

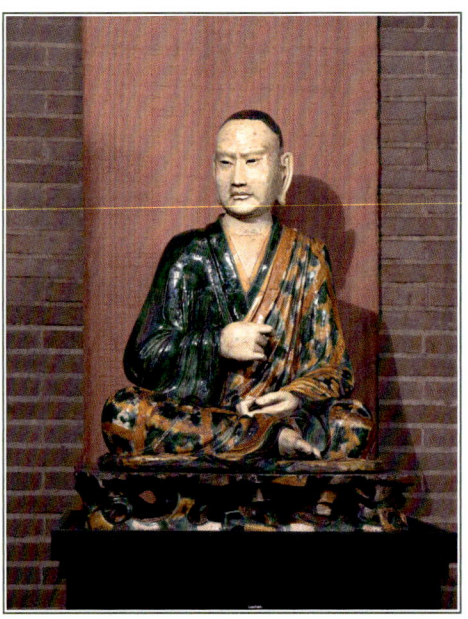

When I was an apprentice in all things, living in New York City, word got around among my friends—they too were apprentices—about a pair of ancient Chinese sculptures that absolutely had to be seen at The Metropolitan Museum of Art. I can't recall my first visit to them, but since then they are part of a continuum untouched by time, works of art I can instantly summon to mind. Here again, photographs cannot do justice. To see them is to be with them. You can't be just anyhow while with them. It's like an audience with persons of great standing. I know of few works that set such a high standard and materially help you approach that standard by virtue of what they are, what they emanate—and these are indeed works that emanate. With them one becomes in the root sense a conspirator, a fellow breather. It is a conspiracy toward awakening in the Buddhist and universal sense. They are *luohans* (Chinese) or *arhats* (Sanskrit), a legendary company of sixteen to eighteen original disciples of the Buddha who are charged with

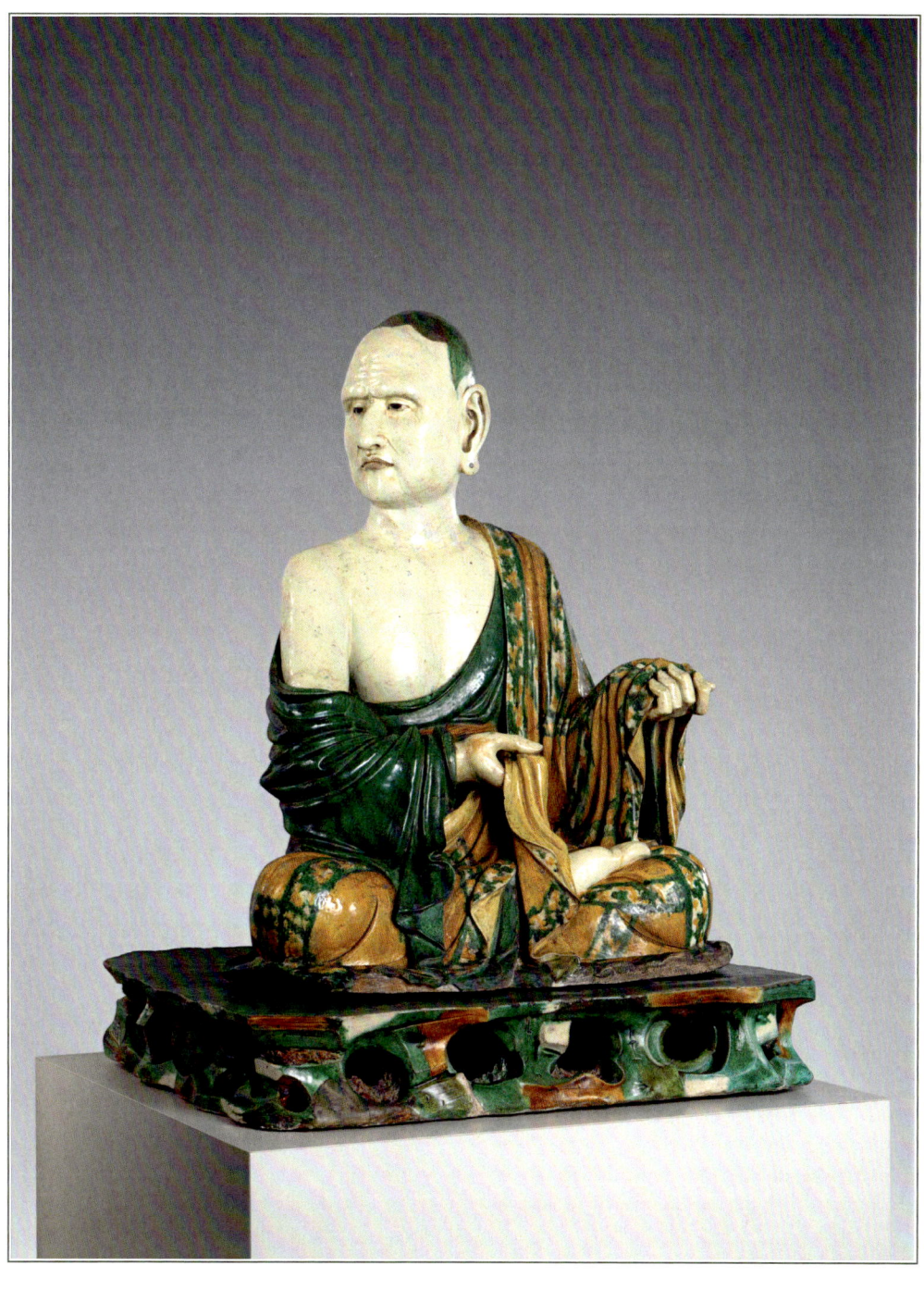

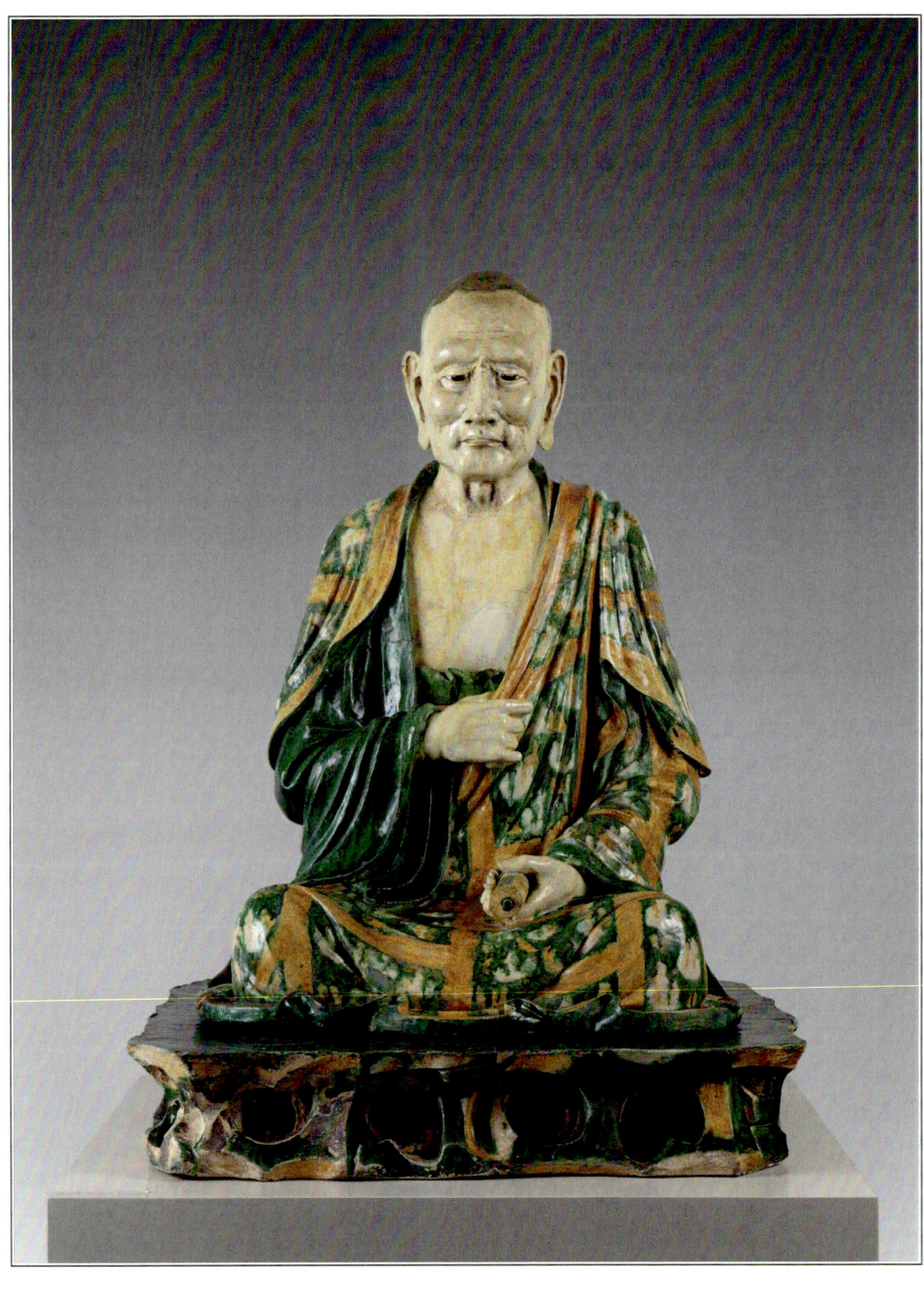

safeguarding the teachings until the arrival in a distant age of Maitreya, the Buddha of the Future.

We apprentices came periodically to be with them, to share a little in their fervor and dedication, to study with them in whatever ways we could manage. It was enough for us to know "ca. 1000," and that they had been discovered with a group of similar clay sculptures in a cave in China in 1912, after which they had been rather clumsily diffused into the art market. As a consequence, the two New York luohans have brothers in museums elsewhere in the United States and worldwide. The wonderfully composed figure in the small illustration just above is in the British Museum. There is an equally fine example in the Penn Museum, Philadelphia (see p. 100), and still others elsewhere. In recent years scholarship concerning the entire group of sculptures has become extraordinarily keen, particularly through the work of Eileen Hsiang-ling Hsu.[19]

As apprentices, we studied the attitudes and natures of the two luohans: the seemingly arrogant younger one, assuring us that we could be less than perfect and still have some place in the world of seekers and questioners; the perfect older one, emanating wisdom, compassion, and inwardness. He was more alive, infinitely wiser than us. What a thing to behold. What a thing to behold them together. Which is it to be, then: remote perfection or knowing and bearing the burden of the human condition? Both figures are luohans, charged with a high task. There must be different ways of going about it.

33. IKKYU'S PORTRAIT: THE PASSION FOR MEMORY

Ikkyu Osho
1481 CE, Muromachi Era
Height of the seated figure nearly 33 inches, painted wood
Shuon-an Ikkyu-ji, Kyoto Prefecture, Japan
Source: www.minamiyamashiro-koji.jp/360vr/ikkyuji/ikkyuji/

I suppose that I would be indifferent to works of this kind, had I not encountered one in a Buddhist temple in Kyoto. I had entered in a light spirit, glad to have a few days off from an assignment in Japan, when suddenly I noticed a man looking fixedly at me. It was a sculpture in wood darkened by the centuries. He was seated in a posture of utmost dignity, with lifelike bone and jet eyes; the treatment of facial detail, robe, and symbols of office was all as it must have been in his lifetime. This was the man himself— no doubt a much-respected abbot—in a highly realistic wooden effigy. Works of this type, characteristic of medieval Japan, must be rooted in a compelling need to remember: to remember *that* person, to retain him among us insofar as pos-

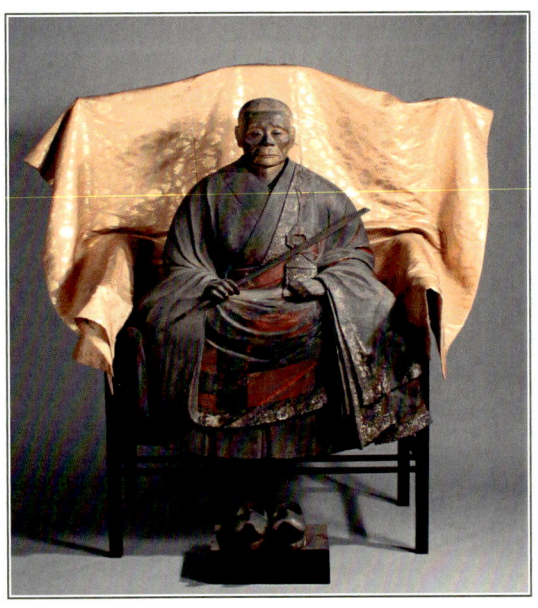

sible, to continue experiencing his influence, again insofar as possible. The example chosen here, the memorial sculpture of Ikkyu Zenji (he had various honorific names), was carved soon after his death, 1481 CE, at an advanced age. It must have been nearly unbearable to take leave of him. Such a work embodies the urgency of remembering, of remaining close. To the point that Ikkyu's own hair was originally threaded into the sculpture—you can see where. We are not far from the Western medieval

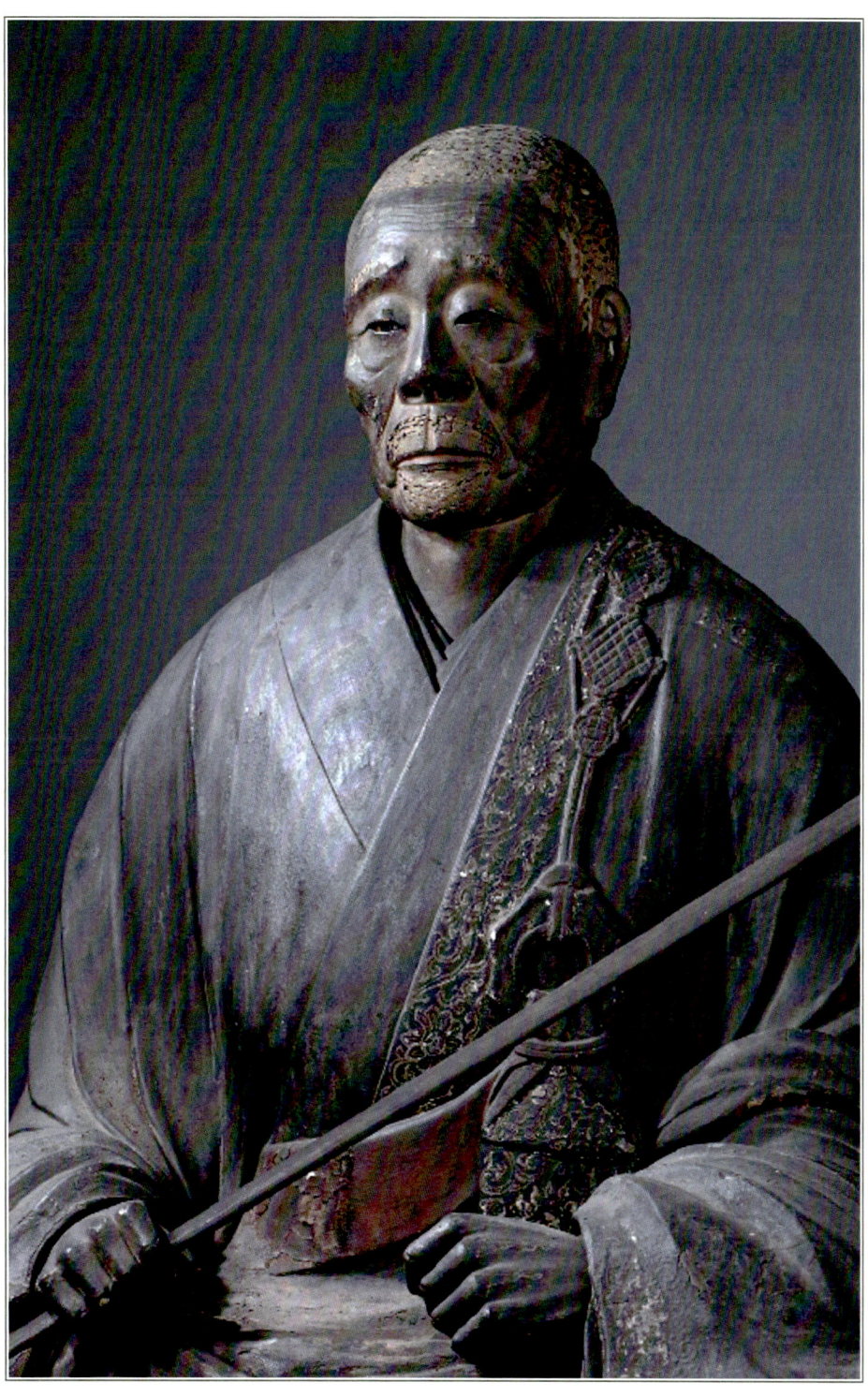

practice of preserving saints' relics and attributing lasting spiritual power to them.

By means of this image I had a definite goal in mind and only one: to point to the fire of memory burning, often unseen, unfelt, still present, throughout the history of art. Encountering works from cultures worldwide, sorted out and understood by scholars who care for them, we cannot help but remember: who we are, what we were, what we remain. At times, as in this memorial sculpture of Ikkyu, the urgency of memory makes itself vividly known. I learned much about remembering from the writings of Elie Wiesel, may his memory be a blessing, and sometimes explore the older corridors of my life with wonder that, like us all in reasonable health, I can remember. The sculpted images of many whom I've known are there. The conversation, the flow of vitality between us, resumes. Memory of that kind isn't exclusively mental; it's a presence inside oneself, the warmest of mysteries, as if we change temperature when we remember.

Now that would have been enough: the passion for memory noticed through a powerful icon. But then there is Ikkyu himself, the rebel Zen student and master, the critic of hypocritical religious practice in his era, the incisive poet lyrical and mocking, the calligrapher of unforgotten refinement, the wanderer from temple to tavern and brothel and back again, finally a recognized religious leader who showed no quarter. What an extraordinary individual. To learn something of him is not a generic encounter: it is to meet a remarkable human being whose example continues to look at us with encouragement and a touch of derision. He compared some of his brother monks to "frogs fighting for respect at the bottom of a well . . . . Right and wrong, myself and others, fussing away a whole life."[20] There need be no great distance between us and him. Memory sets time in place—this is here, that is there—and ignores it.

34. NIO: JAPANESE TEMPLE GUARDIAN

Naraen Kongo, Guardian of the Night
711 CE, clay with wood repairs and traces of paint
Height nearly 12.5 feet
Horyuji Temple, Nara Prefecture, Japan
Source: CNP Collection / Alamy Stock Photo

I ask myself why this sculpture is firmly included here. Isn't its supernatural threat of violence over the top, far over the top? Shouldn't we admire from a safer distance the unknown sculptor's fiery imagination and skill? That was then, this is now? But I can't convince myself of any of this; the figure, its attitude, its message reach across the many centuries and address us still.

We can take refuge briefly in facts. The Nara period in Japan (710 – 794 CE) was formative in many respects. Buddhism had begun to flower after its introduction from China a century earlier. Printing, record-keeping, and characteristic forms of art and literature entered the stream of Japanese culture, as did the design and construction of Buddhist temples and associated buildings at Nara, still a wonder of the world. Horyuji is one of its three major temples. The priests and government officials responsible for it must have recognized the need to give form and force to the divinities protecting it. At one of the main gates of the temple complex, a pair of Nio visibly stand guard—you can't miss them as you approach. The partner of this "guardian of the night" is equally fearsome. They won't spring down from their niches to bar the way to people of ill will, but their magic is evident: things will not go well for you if you violate the spirit of the place.

The Nio embody implacable force—and they are gods. Their lineage goes back to Vajrapani, the mythic defender of the Buddha who manifested the Buddha's power as he invisibly accompanied him. Despite appearances, Nio are religious: our guardian of the night pronounces through nearly closed lips the syllable "un", while his partner through open mouth pronounces the syllable "ah", together pronouncing the great reminder and acknowledgment of the sacred: OM.

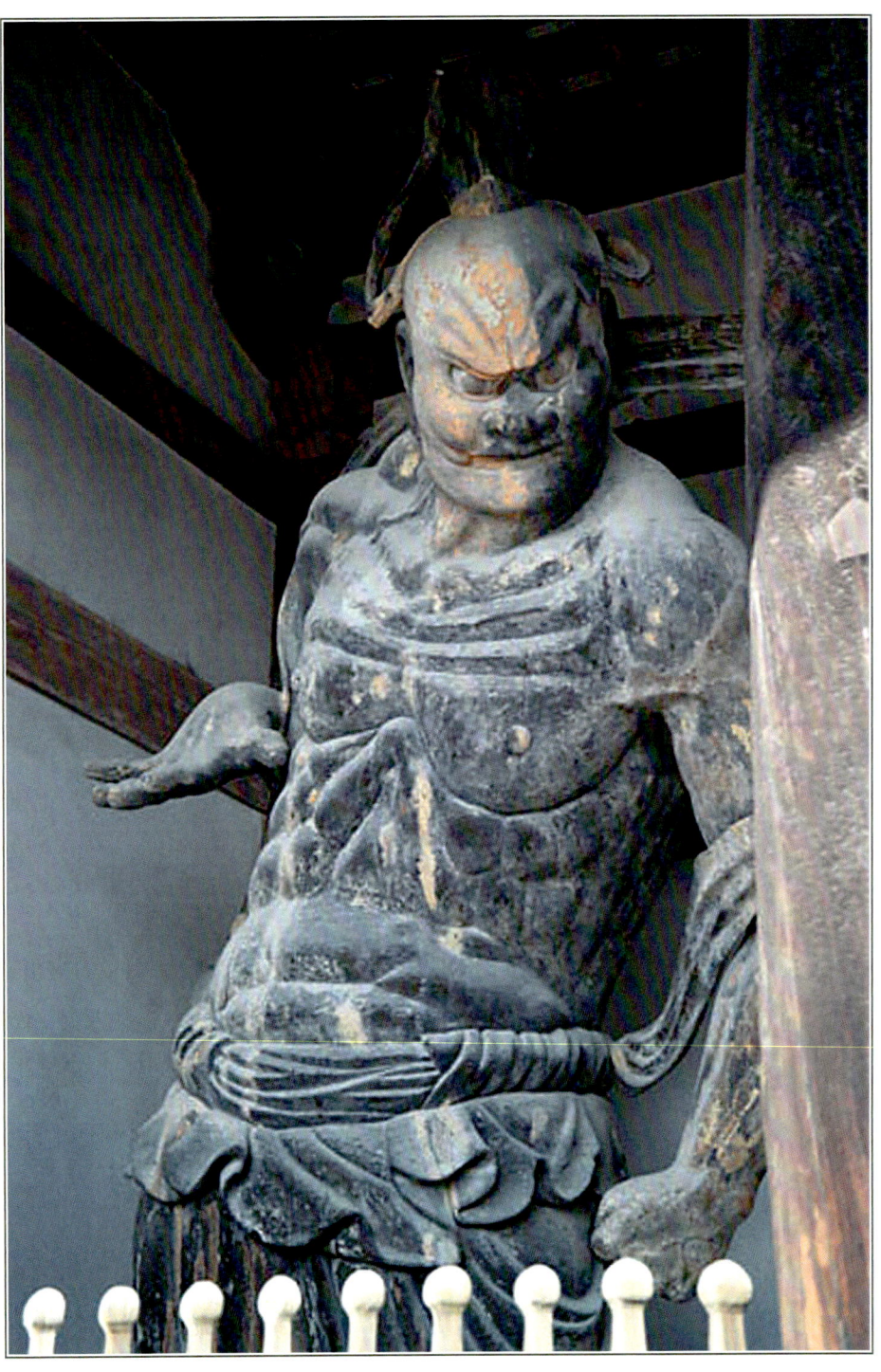

Is there a force like a Nio in us? If so, what does it serve? Are there truths or persons or places which, were they threatened, would draw forth the Nio force? In a world where so much is amiss, can the Nio force be kept in reserve, just in case? Once I asked a musician whether he would, if necessary, die for the sake of preserving the music of J. S. Bach. He replied that he would not. I hope that now, years later, he would reconsider. Nio force is needed in many dimensions of experience. We have the notion of "speaking truth to power"— admirable beyond words, and necessary. Nio suggest something else: opposing power to power. Sometimes there is no alternative.

A petition or prayer: may we have this force of integrity and ultimate concern in reserve—and rarely need to manifest as a Nio. Most often what is needed is not the sword but a mind.

35. RIKYU'S TASTE

Black Raku Tea Bowl
Artist: Chojiro (1516 – ?1592)
Low-fired, glazed earthenware
Early 17th century CE, Momoyama Period, Japan
The Metropolitan Museum of Art, New York
Source: Art Resource NY

Portrait of Rikyu
Artist unknown
Early 17th century CE
Metropolitan Museum, New York
Source: Wikipedia / public domain

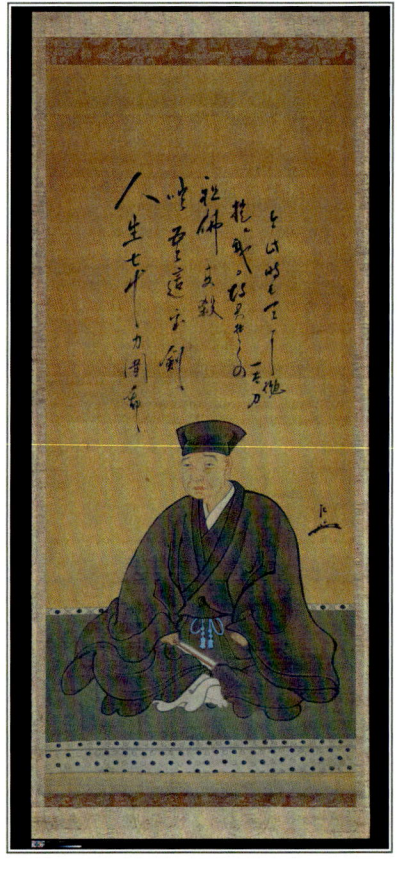

"Whatever utensil you handle, pick it up as if it were light and put it down as if it were heavy." Listening to this counsel, we already come under the spell of Sen no Rikyu (1522 - 1591), the leading tea master of his era whose thought and practice shape the tea ceremony even today. In his tradition, he occupies a position like that of J. S. Bach in the development of Western music: he drew together the best of what preceded him, endowed it with new genius, a unique blend of rigor and improvisational creativity, and passed it on to unforgetting generations to come. Recent scholarship concerning Rikyu and tea is revisionist: what we thought we knew may not be so.[21] Even viewed through the chiaroscuro of uncertain history, this was a

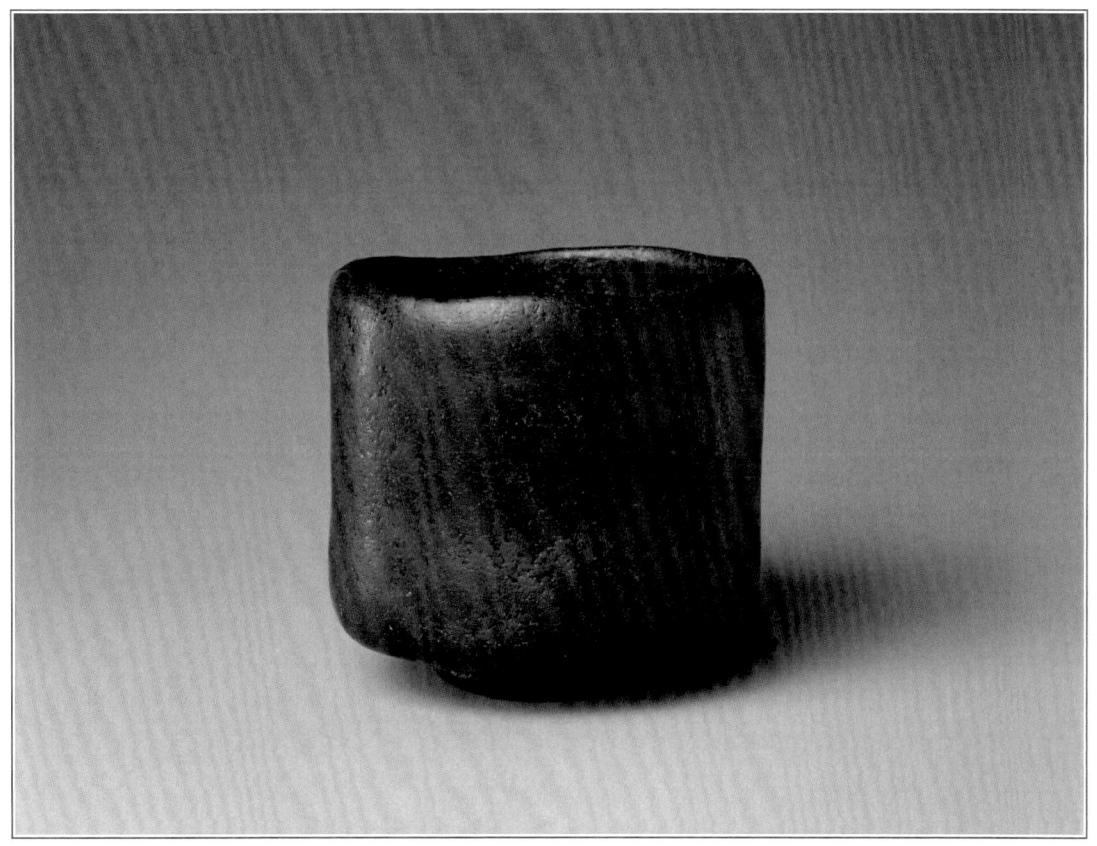

very great individual who contributed fundamentally to the lasting brilliance and depth of Japanese culture. The tea ceremony is choreographed civility, even choreographed consciousness—host and guest briefly tasting life, conversation, and tea as if all is well. It is a ceremony of appreciation. The portrait of Rikyu on p. 100, a somber appreciation, is by the famed painter Hasegawa Tohaku, Rikyu's contemporary.

Tea ceremony utensils are closer to hands, to actual use, than other objects in this book: bowls, caddies, whisks, scoops, ladles and kettles and much else. The extraordinary tea bowl on the facing page, attributed to Rikyu's friend Chojiro, the very first of generations of Raku potters, breathes the spirit of *chanoyu*, the way of tea. Through Rikyu and then many others, Japan evolved an independent aesthetic rooted in Rikyu's *wabi* taste for unpretentious objects and environments, perfect in their imperfection, and in the calm mind of Zen Buddhism (Rikyu was a lay priest). There is nothing like this aesthetic in Western tradition (but see pp. 184-185). To spend time with the objects in the Raku Museum of Kyoto and in museums across Japan, even to encounter such objects in books, is to enter a new world of sensibility. Chojiro's tea bowl is an invitation.

Rikyu was a man of peace willingly conscripted by the warrior ruler of his day, Toyotomi Hideyoshi, to serve tea to the ruler's friends and rivals, to teach tea, and—given his prestige—to conduct diplomacy on Hideyoshi's behalf. When Hideyoshi was quite through with him, for reasons that scholars have I think not yet reduced from surmise to fact, he ordered Rikyu to commit suicide. Duly performed on April 21st, 1591. Two feature films about the life and death of Rikyu appeared in the same year, 1989: H. Teshigahara's *Rikyu* and K. Kumai's *Death of a Tea Master*. Both are marvelous, the latter especially so.

The Japanese friend to whom this book is dedicated once told me that in his view Japan has contributed two unfathomably great figures to world culture: the poet Basho and the tea master Rikyu. I'm sure he's right, though I would add the film maker Akira Kurosawa. Let us drink tea from time to time and remember Rikyu. Traditionally we would drink from the same tea bowl. Why not do so this time?

36. HOKUSAI AND HIROSHIGE AND . . .

Hokusai
Woodblock prints, ca. 1830 – 1832 CE
The Cooper and Mt. Fuji
Red Fuji (South Wind, Clear Sky)
The Metropolitan Museum of Art, New York
Source: Wikimedia Commons / public domain

Hiroshige
Woodblock print, 1838 CE
Birds and Wisteria
Source: Heritage Image Partnership Ltd / Alamy Stock Photo

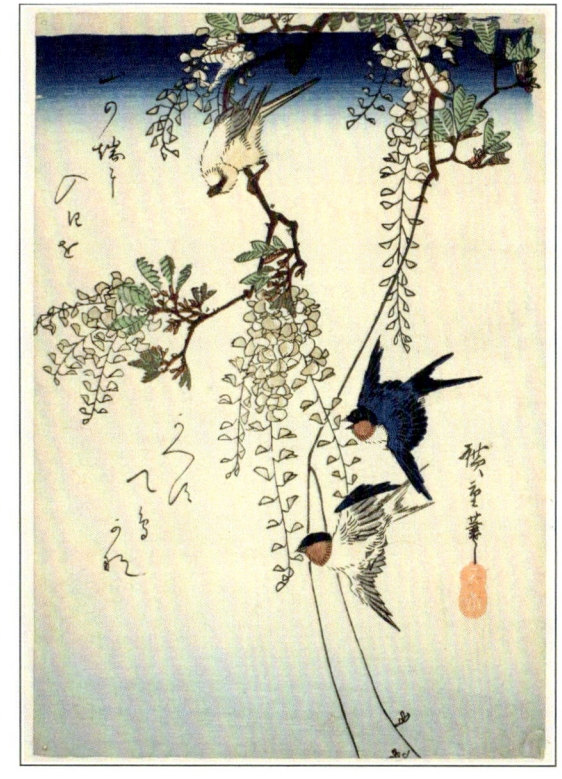

We can easily imagine theater and its audience in Shakespeare's time: the teeming city of London, the stunning variety and abundance of plays and playwrights, the scope of scripts from high tragedy to low comedy, a world mirrored in depth and breadth. Now let us imagine Edo, the teeming city renamed Tokyo in 1868. The popular art of the woodblock print, churned out by some 200 publishers, mirrored with equal verve the life of Edo's people, their humanity, their interests, their admirations, curiosities, refinement and earthiness. There were visual chroniclers in Edo. They make us see their world, even today, and their works

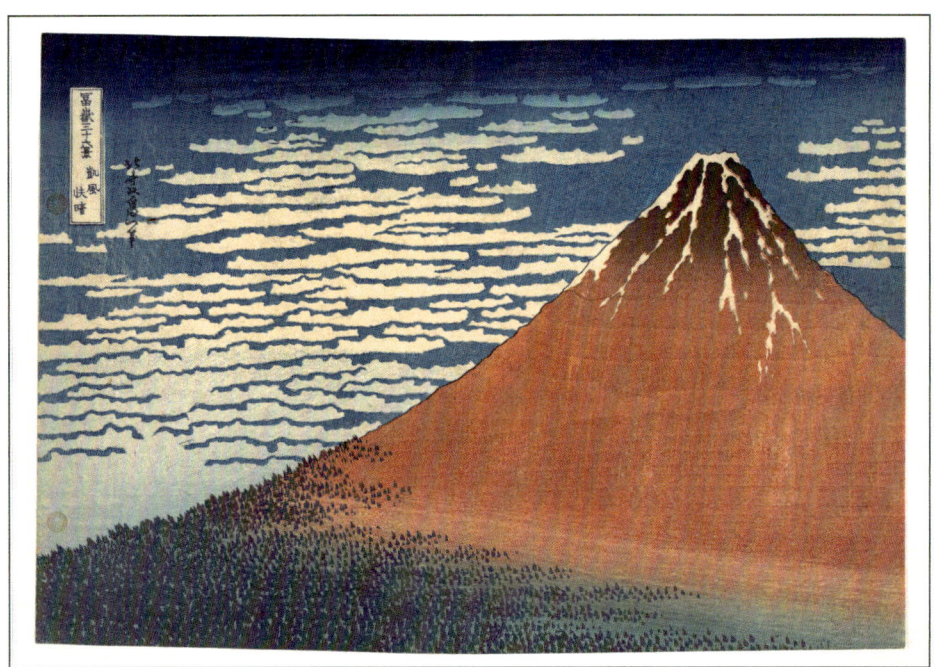

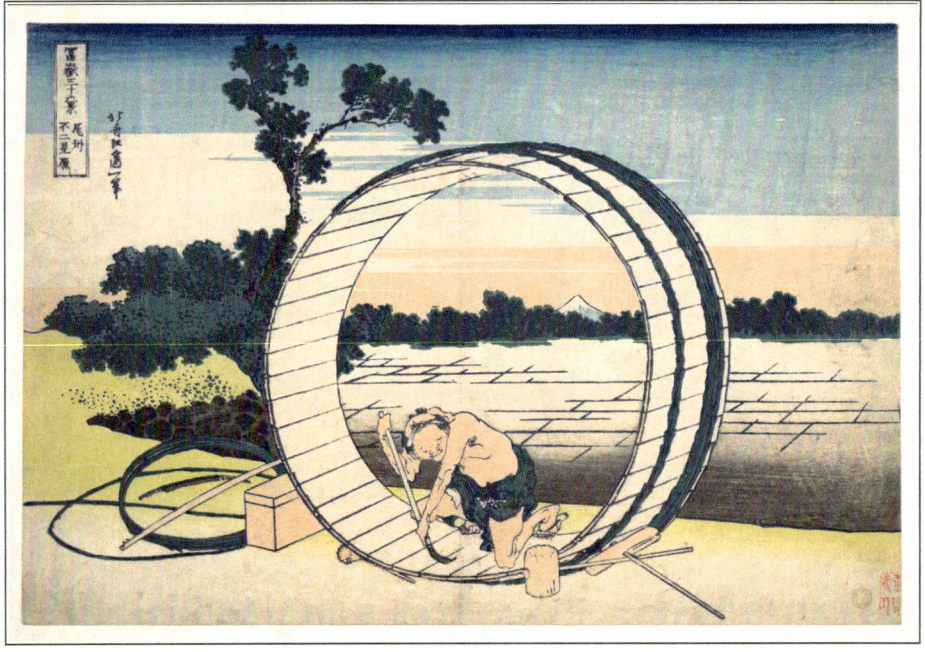

on paper were inexpensive enough that ordinary people could afford them to brighten their homes or add to growing portfolios of prints.

Among the many outstanding artists producing *ukiyo-e*, as this genre is called, I want to focus on just two, Hokusai (1760 – 1849) and Hiroshige (1797 – 1858). The works by Hokusai on the facing page and Hiroshige's exquisite "flowers and birds" on p. 113 offer an invitation to explore an art that is virtually boundless, from prints worth a fortune today to elegant ephemera produced for tailor shops to advertise the latest in kimonos. This art, both popular and aesthetically brilliant, flourished with consistency of style and technique from the mid-eighteenth century to the late nineteenth.

Hokusai was an incomparable chronicler of life and landscape. In old age he spoke of himself as "the old man crazy about painting"; such he had been through a long working life. "Red Fuji", from the series of *Thirty-Six Views of Mount Fuji*, is a work of mastery conveying his veneration of the iconic mountain in an austere but vividly colorful image. The second print again shows Mount Fuji but far off; its focus is a cooper, a humble barrel-maker at work; the point must be to experience both the modest artisan and the sacred mountain in one vision. The barrel's staves encircle the mountain and ensure that we perceive all elements together. Hokusai's many volumes of prints based on sketches from life—an early if not the first appearance of *manga*—preserve an entire population of men, women, and children such as the cooper. Hokusai was a humanist working at the highest levels of empathy, cheerfulness, and generosity of vision. Precisely the same must be said of Hiroshige, a master of his art and friend to all things.

The icon here is the entire tradition of woodblock prints, the self-portrait of Japan.

PARENTHESIS: ISLAMIC ART

Many of us in the West today know too little of Islamic culture. A few favorite works of literature, art, architecture are unreservedly appreciated; the rest is likely unfamiliar. The 13th-century religious teacher, poet, and storyteller Jalal al-Din Rumi is a household name. We have domesticated him under the simpler name "Rumi", and the brilliant adaptations by the American poet Coleman Barks and others have made him a bestselling author. The theater director Peter Brook's production of *The Conference of the Birds*, an extravagantly delightful philosophical tale, has given its author, the 12th-13th century Sufi poet Farid al-Din Attar, his deserved place (C. S. Nott's version of the original in English is well worth finding). Every reader has some acquaintance with *The Thousand and One Nights*, a multitude of tales from the Middle East and adjoining lands, available in numerous translations.[22] When I think of that book I am at once optimistic again, readier for life, in love with "Heart's Miracle, Lieutenant of the Birds", voyaging with Sinbad, laughing again over the persistent reappearances of Abu l'Qasim's luckless slippers (owing to years and years of repairs, "they were so heavy that they had become proverbial throughout all Egypt.") I think also of the many tales of the caliph Harun al-Rashid, the 8th-century ruler in Baghdad: an example beyond compare of vitality, justice, humor, and quickness of mind. Such riches.

In the material arts, who hasn't longed to visit the Taj Mahal, the mid-17th century architectural masterpiece in North India, product of a blend of Indo-Persian taste and skill overseen invisibly, as if from above, by a mathematically guided spirit of harmony rarely seen on this Earth? At the other geographic extremity of the *ummah*, the far-flung Muslim community, is an architectural masterpiece of another kind, the Alhambra palace in Granada, a 14th-century exercise in grace and intricacy unique in the world. And there is so much else to know and care for.

The five works that follow, icons all, speak to us from a vigorous and enduring culture of art and craft that called on many kinds of makers:

calligraphers of refined skill, education, and dedication; court, village, and nomadic weavers; wood and ivory carvers; metalworkers; ceramic artists; and more still. They were participants in what strikes me as a resolutely handmade arts culture, in which the meeting of thought, materials, traditional patterns, and skilled hands created entire environments. The sense of hands at work is never far.

In the West we have thought quite a lot about the *Gesamtkunstwerk*—the total work of art bringing together the separate arts in an integrated whole. Our typical frame of reference has been somewhat narrowly focused on projects in the performing arts and architecture. The art, architecture, and craft of the Islamic world is an integrated whole of the kind we have conjured through the notion of the *Gesamtkunstwerk* but never realized for long. The textile patterns and jewelry of a nomadic woman's clothing bear some resemblance to the decorative patterns of tiles in the great palaces; the calligrapher's art appears both small on the page and large in molded, carved, or ceramic inscriptions on the walls of mosques and palaces. The designs in carpets—for example, a paradise vision of restful pools of water and flowering trees—are literally to be found in the homes and palaces of the wealthy. The modestly sized prayer rug, a unique artifact in a religious culture that calls for prayer five times daily on one's knees, is not for rich or poor, it is for everyone.

There is a center in a unified cultural world of this kind. Because I don't know Arabic I am not well placed to characterize that center, but it is without doubt the Qur'an itself, the revealed scripture traditionally understood to have been dictated by the Angel Gabriel to the Prophet Mohammad in the first part of the 7th century. The chanted language, its rhythms, pitch levels, colors, and repetitions, is said to be the center.

I have another zone of ignorance where I nonetheless know there is much light. Like you, I'm aware of the rapid Muslim conquest of much of the Middle East, North Africa and Iberia, and further still from the mid-7th to mid-8th centuries. What I don't fully grasp is the rapidity of the appearance of arts of immense sophistication and beauty across much of what had abruptly become the Muslim world. True, two ancient civilizations, Sassanid Persia and parts of the Greek-speaking world, entered into the world of Islam and enriched it, but Islam had its own nature from the beginning. There was a passage from the sword to the *qalam*, the dry trimmed reed of the calligraphers; the *qalam* was their pen, an enduring symbol of wisdom and learning. A further expression of the transition from the arts of war to the arts of peace was a new institution sponsored by my favorite, the caliph Harun al-Rashid in the 8th century, and greatly strengthened by his son: the House of Wisdom in Baghdad, a library and meeting place for learned individuals, Muslim and of other faiths. The House of Wisdom was the quiet center where ancient Greek knowledge was gathered, translated, and expanded under official patronage; the Syriac Orthodox Christian translators at work there were the last echoes of the ancient schools of Athens and Alexandria.

It must be time now to enter that House. We are not the first to enter; we won't be the last.

37. THE FIRST THING GOD CREATED: THE *QALAM*

Fragment of a Qur'an in Kufic script
9th – 10th centuries CE, the Abbasid Dynasty centered on Baghdad
Height slightly more than 9.5 inches
The National Museum of Asian Art, Washington, D. C.
Source: The National Museum of Asian Art

Fragment of a Qur'an in an alternative Kufic script
Late 13th – Early 14th centuries CE, the Nasrid Dynasty centered on Granada
Height slightly more than 21 inches
The Metropolitan Museum of Art, New York
Source: Art Resource

Image of a study hall (manuscript illumination)
The *Maqamat* of Hariri, 13th century CE
Bibliothèque nationale de France, Paris
Source: Wikimedia Commons / public domain

We need to imagine something splendid: an entire culture founded in and returning daily to the written word. "Verily, the first thing Allah, the Almighty, created was the Pen. He said to it: 'Write.'"[23] And what it wrote was the Qur'an. Intensely beautiful letter forms and page designs appeared early in the history of the preservation of the Qur'an and continued to appear on a regional basis for centuries to come. Like all histories, the history of Islamic civilization experienced good days and bad, internal strife and external wars, earthquake, fire, and all else, but the steady excellence of the learned calligraphers responsible not only for scripture but also for poetry, history, and other works persisted. I keep in my study a Qur'an fragment from Mamluk Syria, ca. 1280 CE, written in a flowing hand--*khafif al muhaqqiq*[24]—spacious on the aged linen page (such relics are not torn from books, they are rescued from hurt books). I prize it not only for its intrinsic beauty but for its place in history: just a few years prior to the fall of the Crusader fortress at Acre in 1291, which marked the end of the Crusader Kingdom centered on Jerusalem. Somewhere near Acre a master calligrapher was at work. I imagine—many things can only be imagined—that he prayed and took up the *qalam* with a good heart and fantastic skill. The arts of peace must prevail: this is my domestic symbol of a global need.

"Excellent writing clears the eyes."[25] The pair of examples on the facing page are excellent writing. The 9th – 10th century page written in Kufic style, the first in which the Qur'an was formally written down from oral sources, returns us to somewhere near the origin of Islam. The letter forms and their steady pulse across the page are breathtaking. These marks are both voice and silence. Their austerity is lightened by delicate red diacritical signs. This first alphabet of Islam has unmistakable authority.

The second example from a later period and another region shows what Kufic script could become: slender, elegant, nearly weightless, with curved descending tails and verticals like resilient reeds. Again the sheer elegance is breathtaking. One has an impression of the calligrapher's perfect control of a fine repertory of signs. The gold rosettes in both examples mark the ends of verses and add a further element of decoration. Calligraphic art at this level leaves one—I suppose paradoxically—speechless. We are not alone in that respect: a learned calligrapher said of a noble predecessor: "Such writing

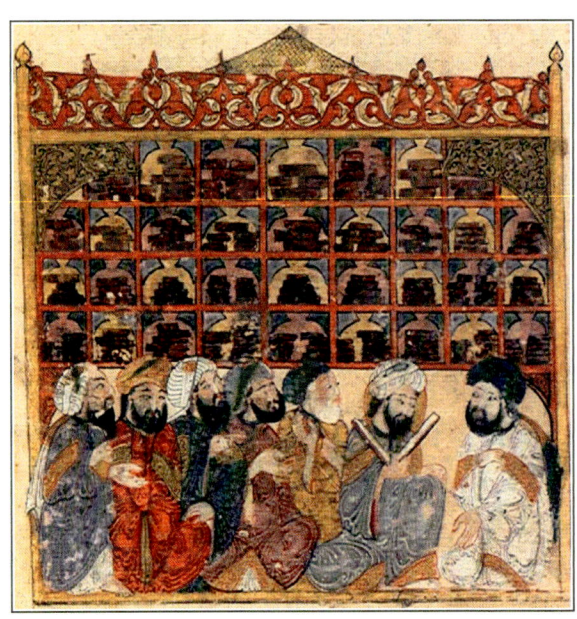

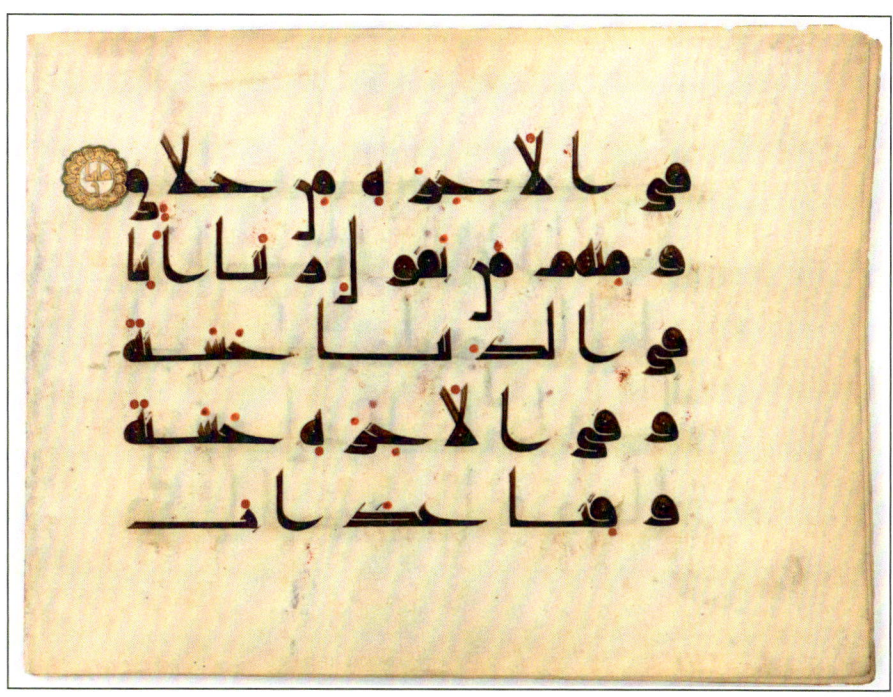

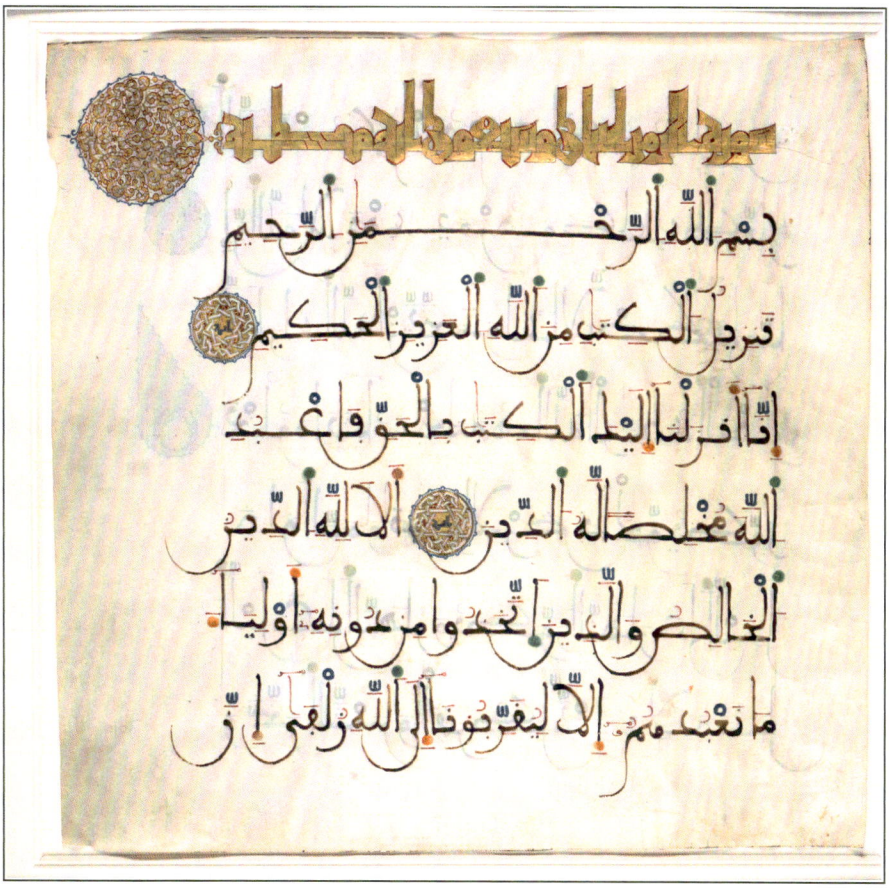

in comparison with the limitations of mankind! That was another pen and another hand!"[26]

The inset image just above of a mid-14th-century library and its scholars, packed together, intently listening, is not only a grace note here. It conveys something of the spirit of what came to be called the Golden Age of Islamic culture. People preserved, expanded, and passed on knowledge, made fundamental discoveries. They didn't mind squeezing together to hear better— always a positive sign. It was a good time to be alive.

38. STARS: MINBAR DOORS FROM MEDIEVAL CAIRO

Pair of minbar (pulpit) doors, ca. 1325 – 1330 CE
Rosewood, ivory, ebony and other materials
Attributed to Cairo
The Metropolitan Museum of Art, New York
Source: Art Resource NY

The majestic art of geometric patterning in the visual culture of Islam can be approached from two points of departure: a search to understand its uniquely beautiful complexity, and a search to relate these patterns to religious and philosophical principles fundamental to the Islamic world-view. Many Western scholars and artists, often inspired by the work of Keith Critchlow (1933 – 2020) and his colleagues at The Prince's Foundation School of Traditional Arts (London), have taken both paths. The analysis of complex Islamic geometries is a lively study today; all that is needed for pattern analysis—it is already a great deal—is a compass, a ruler, a good head, and lately computer programs. That we are using computer modeling to interpret the patterns created by medieval Muslim artists strikes me as an extraordinary homage.

The metaphysical interpretation of complex geometric patterning in terms of unity and multiplicity has been developed by other thinkers of our time, including Nadar Ardalan, Laleh Bakhtiar, and Seyyed Hossein Nasr. Their work is grounded in the pioneering studies of Coomaraswamy and certain of his peers in subsequent generations. Coomaraswamy wrote that "visual symbolism . . ., even more than verbal symbolism is the characteristic idiom of traditional metaphysics."[27] "To have lost the art of thinking in images is precisely to have lost the proper linguistic of metaphysics."[28] We are immersed here in the proper linguistic of metaphysics—and in a work of utmost intellectual ingenuity and artisanal skill.

Islam had two inheritances. From the Prophet Mohammad a proscription against representing living things in art: the most colorfully expressed *hadith*

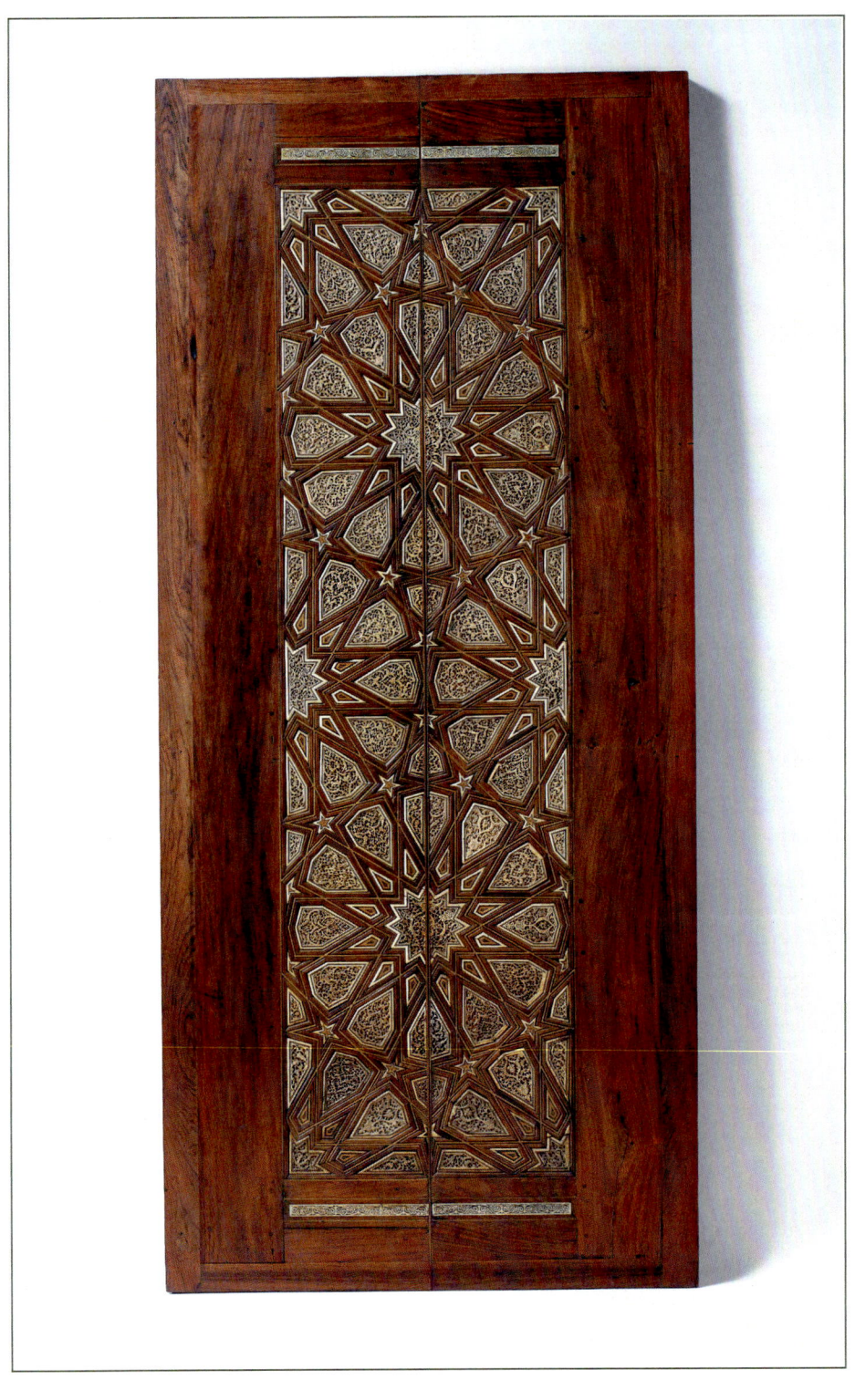

or recorded saying reads, "Angels do not enter the house in which there are portrayals or pictures." From the tradition of Greek science, systematically translated by medieval scholars of the House of Wisdom: the second inheritance, an intensive interest in computational mathematics and geometry. To endow with meaning and enliven the surfaces of architecture and other things made, the proscription summoned a threefold solution: geometric patterning, curvilinear arabesque such as you see in the inset illustration of an ivory panel from the minbar doors, and calligraphy.

I approach these minbar doors as a peasant. My eyes and mind can scarcely encompass their complex design. I am delighted, dazzled, quietened. Two complete twelve-pointed stars on the vertical axis, two half-stars in the mid zone, four quarter-stars at the corners, exquisitely detailed vegetal arabesques at a micro scale in the ivory panels, the stars interacting in an orderly way that defines them both as independent and as subordinate to the larger pattern they generate. Imagine the *imam*, the prayer leader, passing through these narrow doors, climbing the steps of a high pulpit to deliver a few words of truth—and symbolically entering another world where all things are what they are separately, yet bound to each other in unity. The pattern here is an excerpt from a limitless pattern.

I would have wished to speak with the artists and artisans who made these doors, who understood them.

39. EMISSARIES FROM ELSEWHERE: MIDDLE EASTERN CARPETS

The Ardabil Carpet
1539 – 1540 CE, Safavid Period, Iran
Knotted silk with wool pile
Length 34 ft 6 inches
The Victoria and Albert Museum, London
Source: The Victoria and Albert Museum

Garden carpet
Ca. 1800 CE, Safavid Period, Iran
Knotted wool pile on cotton warp and weft
Length 22 ft 6 inches
Harvard Art Museums/Arthur M. Sackler Museum, Cambridge
Source: Art Resource NY

Setting out to evoke the power of Islamic carpets, I remember Jon Thompson, such a friend, English, a world-renowned expert on carpets yet the author of approachable, beautifully illustrated books.[29] Once he joined me in our home. I pointed, no doubt with rosy pride, to a twentieth-century carpet from Khotan, close to the Chinese terminus of the ancient Silk Road. "Wait until you see a real one," Jon said—a factual, not cruel remark. The centuries-old hand looming and circulation of carpets from the Middle East has periods of excellence and decline; artistic centers that outstrip others in quality; village, nomadic, and urban workshops that maintain traditions and standards, others that willingly compromise or unknowingly weaken. Though not destined for a museum, the Khotan on our floor is grand enough.

Carpets and other woven textiles from the Middle East are a unique offering to the rest of the world. They are emissaries from places and peoples unknown, making themselves known through dramatic design and vivid color in endless variety. There is a level of workmanship in some carpets that

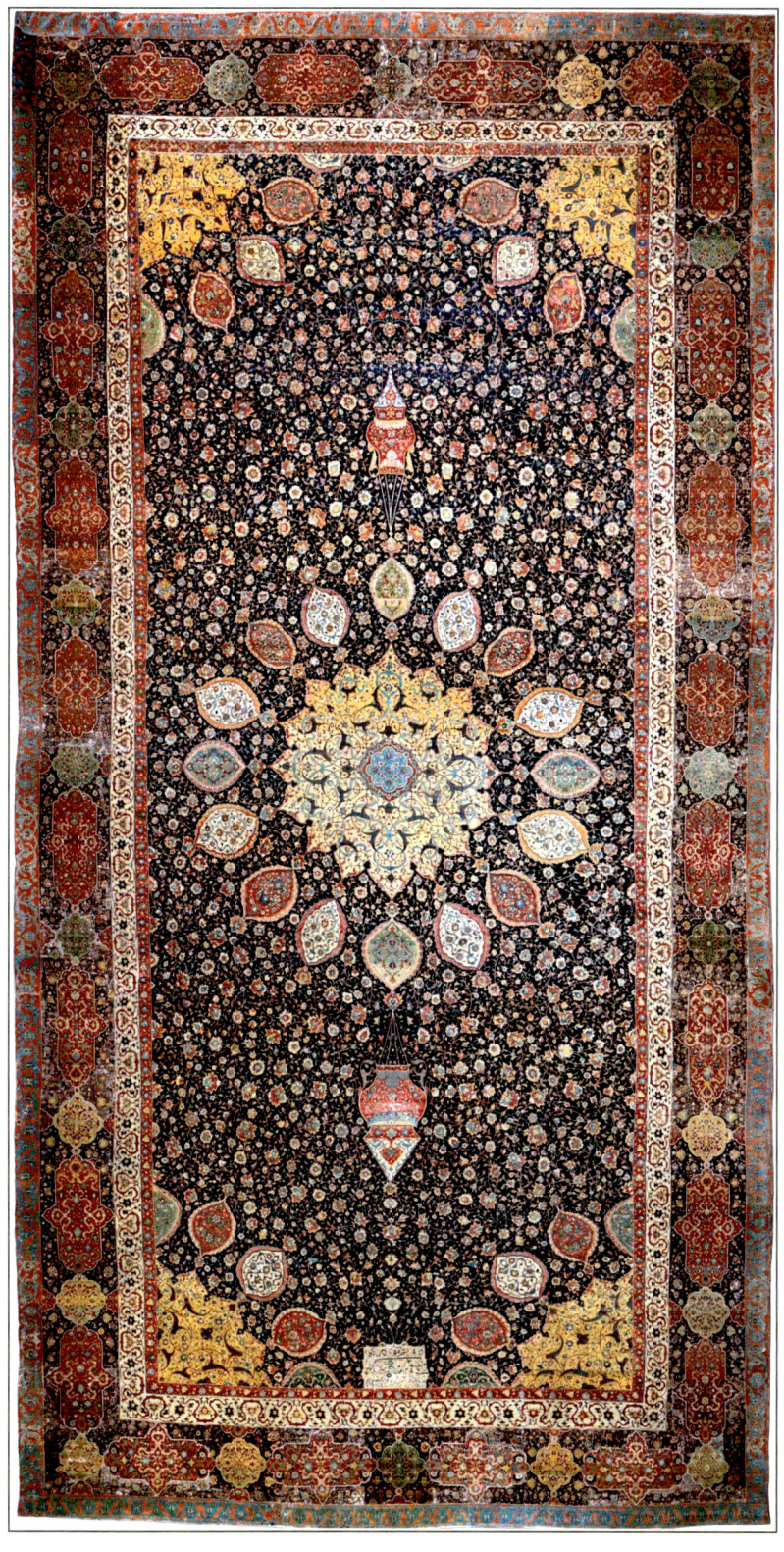

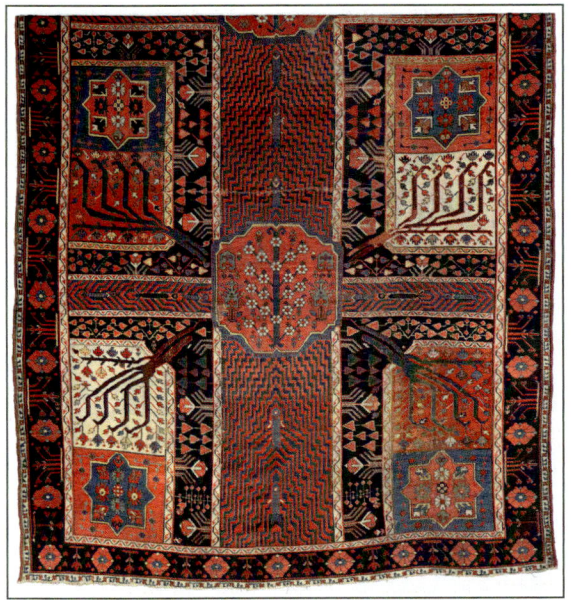

I can only identify as "sigh": the true and deserved response to such excellence is a sigh. The carpets chosen for these pages are at that level. The famed Ardabil carpet, with a density of 300 to 350 knots per square inch, is an overwhelming masterpiece estimated to have taken four years to create by a team of weavers. Its central medallion and quarter-medallions at the corners recall the minbar doors; the floral field gives the impression of a starry night of flowers; the overall color palette possesses subtle, tranquil beauty. How could such a thing exist on this troubled Earth? We should take heart—and take the lesson, however each of us perceives it. For me the lesson is something like "Don't stop now—we have been able to accomplish *such things*, we must accomplish more." This response places art in an ethical context, but that is the nature of icons: they call and encourage, remind and ask of us.

The garden carpet is again Persian but reflecting a different aesthetic, visually more angular, endowed with a charming storytelling quality through the transcription of trees, flowers, water, fish into a visual code. Our word "paradise" passed through Greek and Latin to reach us from an early Iranian source; to this day the Modern Persian and Arabic word *firdaus* means garden or paradise. The carpet represents a garden paradise, a place of rest, abundance, and beauty.

I asked Jon Thompson whether Middle Eastern carpets are encoded with traditional knowledge—be it high Sufi knowledge of the nature of things or village and nomadic knowledge of what matters. He responded that nearly all carpets are copies of copies of copies—that is the nature of the tradition. The archetype, the very first of its kind, may have been encoded, but designs changed over time; one really can't be sure that they mean what they once may have meant. "The people who made these objects, they never told you." As they reach us from distant places, Middle Eastern carpets are beautiful questions.

The icons in the next sequence—from Mughal India, ancient Greece, the Italian Renaissance, and 17th-century Holland— evoke one theme: tenderness for life. They are drawn from "everywhere," in disregard of time, because the theme is everywhere. Some artists turn toward living things not only with keen attention and skilled hands but with love that makes itself felt. Whether they are documenting an unusual animal for an emperor, shaping a small bronze as a temple offering, keeping a book of drawings that may or may not lead to commissioned paintings, or bringing a small bird and its world to life, certain artists are intimately attuned to things with sap, things with blood. The images they create are both elegant and moving. They don't tie us to the world, they show that we are already tied.

40. TENDERNESS FOR LIFE: USTAD MANSUR

Zebra
Ustad Mansur, 1621
Watercolor and gold on paper
App. 10.5 x 15 inches
The Victoria and Albert Museum, London
Source: The Victoria and Albert Museum

The Mughal Emperor Jahangir (reigning 1605 – 1627) was proud of Mansur, an artist long attached to his court whom he honored with the titles "Ustad" (Master) and "Wonder of the Age." Mansur played a role akin to that of a presidential photographer in our time: he was on call to document whatever caught the emperor's interest, and the emperor was demanding: "I ordered Wonder of the Age Ustad Mansur"—so Jahangir wrote several times in his memoirs.[30] Sometimes Mansur seems to have exceeded his brief: Jahangir noted with surprise that while Mansur was traveling with him in verdant Kashmir, the artist made more than one hundred paintings of flowers. Ruler of a vast realm, often at war to defend or expand it, Jahangir was both a classic autocrat and a person of refined taste, even pleased from time to time to meet privately with sages and ascetics.

Jahangir had received the zebra, wholly unfamiliar in north India, as a gift from a courtier accompanying a Turkish delegation that had passed through Ethiopia. Initial suspicion: it was a cleverly painted mule. That doubt resolved, the emperor put Mansur to work, perhaps with the thought of including the image in his memoirs. He was an early icon collector.

Why is this image compelling? Mansur could see and cleanly record what he saw, but so could many others. There is something more. Every visual element is tasteful: tawny background, elegant red bridle and reins, delicate floral arabesque in the frame added later by Jahangir's son and heir. But good taste isn't that rare—there is something more. The tensile quality of Mansur's line, as if it were drawn wire, and his attention to minute detail are notable

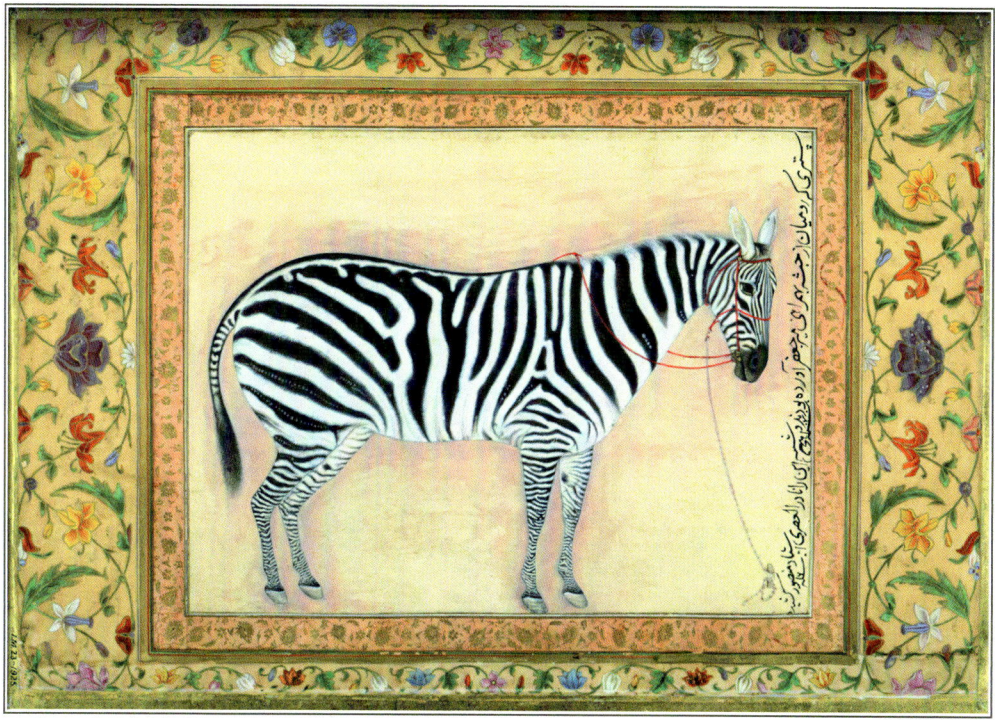

strengths. Then we might notice that Mansur didn't bother to include a patch of ground where the zebra could stand; he permits nothing to distract, nothing anecdotal. The heavy hind quarters and thin legs, the slightly bowed head with its watchful, seemingly patient eye. . . Without insisting, Mansur's art draws us into a felt encounter with not just the form but the life of a magnificent creature, far from home, captive. He is responding to an imperial order but also paying an artist's homage. Mansur's tenderness for life is unmistakable.

The text in Jahangir's hand along the right margin reads in Persian, the court language: "A mule which the Turks in the company of Mir Ja'far had brought from Ethiopia. Its likeness was drawn by Nadir'ul-'asri [Wonder of the Age] Master Mansur."[31]

My mind returns repeatedly to Jahangir, who cannot always have been easy to bear for Ustad Mansur. Difficult or wise, patrons have been large facts in the lives of many artists. Despite his furies and indulgences, Jahangir was not without feeling. Asked by the elderly woman who had raised many of his children for a peaceful place to live out her years, he made all the arrangements and asked the governor of Delhi, where she would live, "to serve and guard her in such a manner that no dust from any road of vexation might settle on the hem of her contentment."[32] In quiet times he and Ustad Mansur must have spoken easily with one another.

41. TENDERNESS FOR LIFE: A GREEK VOTIVE BRONZE

Deer nursing fawn, with visiting bird
750 -700 BCE, Height nearly 3 inches
Probably from the Kabirion Temple, Thebes
Museum of Fine Arts, Boston
Source: Museum of Fine Arts, Boston

Accompanying image: Archaic votive offering, horse
8th century BCE
The Metropolitan Museum of Art of Art, New Yorkf
Source: Art Resource NY

This stunning miniature conveys such tenderness for life that one scarcely wants to know more about it—no history, no religious context, let it be. But it is, after all, a votive offering, a gift made to a temple by a "parishioner" in ancient times who surely had something in mind. A wonderful text compiled in the Byzantine era, *The Greek Anthology*, collects hundreds of dedications that reveal the nature, religious and transactional, of votive offerings. One such, by an anonymous donor of a trumpet to a temple associated with the goddess Pallas: "Preserve, Tritonian goddess, the offerings and the offerer."[33] Another dedicated to the goddess Artemis concerned a humble gift, "this hat from his head, a token of his wayfaring; for thou hast hearkened to his vows, thou

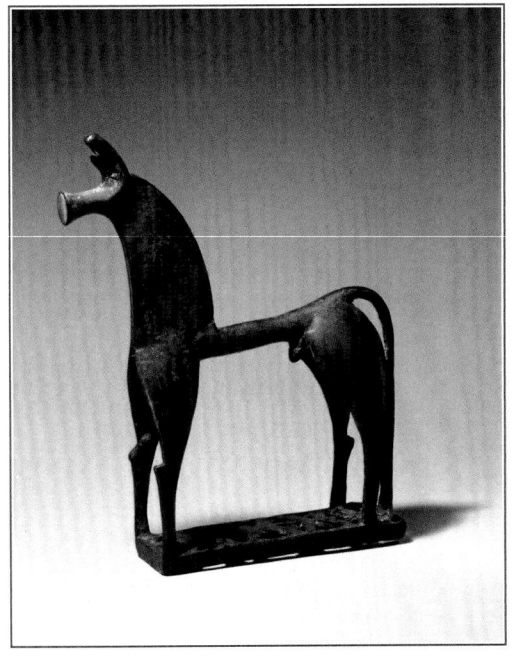

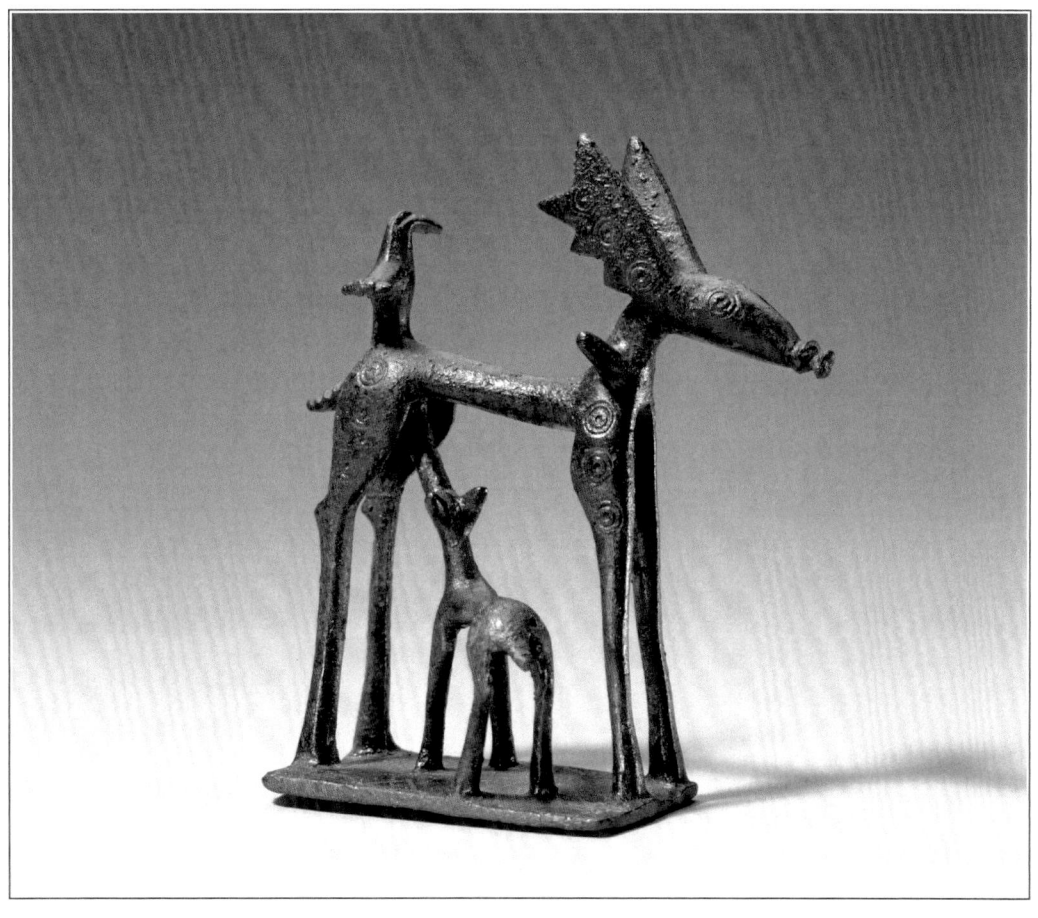

hast blessed his paths."[34] Gratitude. Another donor, to a temple dedicated to three divinities: "I beg from them fine flocks, good wine, and to gather good grain from the ears."[35] That was the nature of votive offerings: objects large and small, grand and humble, deposited in a sanctuary with the hope of benefits in return.

How, then, to understand the superbly tranquil vignette on the previous page, a doe nursing her fawn, undisturbed by a bird comfortably perched on her hind quarters: an episode from the Peaceable Kingdom in an Archaic Greek version. What transaction is implied—I give you this, please grant me that? The temple of the Kabiroi where this is said to have been discovered was an odd place, still not well understood, but what we know raises questions. Hundreds of miniature votive offerings—muscular bulls—have been excavated there. As well, children's toys such as tops, implying that the temple was the site of initiations into manhood for boys who left childish things behind. Pottery found at the site is off-putting: painted with processions of grotesque, seemingly drunken dwarf-like figures with prominent sex organs. What does all that have to do with our little pastorale, this tender icon? I don't know. Perhaps it was offered by a hunter or herdsman, or perhaps after all by a child who had prized it. "The two oxen are mine," reads a farmer's dedication at another temple, "and they helped to grow the corn. Be kind, Demeter, and receive them, though they be of dough and not from the herd. Grant that my real oxen may live."[36] There may well have been a petition of this kind, but for what benefit? Artemis, the virgin huntress, daughter of Zeus, who cared for deer, might have listened more closely than the enigmatic Kabiroi.

The votive offering of a miniature horse in the illustration on p. 132, though from the Archaic period like our deer, could have been sculpted—with pride, with satisfaction—by a number of artists of our own time. These very beautiful works from early Greece have not been overlooked by contemporary and near-contemporary artists. Marino Marini's horses reflect something of the Archaic spirit. So too Susan Rothenberg's unforgettable paintings. And not least, a little-known Sardinian artist, Franco d'Aspro, some of whose small bronzes are votive offerings to gods and goddesses who must still have been nearby in his island home.

42. TENDERNESS FOR LIFE: PISANELLO DRAWINGS

Drawings from life: boar and elegantly saddled mule
Antonio Pisano, known as Pisanello (ca. 1380/1395 – 1450/1455 CE)

Boar: The Fitzwilliam Museum, Cambridge (UK)
Source: Creative Commons

Mule: The Louvre Museum, Paris
Source: Creative Commons

Detail of fresco in the Basilica Sant'Anastasia, Verona
Source: Wikimedia Commons / public domain

P isanello was sought after as an artist by princes and high churchmen. His overwhelming skill, unmistakable in this frontal view of a horse's head burdened by golden armor yet poignantly alive, took him from one city to another, one project to another. His revival of the Imperial Roman prac-

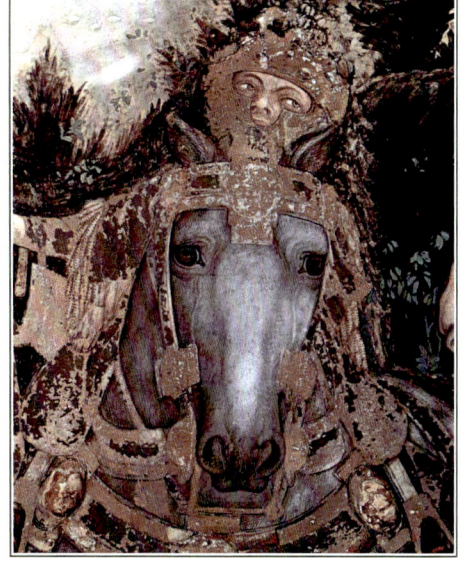

tice of commemorative medallions, typically circular profile portraits of prominent individuals who distributed them as gifts to chosen people, ensured that he never lacked patrons. Although categorized as a participant in the Late International Gothic Style, he was an early and influential instigator of renaissance, the rebirth of Classical norms, style, and meanings in fifteenth-century Italy. There was also a more private artist, evident in collections of his drawings now distributed among several museums.

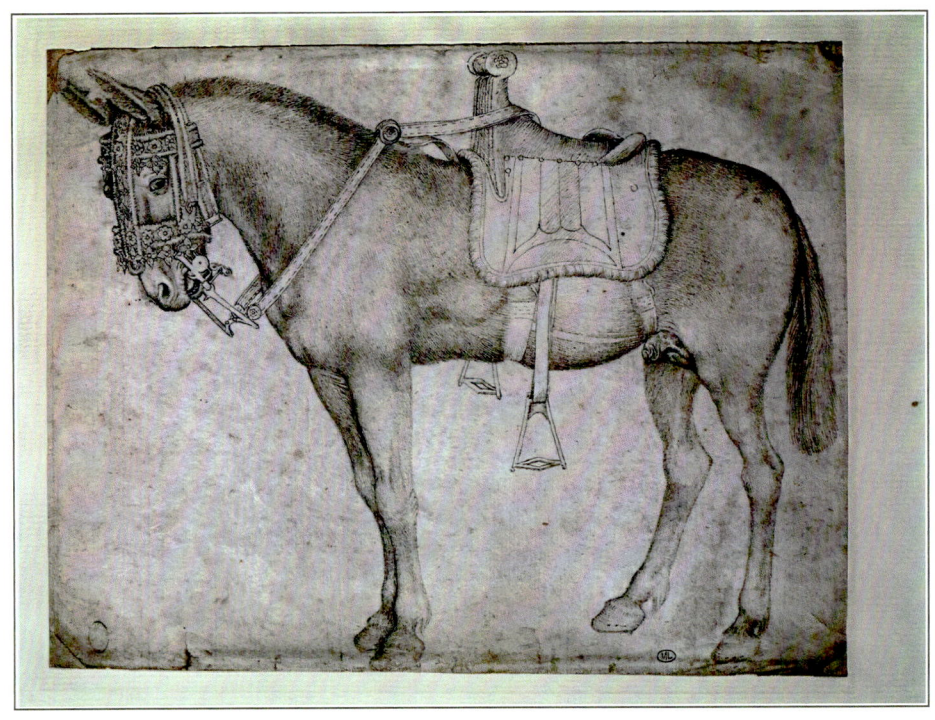

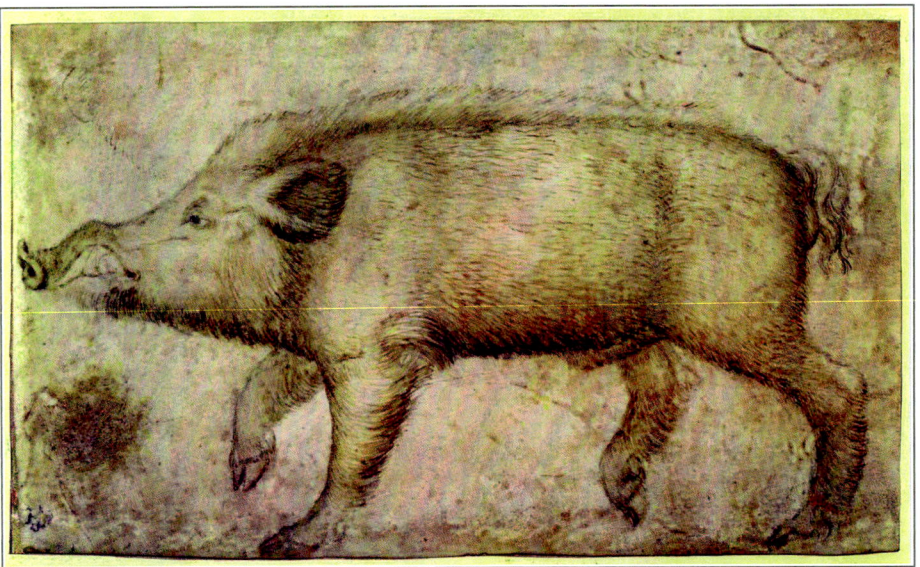

While some of the drawings are preparatory—fully worked out images, often of horses and dogs, appear in the paintings—others reflect a private sensibility and concerns that mattered to no one but himself and perhaps a circle of friends. These works reflect such attention and tenderness for life.

Though in a wholly different time and place, Pisanello is a true peer of Ustad Mansur's. Each is a master of attention. Each is interested in extending the scope of what can be recorded on paper, as if the artist's task is to rescue things from sliding unnoticed away. Each sees into the life of the creatures he chooses to draw or paint. Striking in Pisanello is his unflinching gaze; the boar is our evidence. A homely creature—spikey fur and tusk-like teeth and lidded eye—yet here it is in all its contrarian beauty: one of God's creatures, walking, nearly dancing across the page. The mule, so richly bridled and saddled, tells another story. Its slightly tense, arched neck, the tug of reins looped around the saddle horn, the inquiring cocked ears, the bright eye unmistakably looking at us—all of these details prompt us to read this image both from outside, admiring Pisanello's draftsmanship, and from inside, sharing something of the mule's sense of itself. These are two among many drawings that bear witness to Pisanello's interest in all things alive. I wish that I could show you the cow sitting on the ground—a trivial subject, a classic drawing—and the rabbit leaping, the hooded falcon perched on its master's glove.

The detail of a horse's head (and knight well behind) is from a fresco on the theme of St. George in the Basilica Sant'Anastasia, Verona, dating to the mid-1430s. It is bravura work, bursting with unusual, meticulous detail: a crowded scene of men good and bad, of a beautiful princess in profile as if on a medallion, of animals large and small, of landscape and architecture. Yet while offering this large spectacle, Pisanello is attentive to the inner lives of his cast of characters. Our horse's eyes, the eyes of St. George embarking on a life-or-death mission, and more still, endow this work not just with grandeur but with a sense of identities in play, under stress, present.

43. TENDERNESS FOR LIFE: FABRITIUS' GOLDFINCH

The Goldfinch
Carel Fabritius (1622 – 1654)
Oil on panel, 1654, app. 13 x 9 inches
The Mauritshuis, The Hague
Source: Wikimedia Commons / public domain

Self-portrait, ca. 1645
Oil on panel, 27 x 19 inches
Boijmans Van Beuningen Museum, Rotterdam
Source: Wikimedia Commons / public domain

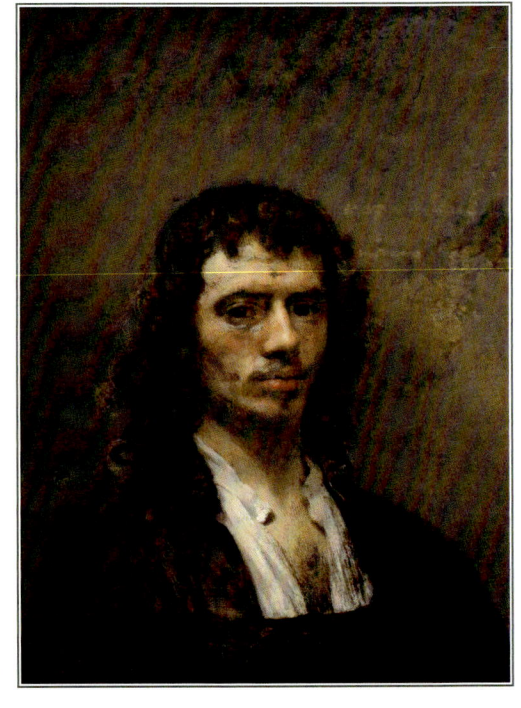

Fabritius' self-portrait provokes a surprisingly direct encounter. He brings the lucidity of his teacher, Rembrandt, to this examination of his own defiance and vulnerability. It dates to the same year as "The Goldfinch," best known among his few surviving works. He could be someone we know now or know of—a rock star in an amazing band, a rebellious writer. The lasting poignancy of this image is that it was painted, like "The Goldfinch," in the year of his death at age 32. He perished with many others in the Dutch city of Delft when a depot of 90,000 pounds of gunpowder exploded and leveled a quarter of the city. The event is known to Dutch history as "the Thunderclap." I have a space in my mind dedicated to the memory

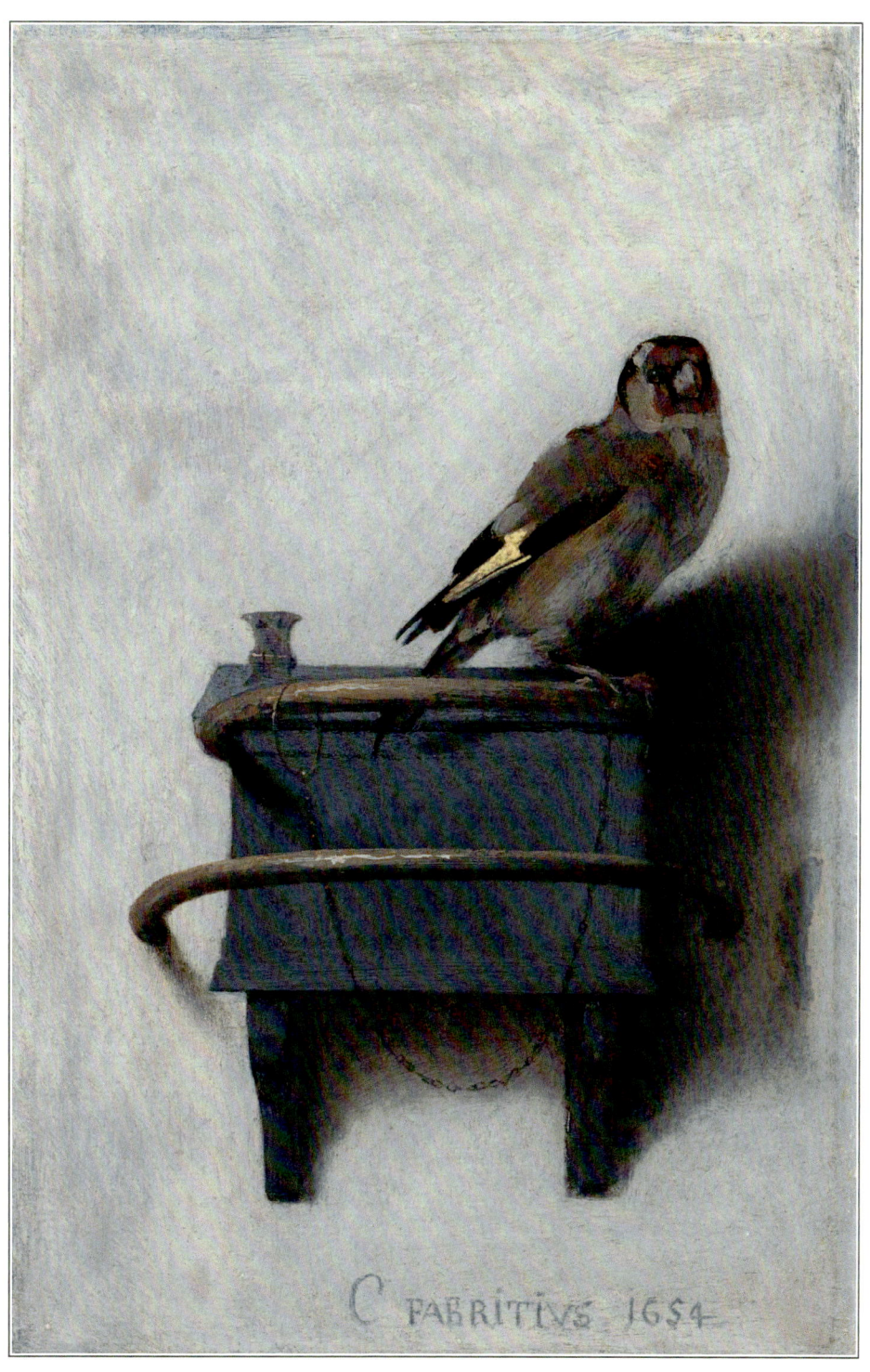

of overwhelmingly gifted people who left long before their time—musicians, writers, statesmen, Fabritius.

Beware of closely approaching the art of seventeenth-century Holland, the Golden Age: you may never return. It offers a complete, inviting world, painted with technical skill, depth of vision, creativity, and love by masters from Rembrandt van Rijn (1606 - 1669) and Johannes Vermeer (1632 - 1675) to Pieter de Hooch (1629 - 1684) and many others. Fabritius offers an introduction to their world. Born to a family of painters, he found his way to Rembrandt's studio in Amsterdam for what looks to be two years of apprenticeship before moving to Delft and joining the painters' guild, where he met Vermeer and de Hooch and is thought to have influenced their development. In those years he found his own style, free of his great master but nourished by all that he had learned from him.

"The Goldfinch" has attracted searching scholarship. Such a seemingly simple painting has its mysteries. Linda Stone-Ferrier, an American art historian, has persuasively argued that the painting was first an illusionistic window decoration—passersby in the street could easily believe that a pet finch was taking the air. Even the artist's grey signature reflects street life in Delft; it is quite like the graffiti apparently common at that time and place.[37]

Why has this painting charmed generations? The little bird with its little chain, perched on its little box and a little alone, immediately stirs empathy—that much is clear. The mastery of three-dimensional representation is fascinating—it gives us back our world, but now we notice its spaciousness owing to Fabritius' art. And there is something more difficult to put into words, though it's a dominant impression. It is the wall and shadows. The quiet color harmony, the interplay of light and shadow, subtle variations in texture—all of that together. Fabritius created a tender homage to life while exploring with dispassionate inquiry the painter's home ground of light, surface, space. The conjunction of love and study endows this painting with its special flavor.

PARENTHESIS: ACCELERATED DEVELOPMENT

Accelerated development in the arts is rare and interesting. It is as if something seizes artists and whirls them forward. What forces are at work? What intelligence? What social and economic conditions that summon greatness? The three examples I have in mind are ancient Greek sculpture; Italian painting from Giotto (earlier fourteenth century) to the High Renaissance and beyond; and music from J. S. Bach to a composer—your choice—of the late nineteenth or early twentieth century. My choice is Brahms (d. 1897), if only because he once said truly "that's how it's done from Bach up to myself."[38] He was both vastly original and a grateful heir. Despite their differences, these examples have much in common. As a preface to the next sequence of icons, can we take a closer look?

I admire consciousness. I admire its power of discovery, its shaping power, and the transition it sponsors from startling discovery to new norms that become simply the way things are done, the way they should be done.

Accelerated development—for example, the transition in ancient Greek sculpture from works that barely suggest the freely moving human figure (p. 4) to works that fully state the figure as a complex physical and psychological presence (p. 39)—relies on the impassioned commitment of generations of artists. The first feature common to periods of accelerated development is virtuoso skill. This in turn implies a tradition of apprenticeship and rigorous training, which is both helpful to the teacher—it brings additional hands to the studio or sculpture yard—and a matter of generosity. Virtuoso skill also implies the ability to recognize the promise of technical innovations—for example, the transition from egg tempera to oil-based paints in the fifteenth century. It opened new worlds of representation and expression.

An accelerated tradition in the arts is self-critical in the best sense: what has come before is subject to discernment. That discernment shows how to continue, how to build on the immediate past without simply perpetuating it.

There occurs a critical embrace: filial acceptance of accomplishments to date, yet with an eye to what more is possible. Accelerated developments scoop up and remember past accomplishments without being dominated by them. Brahms insisted on the importance of studying the works of J. S. Bach and painstakingly edited his predecessor of genius, Franz Schubert; he understood how to immerse himself, without losing himself, in the greatness of the past. The second common feature is critical embrace.

Artists participating in an accelerated development possess a mighty power of concentration. Consciousness at their level of engagement is something like a forge, a hot place of transformation. Of course they rest, they have their pleasures, but they know that their task is to keep the forge in the mind at a transformative temperature. They are questioners, experimenters, makers. Whenever it crops up, they look at their own natural laziness as an entertaining deficiency not to be taken seriously. People who miss nothing amaze me. I've known just a few. And where accelerated development is possible and promising, it is best to miss nothing: no opportunity, obstacle, or submerged reef. The third common feature is concentration.

The fourth common feature depends on the will of the gods or kind fate: individual genius in enough participants to make accelerated development possible. Artists of genius working at such a time meet in fluid configurations: sometimes collaborators, sometimes simply aware of one another's work and advances, sometimes competitors. The situation calls for balance between individuality and shared mission.

Gifted individuals are explorers of the full dimensions of the mind. They contemplate matters in their leisure time or in the studio when they glimpse new expressive or technical possibilities. I have the greatest respect, nearly awe, for the hidden parts of the mind: for the imagination, dreaming, and reconfiguring that occurs when it appears that nothing is taking place. We sometimes move along on a current of fugitive dreams, from some of which the new and needed can emerge in its own time. There is both prose and poetry in every mind. The fifth common feature is openness to understandings coming seemingly from nowhere. This does not undo concentration.

The last common feature to which I'll point, though there are surely others, is responsiveness to context. Artists have patrons and obligations, they bring their gifts to social, political, and religious contexts where expression is needed. Their innovative drive encounters contextual expectation. On occasion they move far past expectation and feel, with disappointment and pride, that their works address the future and in time will be celebrated. Accelerated development in the arts invites artists to note the far edge of expectation and push on from there.

The Italian Renaissance found its ideal chronicler in Giorgio Vasari (1511 – 1574), whose multi-volume *Lives of the Most Excellent Painters, Sculptors, and Architects* (1550) conveys the intensity of learning among artists—learning, collaboration, and competition—in an era of accelerated development. He was aware of the need for gifted individuals who know and know of each other.

> It is a frequent practice of Nature when she produces a person of great excellence in any profession to raise up another to rival him at the same time and in a neighboring place, so that they may help one another by their emulation and talents. This circumstance, besides being of singular assistance to those immediately concerned, also inflames the spirits of those who come after, to endeavor by study and industry to attain to the same honor and glorious reputation which they hear praised every day in their predecessors.[39]

The European works of art in the next sequence, from the overwhelmingly beautiful Late Gothic art of Simone Martini to several works of the Italian Renaissance and the Dutch Golden Age, scarcely begin to reflect the heritage and accelerated development of their eras. Each is, however, an icon and an invitation to explore further.

A question tugs at me. Why have I cared to put before you this schema of accelerated development? I know that it is true enough of every such development, but not comprehensively true of any one of them. Each era has its facts and requires focused scholarship to elicit those facts and array them properly. Behind what I've written is a sense of urgency that we men and women of the twenty-first century need an accelerated cultural and political development in order to keep our world safe. Time is short. Can we learn or relearn what is needed: virtuoso skill, critical embrace, concentration, individuality and collaboration, erasing boundaries of suspicion, responsiveness to context—in other words, deliberate and searching consciousness? It has been possible. It should be possible again. The arts show how it works; this time we need it not in just one domain but across contemporary life from science and society to spirituality.

44. *IL MIO SIMON:* SIMONE MARTINI'S ANNUNCIATION

Simone Martini (ca. 1284 – 1344), assisted by Lippo Memmi (attested 1317 – 1347)
Annunciation with Saints Margaret and Ansanus, 1333 CE
10 ft. X 8.7 ft., tempera and gold on wooden panel
The Uffizi Gallery, Florence
Source: Wikimedia Commons / Diego Delso

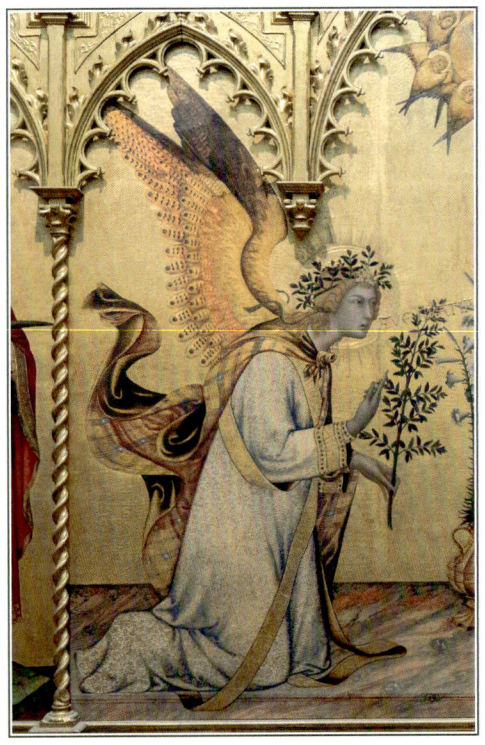

In 1335, not long after this magnificent altarpiece had been completed for the cathedral of Siena, there was an interesting encounter in Avignon. Simone Martini had traveled there at the request of the pope to fulfill a commission. Petrarch (1304 – 1374), the poet of genius and pioneering scholar of ancient literature, had been living in the region for much of his life. Regarded as the founder of Renaissance humanism, Petrarch circulated a book of sonnets, *Il Canzoniere* (The Song Book), that served as a model of verse form and poetic attitude across much of Europe for several centuries to come. His book of songs addressed the theme of his impossible love for Laura, a married woman of stunning beauty who paid him no attention. Here is the nexus between Simone and Petrarch: the poet arranged for the painter to make a portrait of Laura. At least he would have the image if not the reality of his distant

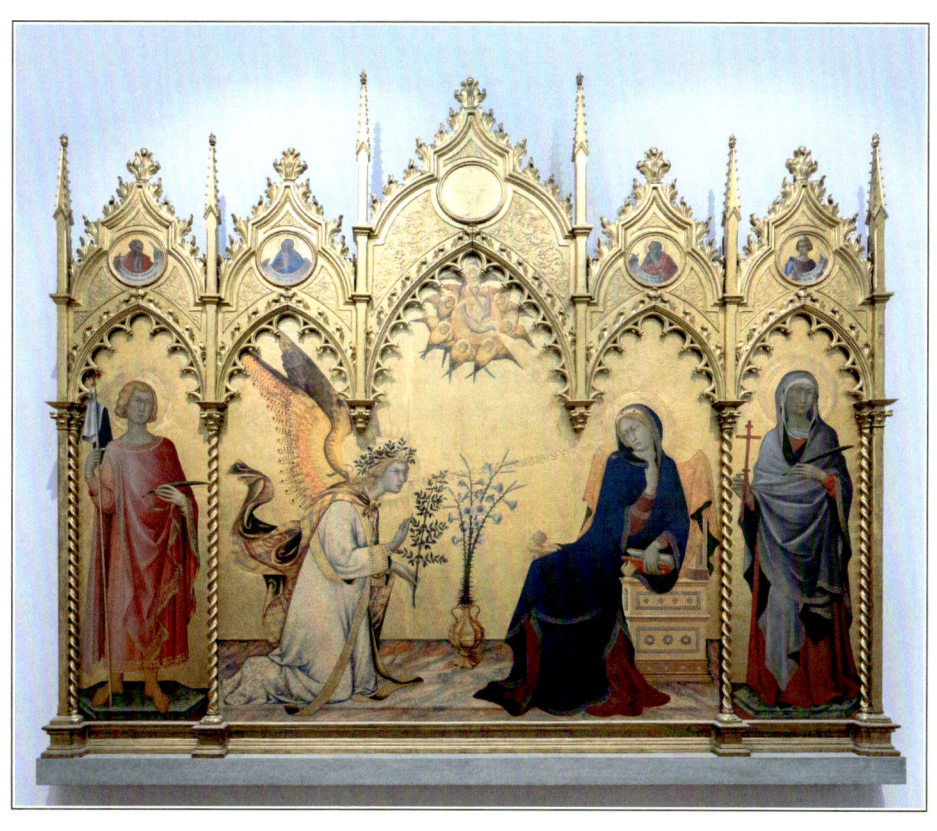

love. The portrait is long since lost, but one of Petrarch's sonnets gives us words that allow us to see Simone's art with the eyes and sensibility of his era. Petrarch speaks there of "il mio Simon"—they must have become good friends—and supposes that Simone had seen Laura's face in heaven:

> L'opra ful bien di quelle che nel cielo
> si ponno imaginar, non qui tra noi,
> ove le membra fanno a l'alma velo.

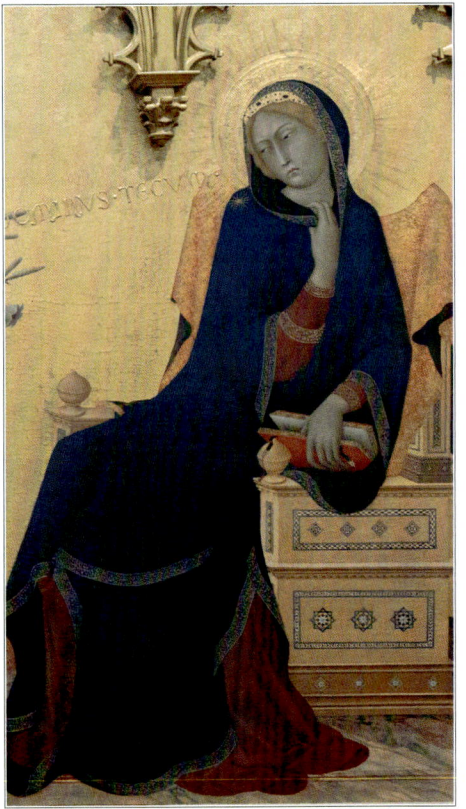

"The work is of the sort that only in heaven / could be imagined, not here with us / where the limbs veil the soul."[40]

These lovely words find their way back from Avignon to Siena, and to the altarpiece. No less than Petrarch, Simone was a humanist. An exquisite craftsman—the altarpiece has jewel-like detail throughout—he also perceived movements of feeling and related gesture as if from within. His vision of the Annunciation is so very beautiful and felt with such noble restraint that one could easily agree: it is a transcription from heaven. Interrupted in her reading by the incursion of the Archangel Gabriel, his wind-blown shawl conveying his sudden arrival, the Virgin recoils with a protective gesture. Yet she sees and listens, hears the words advancing toward her: "Ave Gratia Plena Dominus Tecum"—Hail, full of grace, the Lord is with thee." The Archangel's attitude is as interesting as hers. His expression conveys watchfulness, even apprehension: how will Mary receive the good news that she is to give birth to the Savior?

Simone's portrait of Laura surely had much in common with this unforgettable image, which Petrarch teaches us to see.

45. AN ELEGY FOR MASACCIO

> Masaccio (1401 – 1428)
> The Brancacci Chapel frescoes
> 1425 – 1427 CE
> Santa Maria del Carmine, Florence
> Source: Wikipedia / public domain

I would rather write an elegy than a commentary, as Masaccio died, perhaps poisoned by a rival in Rome, at the age of 26. No greater talent has left earlier.

Scarcely anything is known of Masaccio's early training, apart from the fact that it would have been in Florence. His most decisive master, Giotto di Bondone (ca. 1267 – 1337), had left his lessons on the walls of churches and chapels in Tuscany, where a century later the young artist saw the future in them. Giotto had made the first break with the art of his era, a graceful Italian interpretation of Byzantine art, through a new vision of the figure in space, rounded, naturally posed, endowed with psychological life, placed in a world like our own rather than in a gorgeous hieratic space. Vasari thought of Giotto as "not so much the pupil of any human master as of Nature herself . . . ."[41] Masaccio converted this breakthrough into a tradition; he saw the way forward to an art of "movement, vigor, and life," as Vasari put it.[42] Masaccio's work in the Brancacci Chapel became, in turn, a school for artists. Again Vasari: "All of the celebrated painters and sculptors from

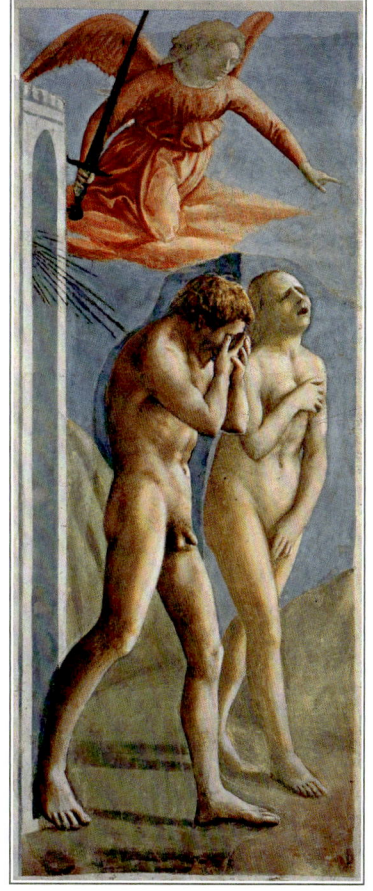

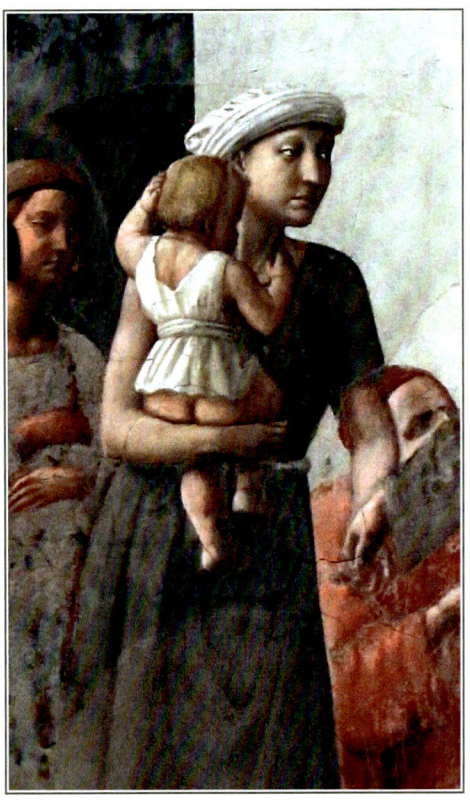

that time until now have become excellent and distinguished by studying in that chapel."[43]

The few illustrations here can only begin to suggest the quiet power of Masaccio's pictorial world. The long and largely lost tradition of Greco-Roman painting, which we encountered in the Pompeian Villa of the Mysteries (p. 42) is reborn here, enhanced by Masaccio's pioneering application of spatial perspective which creates a comfortable, believable perception of three dimensions. The values we appreciated in the Villa of the Mysteries—dignity and restraint, empathy, fluent story-telling—are all here in a new version that would set the course of Western art for centuries more. The dramatic episode on the facing page is from the life of St. Peter, based on Acts 4:32 - 5:5: believers of some wealth in Jerusalem have given Peter money, which he distributes to the poor—here a woman with child—while Ananias, who selfishly held back funds, falls dead at Peter's feet. The woman with child epitomizes Masaccio's art: direct, felt, not fussy, monumental. This vision of the human figure and human presence will wind its way through coming centuries, reappearing for example in the wonderful mid-nineteenth century figural art of Corot and in Picasso at a number of periods in his ever-changing art.

Art in the Classical tradition can easily become declamatory. Not here. The fresco panel showing the expulsion of Adam and Eve from Eden marshals this new vision to tell our tale of greatest woe. Here are our naked father and mother, moving away from heaven on earth, blinded by shame and sorrow. Their nakedness is insistent: they have nothing, they know nothing but their suffering. If there is an encouragement, it is that they stumble toward light, shown us by Masaccio's skill in depicting the play of light and shadow across their bodies. This extraordinary image sets to work Masaccio's new under-standing of the human figure with such power that we stop caring about his art and care only about what is being said. It is a good artist who nearly obliterates his own art.

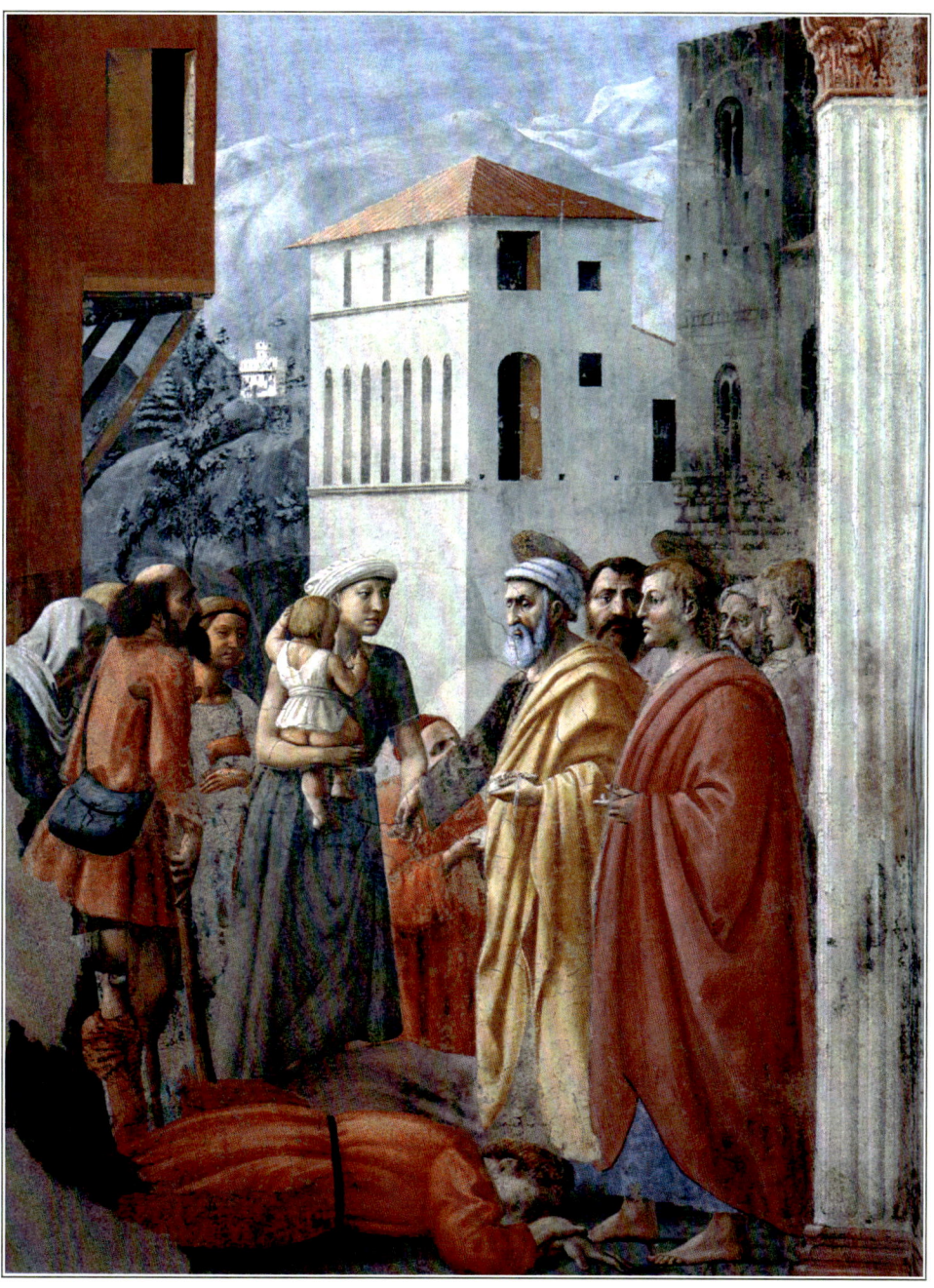

46. A TRIBE LIKE NO OTHER: PIERO DELLA FRANCESCA

Piero della Francesca (1412 – 1492 CE)
The human face (details) from four works, ca. 1442 – 1475
National Gallery, London; Museo Civico, Sansepolcro;
Church of S. Francesco, Arezzo
Source: Wikipedia / public domain

Perspective drawing of the Tempietto di Santa Maria del Colledestro
Published in Piero's *De prospectiva pingendi* (1474 – 1482), Biblioteca Ambrosiana

Piero della Francesca is among the most mysterious and compelling artists in the Western canon. Once encountered, he is unlikely to fade from memory. There is a good range of surviving works to explore on site and in the world's museums, he published several books, we can follow him from city to city, project to project, we know something (though too little) of his friends and conversation partners—the people from whom he learned and with whom he learned. We know that he was intensely interested

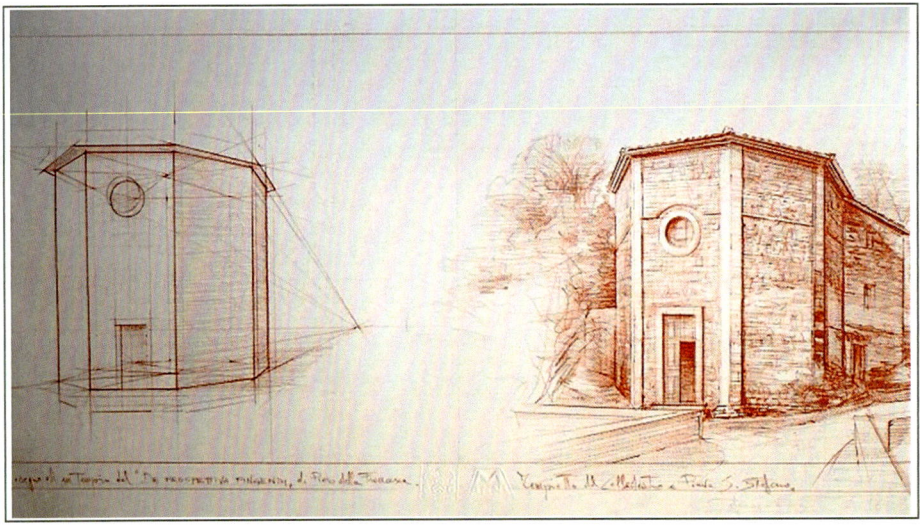

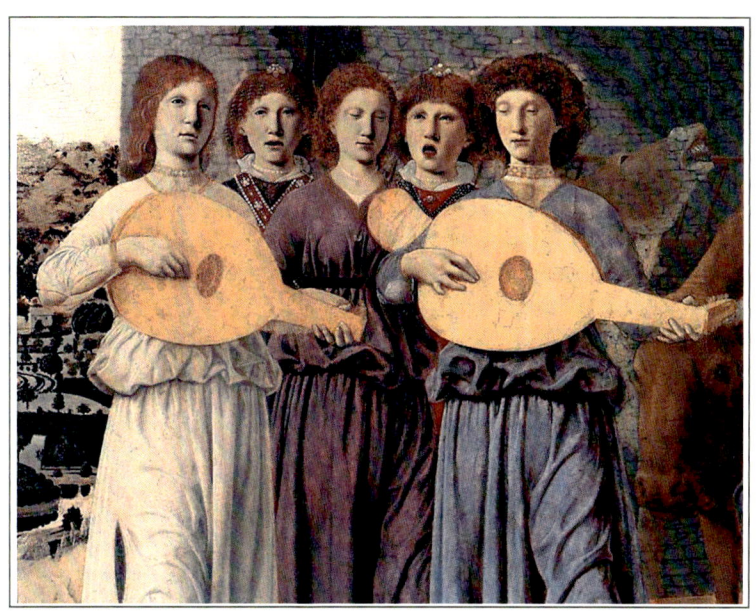

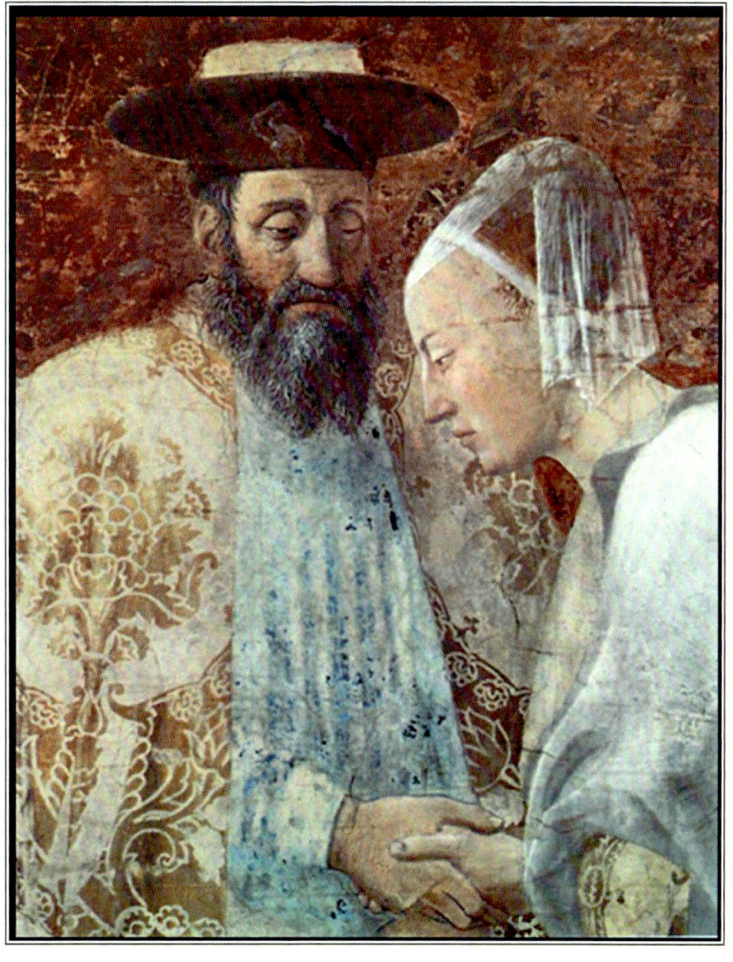

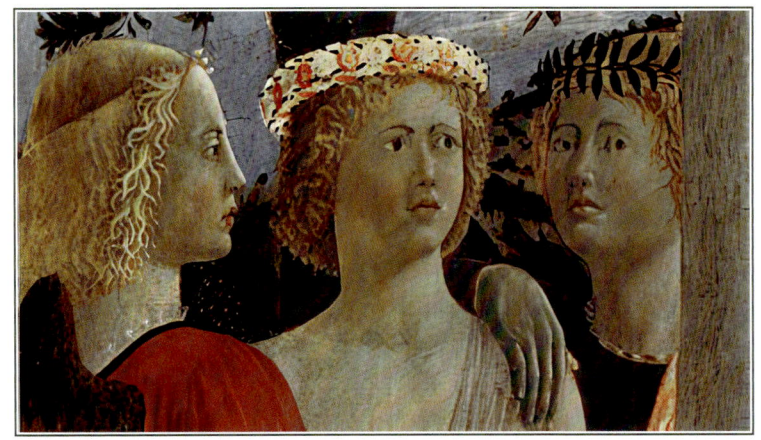

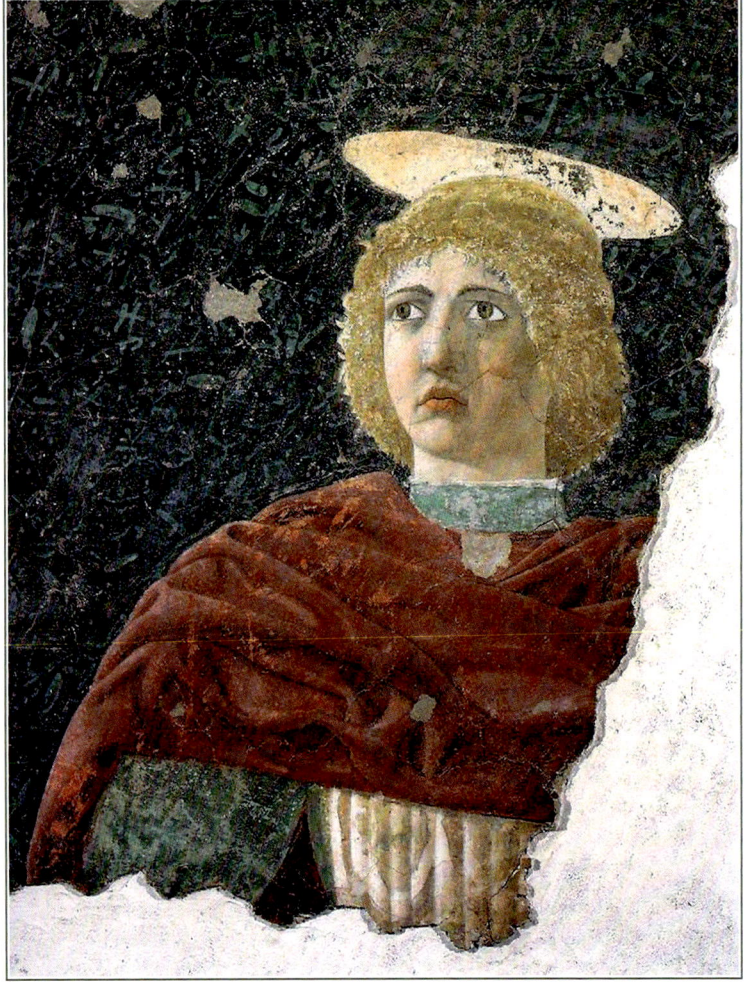

in mathematics and geometry, and we know the kinds of people, learned humanists, artists and architects, translators of ancient literature, with whom that interest would have brought him in touch. In his *On Perspective in Painting*, he collated and advanced not just theory but practice for generations of artists to come (the little study, on p. 150, is from that book). But when we turn back to his works, whether on site or in illustrated books, the sense of mystery resumes. It is as if we are ignorant of some factor, some remarkable X. There is unique beauty, an unmistakable hand—and something stated everywhere in nearly every figure yet uncaptioned, left to us to understand. It doesn't seem to matter if the figure is the Holy Virgin or a common soldier, they share in the same mystery.

On the preceding pages I have collected faces from works nearly spanning his career, from the three angels in the relatively early *Baptism of Christ* (1442) to the encounter of Solomon and the Queen of Sheba in the fresco cycle (1452 – 1455) in the church of San Francesco in Arezzo, the fragmentary St. Julian (1455), and then the choir of singing and strumming angels in the *Nativity* of 1475. Every face is still or nearly so, as if whatever action there is to be will proceed in slow motion. Every face gives an impression of inwardness, of a sense of self. This is not an art that smiles or seeks to charm; it draws us into its own world, insists on what I earlier called X, but perhaps now we are closer to understanding. Piero populates his pictorial world with participants high and low—holy figures, kings and queens, foot soldiers, maids in waiting—whose vast calm restates human nature. Everyone is self-possessed, everyone is awake.

I have no idea why this is so. It doesn't follow from mastery of figure construction and perspective; it's an entirely different thing. It doesn't fit neatly into a schema of accelerated development, as if it represents an advance in logical sequence. No, this is either about Piero himself, his rare sensibility, or about Piero and his friends and teachers, some of whom in later years would have been in the circle of the Florentine scholar, translator, and mystic Marsilio Ficino (1433 – 1499). "The soul exists partly in eternity and partly in time," wrote Ficino. Is that what Piero gives us to see? Not because Ficino said it, but because Piero knew it.

47. "TELL IT SLANT": JOHANNES VERMEER

Johannes Vermeer (1632 – 1675)
Woman Holding a Balance, ca. 1664 CE
Oil on canvas, 16 ¾ x nearly 15 inches
The National Gallery of Art, Washington, D. C.
Source: Wikimedia Commons / public domain

Vermeer's vision of home and persons, light and mood, has been taken to heart by innumerable people worldwide, as if what he said in art long ago is said to us now. In recent decades, exhibitions from London to Osaka have been received by the public as formidable events. Vermeer painted slowly and little—just 34 attested works survive. He spent his all too brief life in the generally prosperous small city of Delft, where he certainly knew and perhaps studied with Carel Fabritius (ten years his senior), and where he later served as director of the local painters' Guild of St. Luke. With eleven children in the family, he made ends meet in part by dealing in works of art like his father before him, and he likely had a local patron who purchased many of his paintings. After his passing, he was all but forgotten until the mid-nineteenth century, when a French art critic was thrilled by a painting he encountered and set about reassembling and publishing Vermeer's work.

Vermeer was an *intimiste*, almost always a poet of modest things and quiet moments endowed with a stir of psychological resonance. What we are shown is simple, quiet—and not so. On the page opposite, a woman stands alone by a window holding a jeweler's delicate balance. She is beautiful (and no doubt well along in her pregnancy); she surveys her treasures on the table before her; her gestures—for example, the weight of her hand on the table—and the tilt of her head are so light and sensitive that one senses them through one's own body. In a somewhat ominous theological echo of this lovely moment, behind her is a painting of the Last Judgment, another and more fateful weighing in the balance. A small mirror faces her across the table, should she care to look

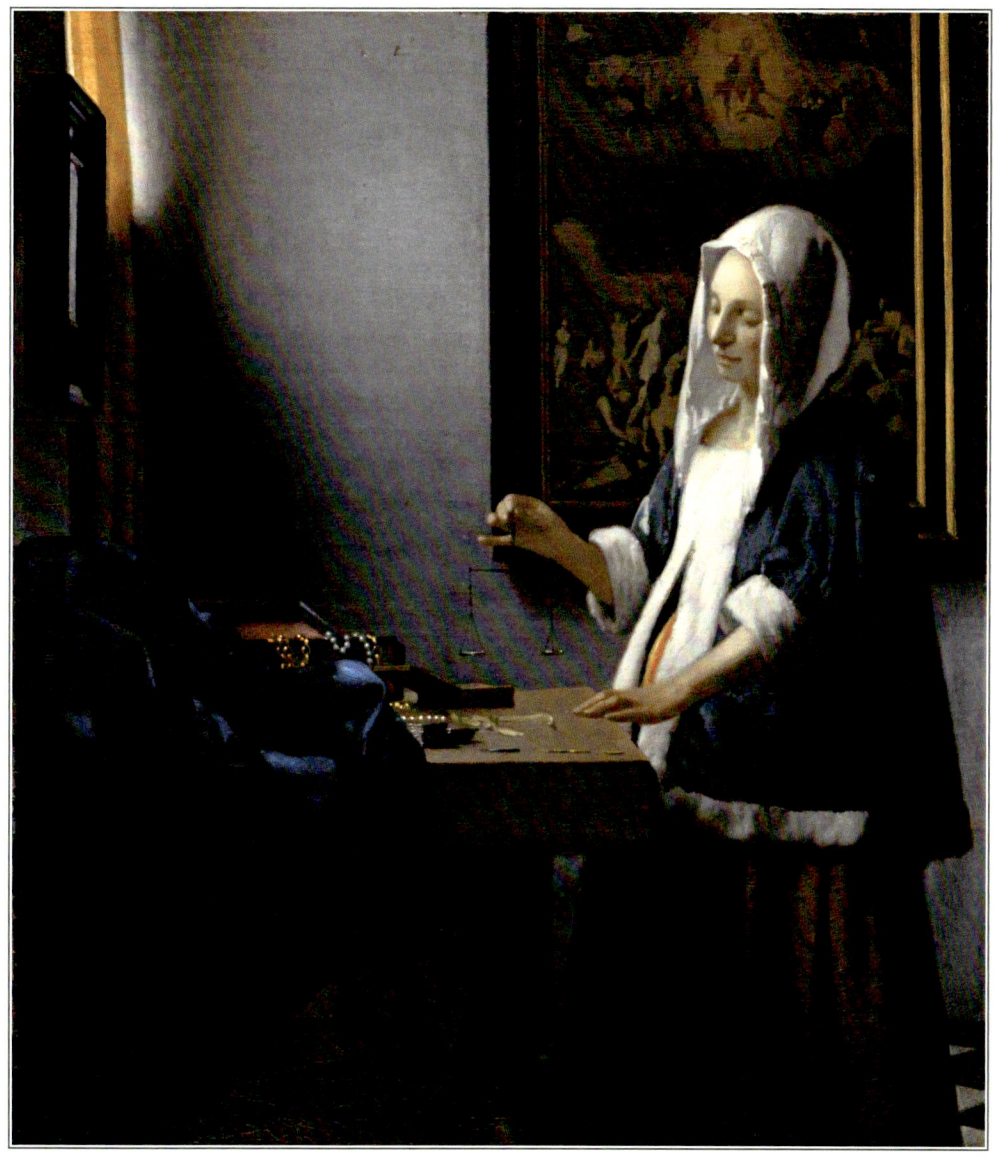

up, but this is not a strident Vanitas image of a kind well known in European art. As we stay with this painting, our eyes travel everywhere to appreciate the transformations of light moving through and past the curtain and across the wall, the realistic—and yet not so—rendering of her fur-lined jacket, the bright edge of her shawl, the beautifully rendered highlights on gold, silver, pearls.

There is something at work in this painting, and others like it from Vermeer, that I have so far put awkwardly into words as "not so." It is time to turn for insight to another *intimiste*, the mid-nineteenth-century poet of surpassing genius, Emily Dickinson. She too lived a circumscribed life; in later years she scarcely left home, and in her lifetime published almost nothing. One of her best-known poems is nearly a commentary on Vermeer's art:

> Tell all the truth but tell it slant —
> Success in Circuit lies
> Too bright for our infirm Delight
> The Truth's superb surprise
> As Lightning to the Children eased
> With explanation kind
> The Truth must dazzle gradually
> Or every man be blind —[44]

Vermeer's pictorial poetry is of this kind. The world he offers is more beautiful, more tender, less hard-edged and abrupt, than his world or ours. The harsh lightning of life is eased. Vermeer tells the truth but tells it slant. I don't know that anyone before or since has seen as he saw, but through his works we are granted access. When one allows one's eyes to receive, one's own home occasionally looks like this, too: it dazzles gradually.

48. "ALL HONOR TO THEE, MY REMBRANDT!"

1 Self-Portrait Leaning on a Stone Sill, 1639
Etching, 8x6½ inches
Rijksmuseum, Amsterdam
Source: Wikimedia Commons / public domain

2 Self-Portrait, 1658
Oil on canvas, app. 52x41 inches
The Frick Collection, New York
Source: Wikimedia Commons / public domain

3 Portrait of Jan Six, 1654
Oil on canvas, 44x40 inches
Six Collection, Amsterdam
Source: The Yorck Project (2002) / Wikimedia Commons

4 Self-Portrait, 1659
Oil on canvas, app. 33x26 inches
National Gallery of Art, Washington, D. C
Wikimedia Commons / public domain

5 Self-Portrait as Zeuxis or Democritus, 1662 – 63
Oil on canvas, app. 33x26 inches
Wallraf-Richartz-Museum & Fondation Corbond, Cologne
Source: Wikimedia Commons / public domain

"All honor to thee, my Rembrandt!" So wrote Constantijn Huygens, who visited Rembrandt's first studio in Leiden in 1629, some years before the artist moved to Amsterdam. They were young: Rembrandt an emerging artist of growing reputation, Huygens a diplomat and poet destined for a remarkable career. Rembrandt's art would change and change again over the decades, but Huygens' prescient words speak to all that was to come.[45] Huygens had been looking for artists who could reflect back to the nascent, proud Dutch Republic all that it was, all that it cared to be. He had found his man.

We need more biography than usual in these pages, and more pages, as the foundation for what I hope to express before we're done. This book is not a mandala, with a god or primal mountain at the center and a well-populated periphery of everything else, but if it were designed in that way, Rembrandt would be at the foot of the mountain, or the mountain itself. He was a great soul; not at first, it takes time and suffering and reflection to make a great soul. But in the end, yes, he became a great soul. These few words ask for time and exploration.

Rembrandt van Rijn (1606 – 1669) was a miller's son, one of nine chil-dren, promising enough to be sent to Latin school in his native Leiden and then on to the University of Leiden for several years before his inclination to the visual arts led to a three-year apprenticeship with a local artist of consid-erable excellence. A further six months' apprenticeship with the well-known Pieter Lastman in Amsterdam completed the young man's grounding in the demanding studio skills and repertory of ideas and standards he needed to set his own course. Rembrandt settled in Amsterdam in 1631 as the house guest and working partner of an art dealer, who helped him rapidly become a sought-after portrait artist in an increasingly affluent society that had a taste for decorous self-representation. Scanning through the many portraits of these years, you could easily gain the impression that he painted portraits of *everybody* in Amsterdam, painted with acute but non-intrusive awareness of the sitter's character, of his and her sense of social position, of how they wished to be seen. This was not his only offering. He was immensely skilled in the creation of paintings, large and small, on historical and biblical themes for which there was endless demand. And then, he was equally skilled and inno-vative as a graphic artist whose etchings on a vast range of subjects circulated at home and in other countries.

Married in 1635 to lovely Saskia, the art dealer's cousin and a person of some familial wealth, the couple acquired a large home, now the Rembrandt House Museum. By 1639, the miller's son had become what we see in the etch-ing (1): a man of the world, an artist of the world adopting a confident posture and attitude familiar in High Renaissance portraiture. He had as many paying students as he could teach and incorporate into the routines of a busy studio. He had enough disposable cash, or so he imagined, to add continuously to a

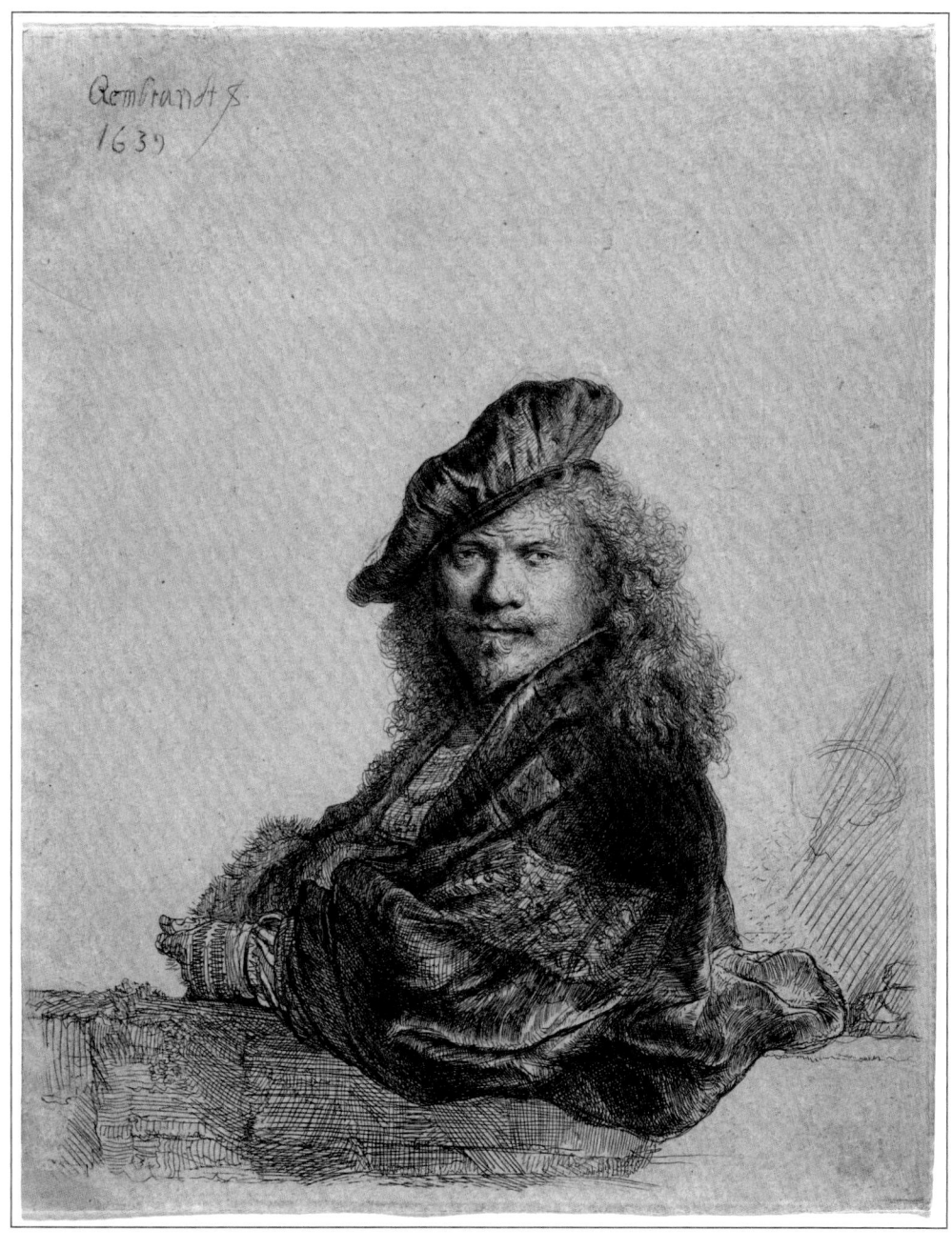

collection of prints, paintings, copies of Antique statuary, things of wonder from around the world, and a range of garments and wraps suggesting biblical times, all this with much else that found its way into paintings. It would be a good life, an easy life.

From the beginning, Rembrandt had two compelling interests: self-portraiture (the first an etching, 1629) and sketching from life. He would spend time among plain people, even beggars, he would wander in the countryside and later convert some of his sketches and vivid memories into etchings. In the end there would be some 75 self-portraits. Many of the early etched self-portraits are evidently experiments; he would try out various, often extravagant facial expressions and effects of lighting and posture on the nearest model at hand, himself. Others from the early years in Amsterdam were "advertisements for himself," demonstrating his skill to prospective clients and attracting connoisseurs interested in artists' self-portraits. But there was something else at work, a self-inquiry in paint and ink as sustained and relentless as the self-inquiry of Michel de Montaigne (1533 – 1592) through his brilliant essays. Montaigne happens to have been an author familiar in Leiden; one of the university's founding professors, Justus Lipsius (no relation, unfortunately), had met Montaigne and made his works known. As there was no Dutch translation of the *Essais* until 1679 and, as far as I know, Rembrandt had no French, the artist would have heard indirectly of Montaigne, perhaps discussed him with Huygens, who admired his writings. Montaigne is relevant simply to illustrate that sustained self-inquiry shouldn't surprise us at this or any period. One of the most memorable professors of my undergraduate years, Harold Bloom, insisted that Shakespeare "invented the human"—so well argued, such a splendid polemic, though untrue. The human has been explored and "reinvented" time and time again, among others by Rembrandt, who was born in the year Shakespeare wrote three of his great tragedies. The human is uninventable, it is already there; as soon as we look toward it, it stares back at us.

The year 1642 is generally recognized as a watershed in Rembrandt's life. In that year Saskia died of tuberculosis soon after the birth of their son Titus, the only child of four destined to survive infancy. The intimate sorrow of her death coincided with delivery of Rembrandt's greatest large-scale painting, "The Night Watch," a treasure to this day of the Rijksmuseum, Amsterdam. Every student of art history is introduced to this vast canvas depicting the militia company of Captain Frans Banning Cocq, crowded together, handsome fellows ready for battle, many in the dark background, their commanders in a bright foreground, bravely marching forth, broadly gesturing,

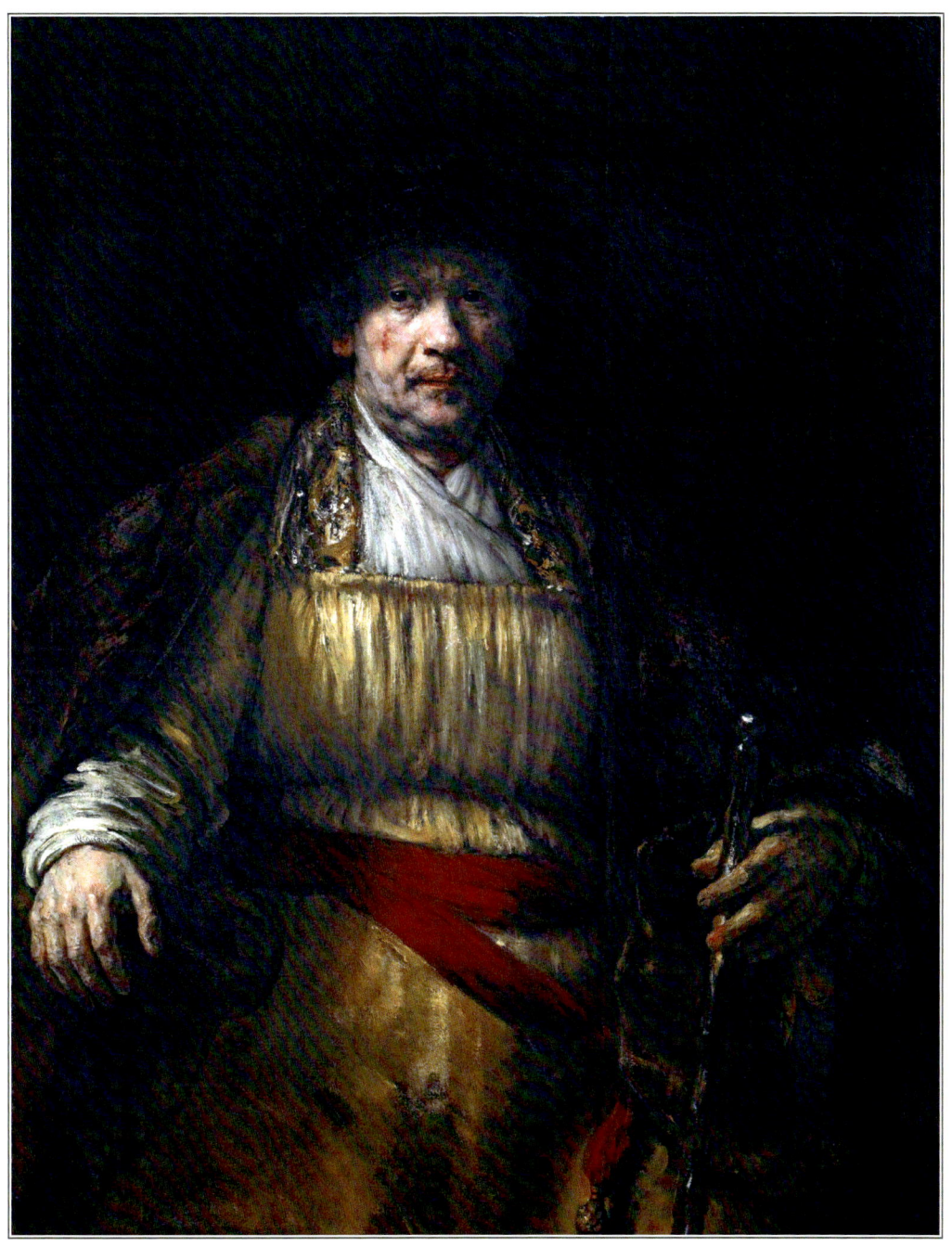

exchanging glances: so very alive. There had never been anything like it; what you were supposed to do with such a commission was line everyone up, make them all visible in good likenesses, add weapons and manly accoutrements, no dramatic action required or expected.[46] Captain Cocq and his companions were apparently pleased with the painting, but elite public opinion wasn't uniformly pleased.

Here we encounter the Rules of Art. In "The Night Watch" and many other paintings, Rembrandt was fulfilling to perfection just what Huygens had foreseen years earlier: he was endowing the Dutch Republic with a powerful identity—but doing so in his own way. You see, he hadn't visited Italy. His earliest biographer, the painter Joachim von Sandrart, writing in 1675, understood that Rembrandt deserved notice for his accomplishments, but "[Rembrandt] stuck with his own manner of painting, and did not hesitate to oppose and contradict our rules of art such as anatomy and the proportions of the human body, perspective and the usefulness of classical statues, Raphael's drawing and well-judged composition, and the academies which are so particularly necessary for our profession. In making this choice he argued that one should be guided by Nature alone, and by no other rules."[47] I want to translate this comment into a common experience: how many times in the world's museums have you walked rapidly past walls of paintings that obey the Rules of Art—so skilled, so dull—toward one or two canvases by Rembrandt where you know that you will linger? The Rules of Art were alive when they weren't rules yet—when Raphael and a fantastic company of Italian and Northern European artists were feeling their way, creating visions that still stop us. In Sandrart's comments you hear what the poet William Blake called "the horses of instruction" bearing down on a unique talent.

There was another problem with Rembrandt. You'll recall that even in early years he would on occasion sketch and etch and paint unbeautiful people whom he found beautiful or touching. He was not one to avert his eyes. In later years he painted nudes, sometimes in the context of biblical narratives and classical myth, sometimes as an homage without context to womanliness. But he disregarded the Rules of Art. His nudes were the women he knew, fleshy, proportioned not quite in keeping with classical ideals. This too is beauty. Arnold Houbraken, another of the early biographers (1718) who wrote to harm Rembrandt's reputation: "As to his female nudes, the noblest subject for the artist's brush, the representation of which earned the fullest attention of the most celebrated old masters, well, as the proverb says, 'too sad a song either to be sung or to be played'. His nudes are all sickening displays and one

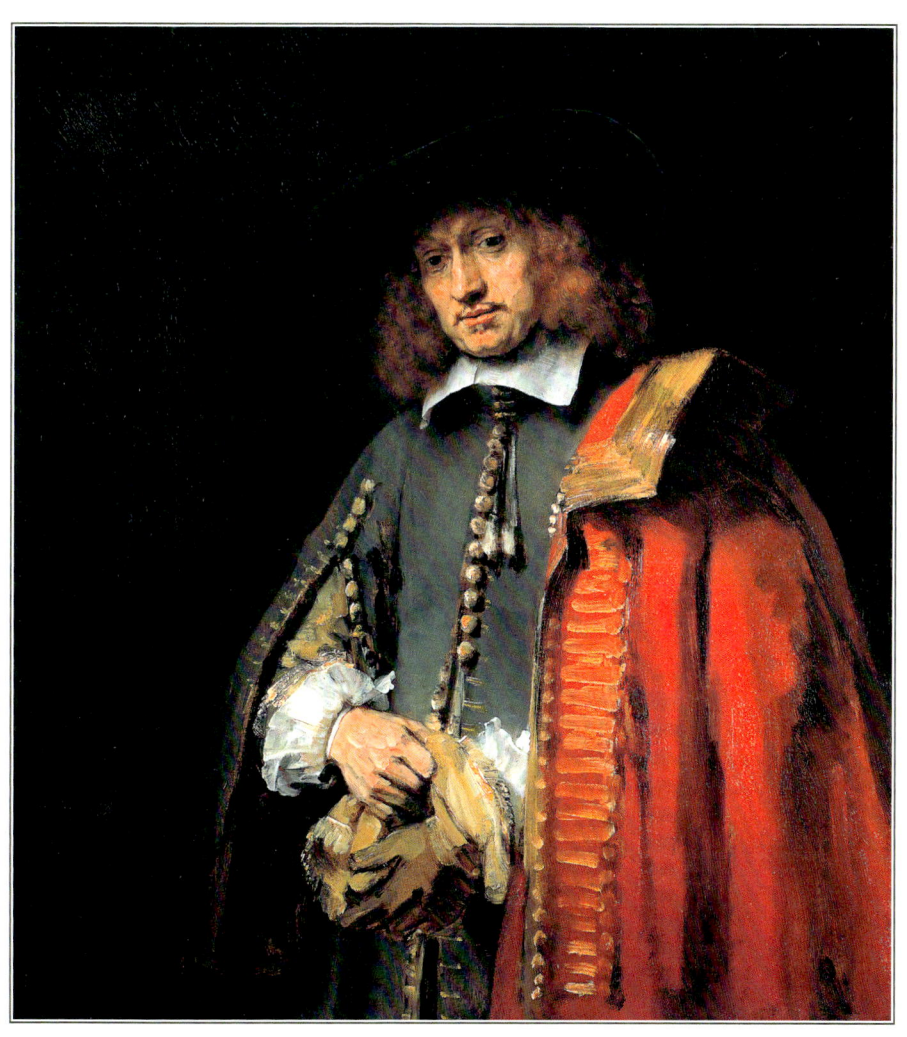

is astonished that a man of such talent and imagination could have been so perverse in his selection of what to paint."[48]

And then, he tended not to complete his paintings, or so it seemed to his critics. Rembrandt is said to have asserted that "a painting is completed if the Master has achieved what he set out to do."[49] There was another charge against him—here the invidious biographer is Filippo Baldinucci (1686), a fastidious Florentine historian of Northern art: "He was a most temperamental man and despised everyone. The ugly and plebeian face by which he was ill-favored, was accompanied by untidy and dirty clothes, since it was his custom, when working, to wipe his brushes on himself . . . . When he worked he would not have granted an audience to the first monarch in the world. . . ."[50] This written by a man who might well have seen Rembrandt's canvas, "The Jewish Bride" (1669), one of the tenderest double portraits of bride and groom in the history of art. All three of these mostly damning biographies are posthumous, but they must capture currents of opinion, not universal but not uncommon, in the last few decades of Rembrandt's life.

There were fewer commissions in the decades after "The Night Watch," but Rembrandt never lacked clients and apprentices as time went on. After Saskia's death, he found it difficult to sort things out. The woman he hired to care for young Titus, and whom he took into his bed, was apparently ill-suited to both roles; the outcome was an ugly legal battle no doubt noticed by the gentry of Amsterdam. There were increasing financial difficulties; Rembrandt was never to be free again of money worries. The great house where he lived carried what had turned out to be insuperably heavy debt, and he was some-what spendthrift, not an ideal steward of his funds. His difficulties culminated in a painful declaration of bankruptcy in 1656, and the sale at auction of vir-tually all his possessions, notably including his own work in all media, works by other artists, and marvelous objects of all kinds, the world of things he had brought into his world.[51] The scope and variety of his acquisitions are simply stunning. Among much else the surviving auction inventory makes clear that Rembrandt had had no need for a remedial study tour in Italy; he had brought the Italian masters to his studio through paintings, prints, even sculpture.

Rembrandt eventually sold the great house that so suited him and moved to rented quarters in a more modest neighborhood with Titus and the woman who now meant much to them both, the sturdy and loyal Hendrickje Stoffels. We know Hendrickje, as we knew Saskia, through his art. To preserve cer-tain benefits stipulated in Saskia's will, the new couple never married, and this in turn occasioned yet another humiliation, condemnation by her church

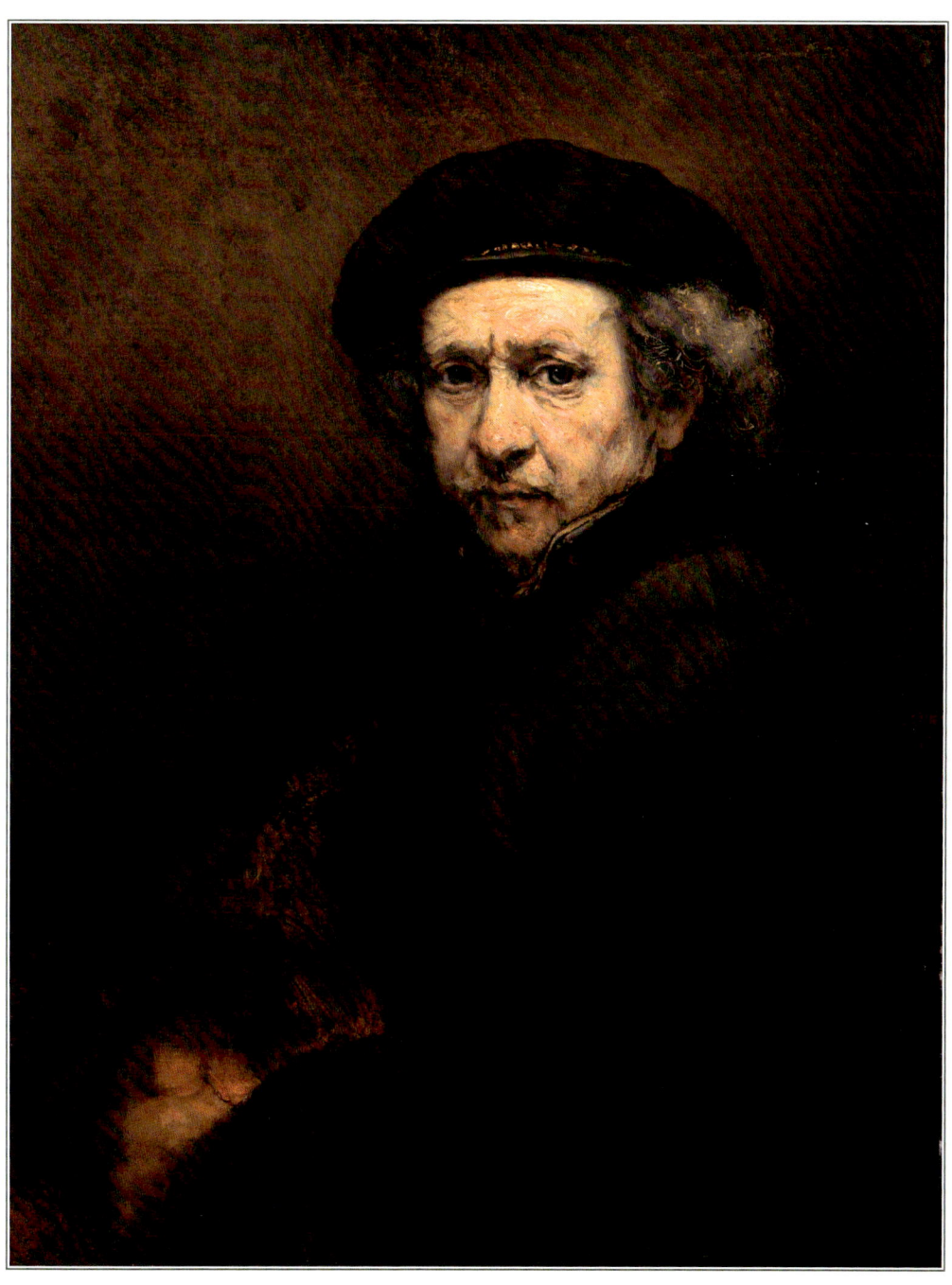

for "fornication." They continued their life together until Hendrickje's death, another profound loss, in 1663.

We have reached the years of Rembrandt's late style. He was now incomparable in his command of the brush, of lighting and space, of the colors and textures of life, incomparable in his psychological sensitivity. After a hiatus of some years in the 1640s, he resumed making self-portraits, but they show a different man in a different way, with a different depth of humanity. Our example—there could be others from earlier in the 1650s—is the magnificent self-portrait of 1658 in the Frick Collection (2). Measure the distance between the 1639 etched self-portrait with which we began—that portrait of youth, success, style, and ambition—and this magisterial image of nearly two decades later. In 1658, after the fourth and final auction of his possessions, Rembrandt had lost nearly everything, yet here he presents himself as nothing short of a monarch, richly gowned, seated as if enthroned, with an ornamental cane in hand that reads as a staff of office. Which is the truth: social humiliation or radiance? Both are true. In his eyes is a degree of defiance—I am still here, more than ever—and a degree of doubt. Time and events weigh on him. This is now a man nearly old, acknowledging what he has become.

There is something more, the very thing I have wished to approach through this extended sketch of his life. The eyes of Rembrandt's people, including himself, now make their presence known. His sitters, his subjects are *there*, filled with quiet life. This is the most vivid impression of all: from the early 1650s to the end of his life, Rembrandt endows his people with unmistakable, reticent presence. It is in their eyes. We were noticing some pages ago that Piero della Francesca also discovered and conveyed this quality of presence, but it differs in his art: his people are remote. Rembrandt's people, including himself, belong here. They are of this world, not another. Some, like him, have been harmed; for that reason his steady presence to himself and to the world is a kind of triumph. Others, like the civic leader Jan Six in the wonderful portrait of ca. 1654 (3), have made their way well in the world, but they too are present in some mysterious way; it is in their eyes.

We come now to the self-portrait of 1659 in the Washington National Gallery (4), which years ago so forcibly reminded me of what I care for. Rembrandt is now his own best witness, entirely free of envious critiques by other artists, of whatever social disapproval lurked among the good people of Amsterdam. He is defeated, aged, saddened—and not. He knows what he is about: he will show us the truth with both love and objectivity, without

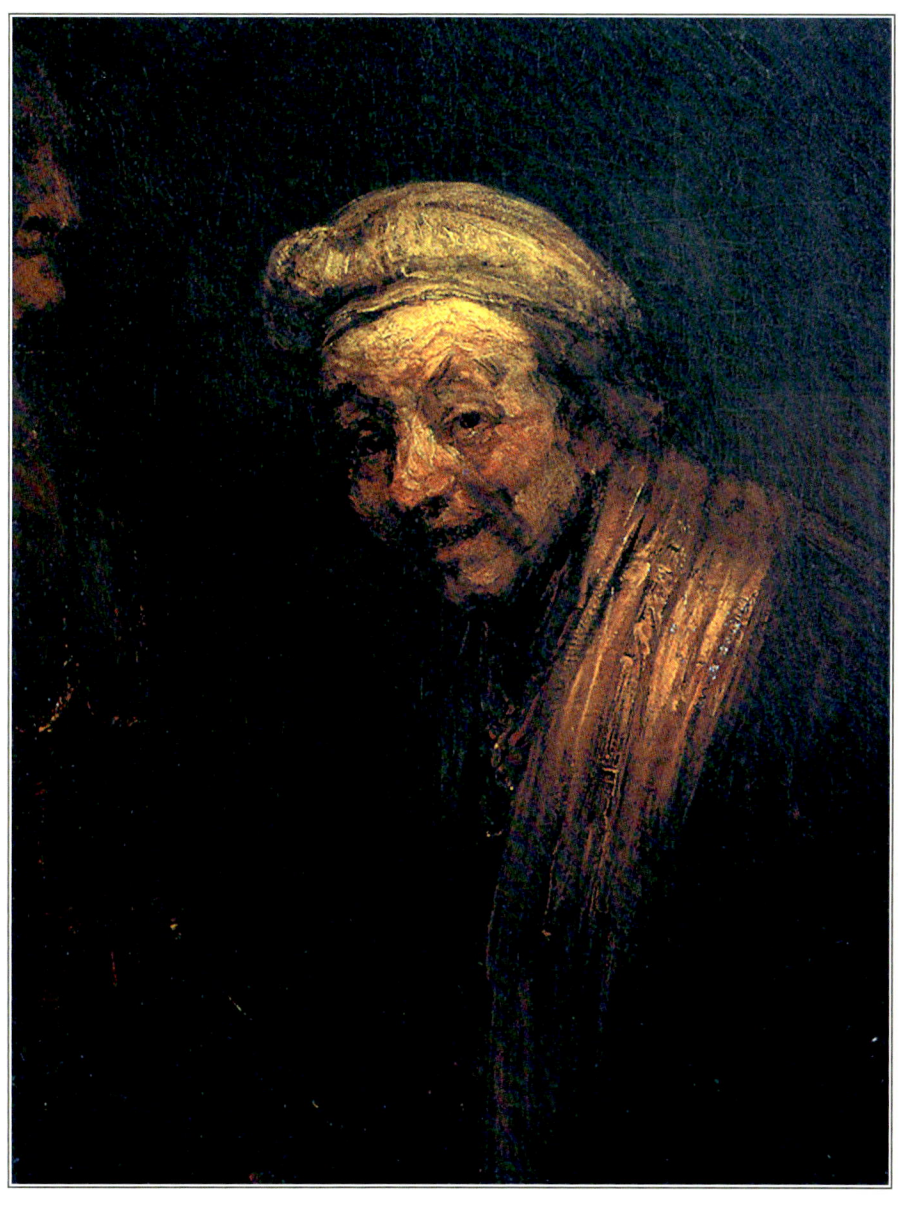

flinching or dissolving in sentiment. He had become an artist without limits, a seer; the only limit was set by time.

One of the last self-portraits, dating to 1662 – 1663, has puzzled interpretation (5). It is generally taken to represent Rembrandt as Zeuxis, the ancient Greek artist of unsurpassed fame in his era—no works have survived—who is said to have died laughing while painting the portrait of an old woman who insisted on modeling for the goddess of heavenly beauty, Aphrodite. Is that her profile at left in the painting? Simon Schama, in his outstanding book *Rembrandt's Eyes*, thinks the classical reference is more likely Democritus, the laughing philosopher who mocked people for their weaknesses of character and mind. Be that as it may, the portrait cannot help but burn through us. Rembrandt seems to be receding into the darkness characteristic of his art over the decades, but a golden light still graces him, and he looks out at us. What comes to mind is Proverbs 31:25; he too can "laugh at the time to come." The final victory is not to fear death. I don't know whether that is the underlying theme here; it seems so.

What is a great soul? There are many more than we might imagine, though few possess the means at Rembrandt's disposal to express their understanding. They have experienced everything that life offers and imposes, from great joy to great sorrow, from self-inflicted humiliation to injustices not of their own making. They have not abandoned, never succumbed for long. They have matured from their point of departure, likely self-centered and brashly seeking, to something close to universal understanding and love. Their sorrows and joys, their vivid day-to-day experience of the gift of consciousness, and what they see of others' sorrows and joys, follies and clarities, have nourished their reflection on the human condition. That reflection is evident in their eyes. They look out from their inner worlds with eyes like those of Rembrandt's people. They are deceived neither by life nor by themselves, but that absence of illusion does not prompt them to withdraw. They have their own inner space, but they continue speaking or making images that speak.

All honor to thee, our Rembrandt!

49. ROBERT FLUDD: THE THEORY OF EVERYTHING

Robert Fludd (1574 – 1637 CE)

Diagrams from *Utriusque Cosmi* and *De musica mundana*, 1617 – 1621 CE

Engraved and printed by Johann Theodor de Bry from drawings by Fludd

Source: Penta Springs Ltd. / Alamy Stock Photo;

World History Archive / Alamy Stock Photo

I'm not sure which would have been more delighted by today's particle physics: Robert Fludd, the brilliant seventeenth-century hermetic thinker, or Johannes Kepler, his contemporary and adversary, painstaking discoverer of the laws of planetary motion. Fludd would have found the complexity and detail of particle physics akin in some respects to his own vision of cosmos and the nature of man—not lofty enough, but complex enough. The names and behaviors of quarks, let alone all else in the "particle zoo"—up, down, charm, strange, and so on—would have stunned him. It was quite Fludd-like. In his time and place, he converted all that he saw and conceived, from God on high to everything else, into dazzling diagrams; like some physicists today, he sought (and felt that he had found) a Theory of Everything. On his

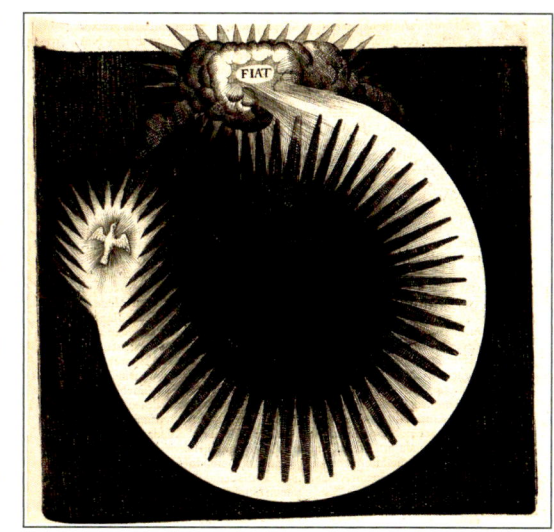

side, Kepler would have deserved to experience grave contentment that his early struggle to develop mathematics as an essential part of scientific research has borne such fruit. Kepler took what you might call the righthand path toward empirical science, while Fludd at that historic crossroad took the ancient lefthand path toward esoteric vision. Except among scholars, Fludd might be forgotten today had he not possessed a genius for visualizing his thought.

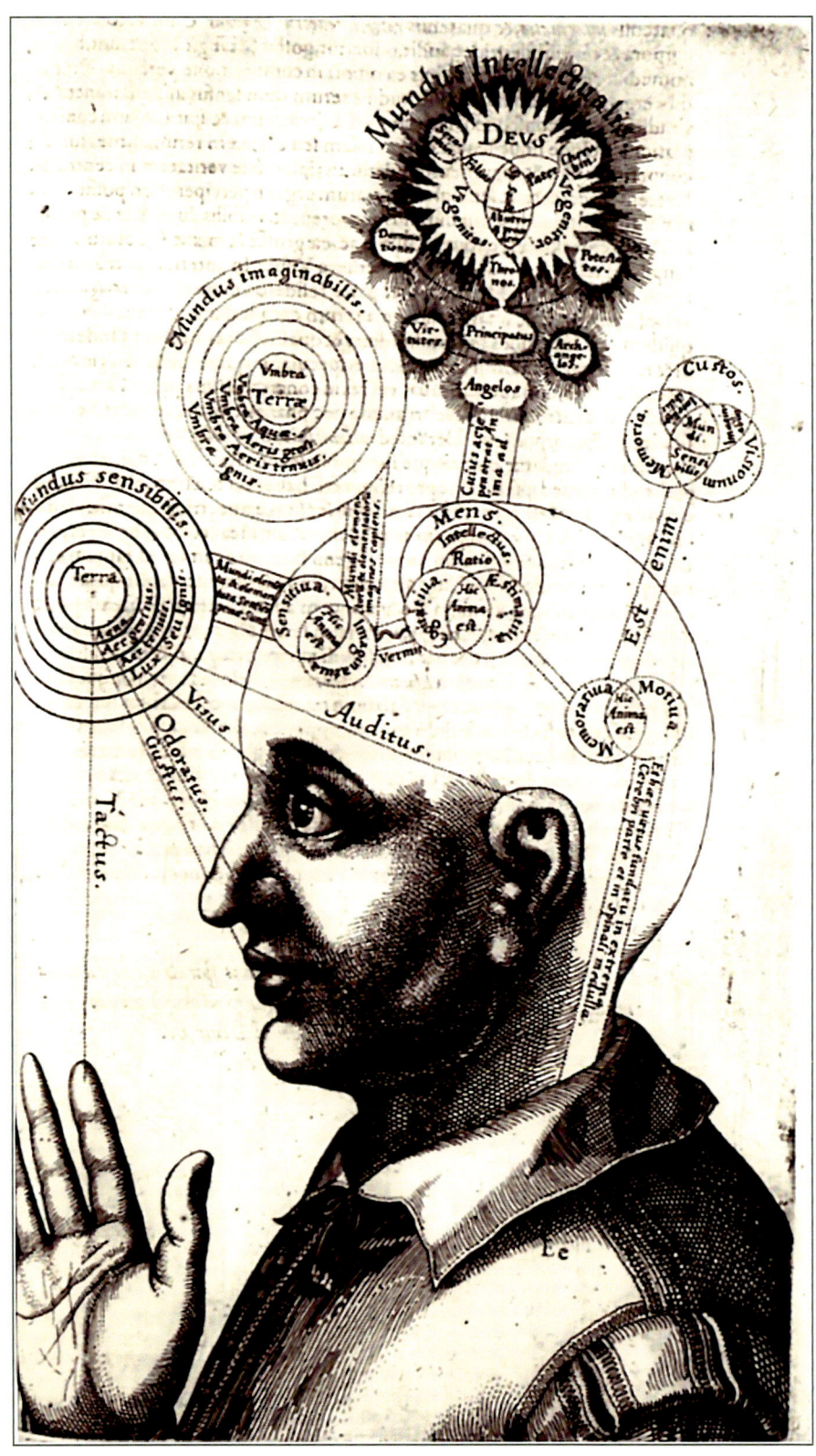

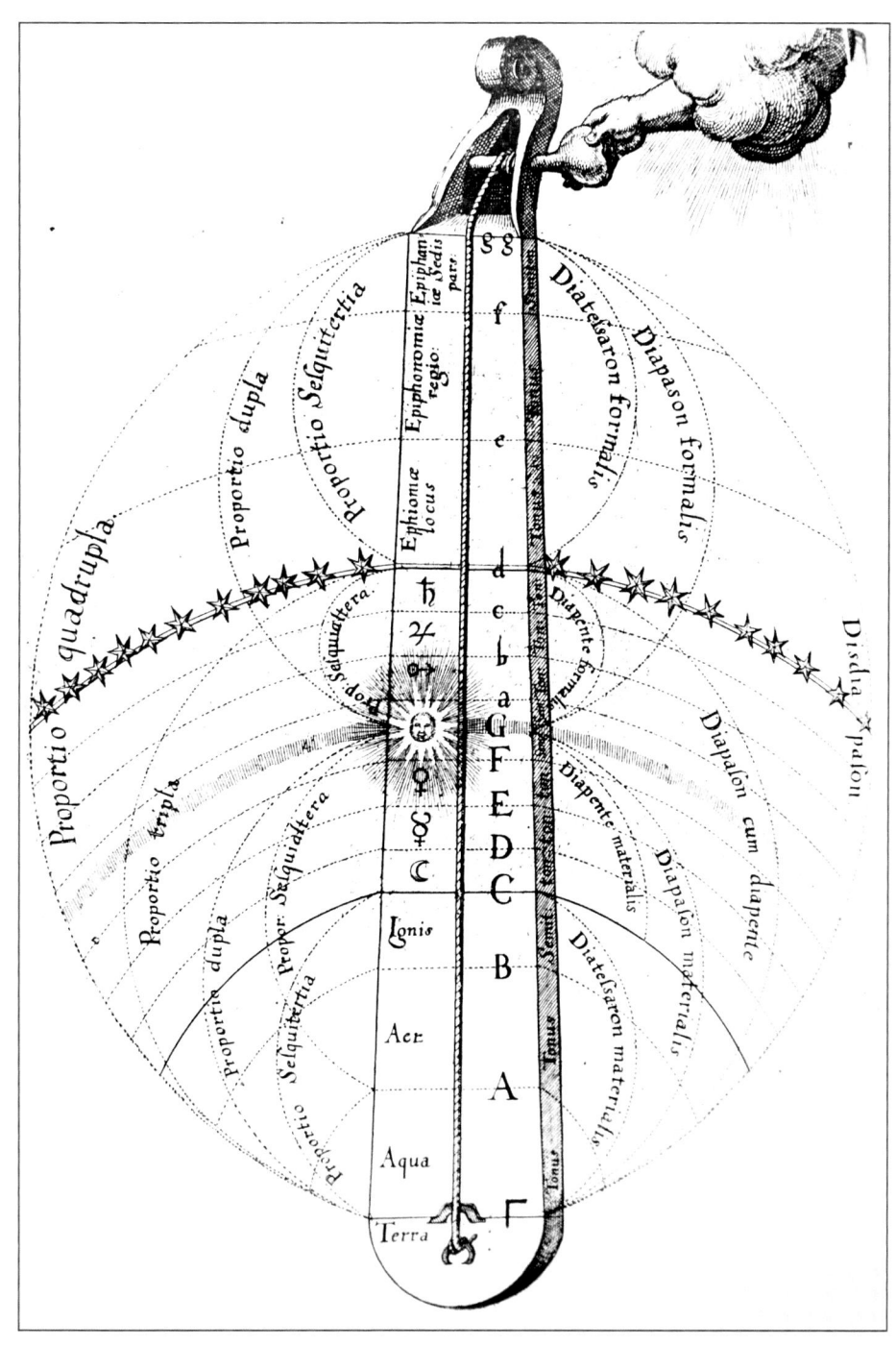

In that regard, there is no one like him and, once encountered, he tugs at one's memory. Some of his pages are icons that stir admiration for his imaginative powers but also something more hidden—a barely detectable, deep-seated longing for a Theory of Everything that grants humanity a dignified place and serene belonging in the scheme of things.

Born to a high official in the court of Queen Elizabeth I and educated at Oxford, Fludd soon proved to be a polymath, an individual of seemingly unlimited intellectual capacity who became a sought-after London physician while absorbing everything available of alternative thinking and practice—Paracelsus not Galen for his medical practice, Ficino's Neoplatonism, the late Antique mystical writings attributed to Hermes Trismegistus, alchemy, Kabbala, astrology, medieval mysticism, all of which was contained by firm Christian faith. When he began to publish, it was evident that he thought in both words and images; overwhelming conceptual and verbal complexity on the printed page resolved into approachable and often strangely inspiring patterns. Apart from practical writings such as a pharmacopeia for fellow physicians, his masterpieces were the *Utriusque Cosmi* (in full: *The metaphysical, physical, and technical history of the two worlds, namely the greater and the lesser*) and *De musica mundana* (let's say: *The World's Music*). The illustrations here are from those books.

The Divine, or Cosmic, Monochord assembles in one diagrammatic vision several categories of knowledge and speculation: the measured musical scale, the four elements, astrologic symbols for the sun and known planets, and the Good Lord keeping all things in tune. A splendid vision. In the adjoining image, there we are—our senses and imaginative and intellectual capacities, linked upward and again sovereignly touched by "Deus," the Good Lord. This may well be the first map of the mind. What a brave attempt.

50. PIRANESI: THE RULES OF ART IN RUINS

Giovanni Battista Piranesi (1720 – 1778 CE), etchings
1. Via Appia and Via Ardentina, from *Le Antichità Romane*, 1756
2. The Campidoglio, from *Views of Rome (Vedute di Roma)*, 1748 – 1774
3. Imagined Prison, from the *Carceri d'invenzione*, 1761, plate VII
    Sorces: Album / Alamy Stock Photo; The History Collection / Alamy Stock
    Photo; Peter Barrett / Alamy Stock Photo

In Vienna's inner city I have had the impression of walking among dino-saur bones. The massive administrative buildings of the long-departed Habsburg Empire seem out of all proportion to the needs of Austria today. Piranesi, whose etchings defined Rome pictorially for successive generations, may have had a similar impression. The grandeur of Imperial Rome was evi-dent across the eighteenth-century city but for the most part in ruins. An architect with a knowledge of scenic design for theater and a native Venetian taste for elaboration and extravagance, Piranesi pursued three unlike visions simultaneously: to document the surviving architectural glories of Rome with an archeologist's precision and care, to reimagine what was missing in a manner all his own, and—not least—to mirror the squalor of life among the city's poor and the insouciance of the city's comfortable classes. The result was extraordinary. Piranesi has struck many as the first Modern artist, the first to reflect in his work an atmosphere of uneasiness, strangeness, and menace, as if something is breaking and cannot be repaired. His brilliant *Imagined Prisons*—14 plates published in a first version when he was thirty years old and in a second, enlarged version in 1761—freed him from specific monuments to explore the dark side of his vision. Like many people I was initially drawn to the *Prisons*—they are the icon, the work of a ferocious mind—but now I see that Piranesi's Rome has much in common with them. The Rules of Art lay in ruins: he knew them all, they lived in his hands and mind, they could not constrain his imagination.

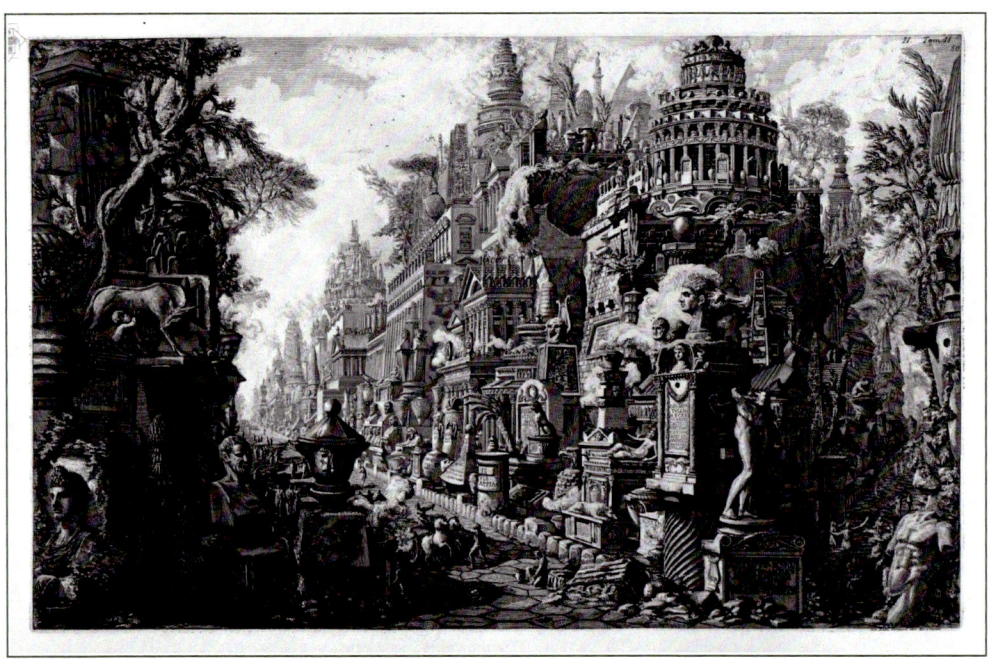

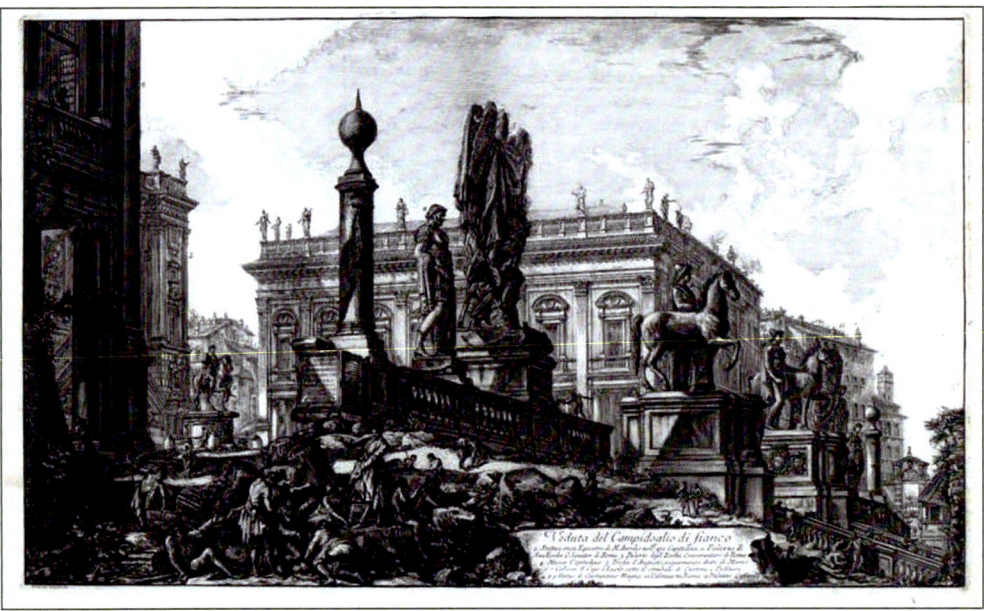

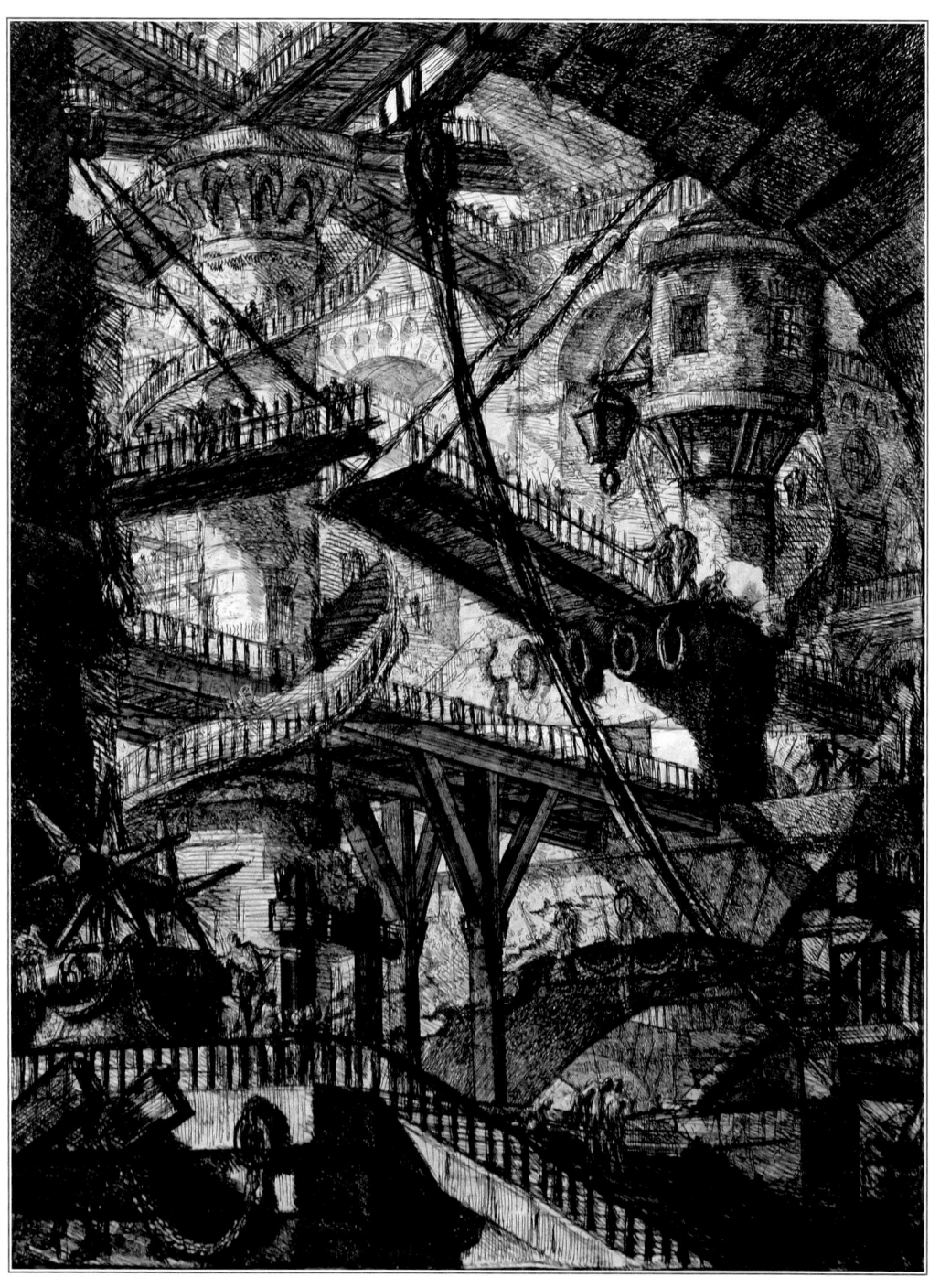

After his initial, not unusual difficulty finding patronage and place in the city's cultural milieu, Piranesi enjoyed great and lasting success in Rome. Produced on his own press from a shop that also dealt in transportable antiquities and restorations, his prints were coveted souvenirs carried home particularly by young Englishmen embarked on the Grand Tour of Europe, an all but obligatory part of their education. What they took home is in part what we see here. The first image here gives us Piranesi when he didn't have much physical evidence to go on; his Appian Way is sheer imagination, a great clutter of great things, fascinating in detail and complexity. The image is deeply strange, a mash of architectural and sculptural fragments—the work of the first Surrealist.

The view at the edge of Michelangelo's magnificent Piazza del Campidoglio isn't magnificent at all: towering, oversized sculpture share the space with a wretched crowd, mostly in rags, strewn among the dislocated cylinders of a fallen column. A well-dressed fellow, perhaps an architect, makes a broad gesture toward who knows what, echoed by similar gestures from ragged figures. Throughout the *Views of Rome* (some one thousand images), there are such figures making broad, senseless gestures in a kind of theater of the absurd. And should we somehow miss the point, in the foreground a figure in rags points his bottom at us. This is chaos, and the pair of well-to-do figures conversing at the right couldn't care less. Imagine the noble world of ancient architecture inhabited by characters from Samuel Beckett's plays—no need to imagine, it's here in Piranesi.

And then the *Carceri*, Plate VII of the *Prisons*. A vast, menacing architecture with stairways leading nowhere, sinister figures peering over balustrades, terrible machines, intimidating chains: this too is chaos. It is inhuman. Some have said that Piranesi was simply playing with the elements of architecture. I don't think so. He was looking at something in his nature, and in the nature of us all, and giving it expression as never before. What furious daring.[52]

51. CHARDIN: "HERE YOU ARE AGAIN, GREAT MAGICIAN!"

Jean Siméon Chardin (1699 – 1779 CE)
Still Life with Jar of Olives, 1760 CE
Oil on canvas, app. 28 X 35.5 inches
The Louvre Museum, Paris
Source: Wikimedia Commons / public domain

Boy with a spinning top (portrait of Auguste Gabriel Godefroy), 1738
Oil on canvas, app. 26 X 30 inches
The Louvre Museum, Paris
Source: Wikipedia / public domain

In an era of vast statement in painting and sculpture, of dramatic scenes from myth and Bible, and equally an era of Rococo charm, of gardens and swings, petticoats and glances, Chardin would have none of it. His was the world of still life and genre—the latter referring to scenes of daily life and common activities. In the annual or bi-annual Salon at the Louvre, sponsored by the all-powerful *Académie royale de peinture et de sculpture*, which both trained from an early age and later exhibited its most accomplished artists, Chardin's works, included whenever he wished, were different. They were generally small in size; you moved toward them and entered their field of privacy. While many other works on exhibition shouted for attention and yearned to impress, his had a quiet voice. The leading art critic of the era, Denis Diderot, co-editor of one of the greatest Enlightenment projects, the multi-volume *Encyclopédie* that aspired to encompass all knowledge, was a steadfast admirer of Chardin's work and a personal friend. We know something of Chardin's thought and language largely through Diderot's so-called *Salons*, his exhibition accounts from year to year.[53] When Diderot encountered works by Chardin after a long, often arid journey past works by many others, he later wrote, "Here you are once again, great magician, with your mute compositions!"[54] That was his best term for Chardin's art: magic.

Chardin hadn't trained in the Academy school—he had had more modest teachers—but he had been accepted early in his career as a member of the Academy in the ranks of painters of fruits and animals, a rating far below the lofty painters of so-called history scenes. However, because he was no competition in that sphere, and surely also because he was a lovely person who got on well with his fellow artists, for many years he was entrusted with the role of *tapissier*: he designed and hung the exhibition, the myriad of canvases from floor to ceiling, the endless works of sculpture and graphic arts. His approach was both fair-minded and, in part, discreet sermons on what is good, what not so good, achieved simply by placing some works high and nearly out of sight, others juxtaposed with instructive comparative works. Diderot was well aware of these quiet editorials and enjoyed decoding them.

Art historians, even to this day, have struggled to find language that sheds light on Chardin's art. "You stop in front of a Chardin," Diderot wrote.[55] He was awed by what he understood as Chardin's realism: "The colors crushed on your palette are not white, red, or black pigment; they are the very substance of the objects. They are the air and the light. . . ."[56] Later critics and scholars accentuate Chardin's closely calculated compositions; Pierre Rosenberg, the dean of Chardin scholars, has written that Chardin invented pure painting[57]— realistic, yes, but concerned with the nature of representation. The lessons he offered would be important to many in later eras, notably Cézanne.

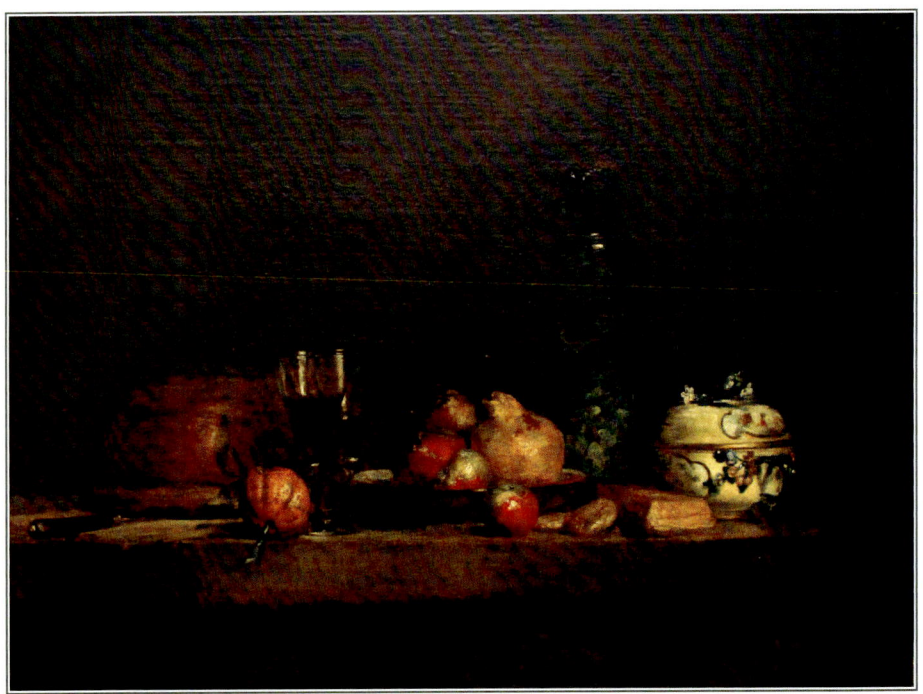

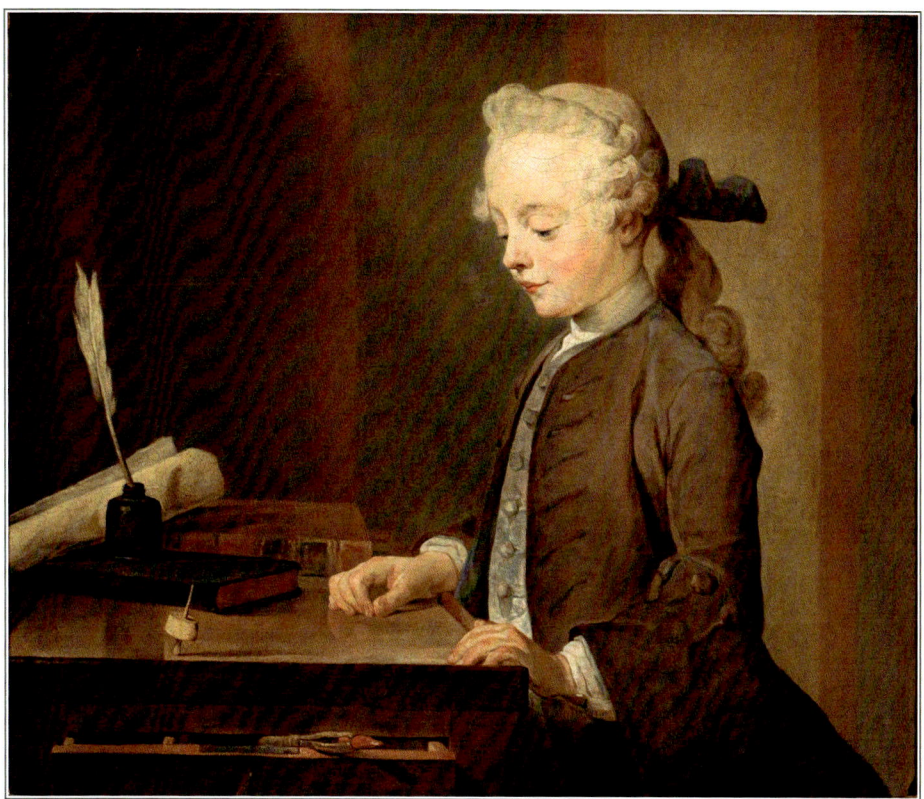

Chardin had the quietest, clearest eyes and mind in his era—an example for any era. He attended to sensation: the sensation of colors and their interactions, the sensation of shapes and textures, the sensation of light, the sensation of space. And the simple goodness of people, such as the boy taking an idle moment from his studies to watch a spinning top. Chardin practiced a kind of eighteenth-century Zen, untutored by any doctrine other than his native commitment to perceiving and sharing the sensations of life. Rosenberg, and not only he, has pointed to one of Chardin's best remembered statements: "I must forget everything I have seen, and even forget the way such objects have been treated by others."[58] Chardin practiced a discreet *askesis*, a stripping away of unnecessary reflection and inheritance. A term from Buddhist scripture and aesthetics comes to mind, though it is hardly fair to impose an Eastern concept on a Western artist: *tathata*, translated as "suchness" or "thusness." It has something of the same force as our word "behold." But even this large word would need to be spoken quietly near a Chardin still life, so as not to disturb the magic. People around Chardin, including Diderot, mentioned that they had never witnessed him at work; his studio was entirely private. I don't suppose that there would have been much to see: attention of the kind he lovingly mastered offers scarcely any spectacle.

PARENTHESIS: XIX AND XX

Tiffany Studios

Vase, 1904 – 1906
Height, app. 9 inches
Musée des Arts Décoratifs, Paris
Inv. No. 1324
Source: Musée des Arts Décoratifs, Paris

Vase, ca. 1900
Height, app. 6.5 inches
The Museum of Modern Art, New York
Inv. No. 601.1965
Source: Art Resource

Arthur Rackham (1867 – 1939)

"King Edward VII's Stroll"
Illustration for J. M. Barrie, *Peter Pan in Kensington Gardens*
(London, Hodder & Stoughton, 1906)
Source: Walker Art Library / Alamy Stock Photo

"The Princess Alerted"
Illustration for "The Ballad of Young Bekie" in *Some British Ballads*
(London, Constable, 1919)
Source: Historic Illustrations / Alamy Stock Photo

Edmund Dulac (1882 – 1953)

"The Alchemist"
Illustration for "The Story of Waldemaar Daae and his Daughters, Told by the Wind"

Tales of Hans Andersen (London, Hodder & Stoughton, 1911)
Source: Tibbut Archive / Alamy Stock Photo

When I think of XIX—the nineteenth century—my mind teems with admirations. It is the century next door, or nearly so; many of its conversations and achievements still feel current. Artists from William Blake at the turn of the nineteenth century to Gustav Klimt at the transition to the twentieth are more fully known and documented than many artists and periods in earlier pages. The richness of available detail is astonishing. Further, it takes scarcely any effort for me, and likely for you also, to see in my mind's eye a pageant of nineteenth-century works and artists: Delacroix's unfinished portrait of Chopin, the best image we have, and by far; Corot's landscapes but more to my taste his renewal of the classically conceived figure, Masaccio-like, sturdy and vulnerable; Gustave Moreau's fascinating exoticism, his jewel-like pictorial world; and then the Impressionists and Post-Impressionists—who can forget the canvases of Manet, Monet, Degas, Gauguin, van Gogh, Seurat, Cézanne; and as if in a waning light, the pale classicism of Puvis de Chavannes. I have crisscrossed Vienna with my wife to visit all of the museums showing the works of Gustav Klimt, generally understood to belong to the twentieth century but there were already masterworks in the late nineteenth.

Yet it is not my century. I have immense appreciation for the work of these artists and many others, but no works of their period have possessed me, none has insisted on staying close as a lasting clue to identity—as an icon. I wouldn't have known this in advance and cannot fully account for the gap. Is there a trace element missing, some nutrient to which I respond without consciously recognizing its presence or absence? Or is the mystery altogether different: have I, and many of us, so thoroughly absorbed the imagery and sensibility of Van Gogh, for example, that his work has a kind of permanence inside? The starry sky, flowers, portraits, fields, and narrow special room where he lived for a time may all be so deeply written in me, and in many of us, that they no longer have a strongly separate life. I have been stirred with admiration, even fascination, by the art of the so-called Nabis, the late-nineteenth-century circle of brilliant French artists: the young Pierre Bonnard and Edouard Vuillard, the somewhat forgotten Maurice Denis, and others—what compelling visual experiences they offered in their brief moment of shared enterprise. But admiration and fascination are one thing, while works that speak to one intimately and press against one's identity are another. Icons raise lasting questions. They tug at you, they refuse to be forgotten.

The twentieth century is a different matter. It may well be that artists early in the century shared something of my attitude—though I am puzzled and they were not. Picasso's "Demoiselles d'Avignon" (1907) slammed the door loudly on nineteenth-century classicism, and the Cubism he developed in concert with Braque slammed the door on pictorial norms cultivated since the Renaissance. The Vienna Secession, with Klimt at its center, gave the first decades of the century a daring new visual language that mocked the proprieties of the past but had its own brilliance and deep messages.

The art of the twentieth century is an essential part of my home culture (see pp. 84–85 for discussion of this idea). It is full of surprises, beauty, and an all but unrecognized spiritual quest to which I felt compelled to bear witness through a book that has remained in print for more than thirty years: *An Art of Our Own: The Spiritual in Twentieth-Century Art.*[59] Its 121 illustrations constitute in large part a further icon collection. Those works have been teachers, "reminders and supports of contemplation," to return to Coomaraswamy's austere concept. In this book there is no need to revisit those artists, movements, and leading ideas. But I do want to spend a moment now with works that I scarcely recognized thirty years ago: certain works of the Tiffany Studios and, in another zone, pages from the Golden Age of children's book illustration in the years before World War I and some years afterward.

There has long been an intriguing question about the sources of twentieth-century abstract art. Where and why did this idea and taste originate? Were there multiple sources? These questions have been much explored and well answered. Certainly Kandinsky's groundbreaking book of 1911, *On the Spiritual in Art*, gave voice and concepts to the movement toward abstract imagery. The revolutionary Cubism of Picasso and Braque moved in the same direction and inspired more than one generation. Malevich's "Black Square" of 1915, and subsequent works, demonstrated another approach to the same goal. There is much more to say of all this—endlessly more—but the small point needed here is that the emergence of the abstract aesthetic is well charted. Imagine, then, my surprise not long ago to encounter glass vases from the Long Island (New York) studios of Louis Comfort Tiffany (1848 – 1933) like those illustrated in the next pages: works of ca. 1900, the creations of designers and craftspeople working anonymously at the time in the vast and vastly successful Tiffany Studios. Vases of this kind were termed "lava glass" for good reason:

many examples have colorful flows of glass resembling the flow of lava down a volcanic slope. The result can be quite soupy, yet there are masterpieces. The two vessels illustrated (and others like them) seem to have originated in part through workshop experiments with forms, techniques, and glass chemistries, and as something like afterthoughts prompted by what else was going on in the Studios. They appeared considerably earlier than the key dates of 1911 and 1915 mentioned earlier, and appeared without an ideology or artist's manifesto to justify or explain. I may be missing something, but I know of no reason to consider glass works of this kind to have exercised an influence on the larger movement of art at the time. They appeared on a side road, a byway; this was "craft," not art.

Louis Comfort Tiffany himself was a celebrated arts entrepreneur, painter, and designer. He had the manner of Mark Twain in the author's later years—the meticulous white suit, the calculated elegance, the aura of specialness which was not misplaced: he was an extraordinary figure. The entire output of the Tiffany Studios carried his name; his taste and business sense dominated, although actual execution was in the hands of the skilled workforce. Leaded glass pictorial lamp shades with well-matched bases, iridescent glass objects of every description from flower vases to desk utilities, jewelry, ceramics, metalwork, and beautifully crafted, sometimes exquisite windows for churches and other solemn sites were sought after by customers virtually worldwide. The first of the two vases illustrated here was a gift by Tiffany to the Musée des Arts Décoratifs (Paris) after it impressed in an award-winning exhibition.

Like all else from the Studios, these proto-abstract lava glass works—the best of them beautiful beyond imagining—owe some part of their conception to Tiffany himself. During his customary Monday morning visits to the factory, he would have approved and encouraged this experimental direction. The vases were the work of a team headed by Arthur J. Nash, a creatively gifted and meticulous senior craftsman, and later his son Leslie Hayden Nash, whose account of life and work in the Tiffany Studios was published belatedly in 2001. It demonstrates beyond doubt his father's central contribution to much that went on, including the slow and technically challenging development of lava glass.[60]

We should look at the two works on the pages that follow, but words won't help much, just as we found that words circled but didn't really touch the ca. 1600 tea bowl reflecting Rikyu's taste (see pp. 110–112). Words cannot help but be pitifully plainer than the objects themselves. Yes, in the first example there are wave-like ripples of lustrous gold glass and what Nash father and son called pebbles. There is overall a soft aesthetic, as if the vessel remains upright more by a steady breeze than by structural strength. But none of these words captures what is before us. As the glass historian and curator Jane Shadell Spillman first conjectured, we are looking at a modern Western echo of traditional Japanese tea taste—particularly in the era after Rikyu, when tea masters preferred markedly eccentric, irregular forms.[61] Tiffany's personal collection of Japanese art and craft may well underlie these bold works, but there is considerable distance between Rikyu's Japan and Tiffany's America. With transformative imagination, someone leaped that distance.

The second example, in the collection of the Museum of Modern Art (New York), is no less beautiful and comparable in its elements. What delights me here beyond words is the origin of these truly brilliant works of abstract design in a factory dedicated by and large to other things, at a time in the art world when there was still no concerted movement toward abstraction. If ever I, or you, were to doubt the expressiveness of abstract art—its ability to give rise to waves of thought and perception, to a strong sense of encounter—these are works to check back with. It is all already here. This is high art, grand art, modestly willing to be called craft, should someone insist.

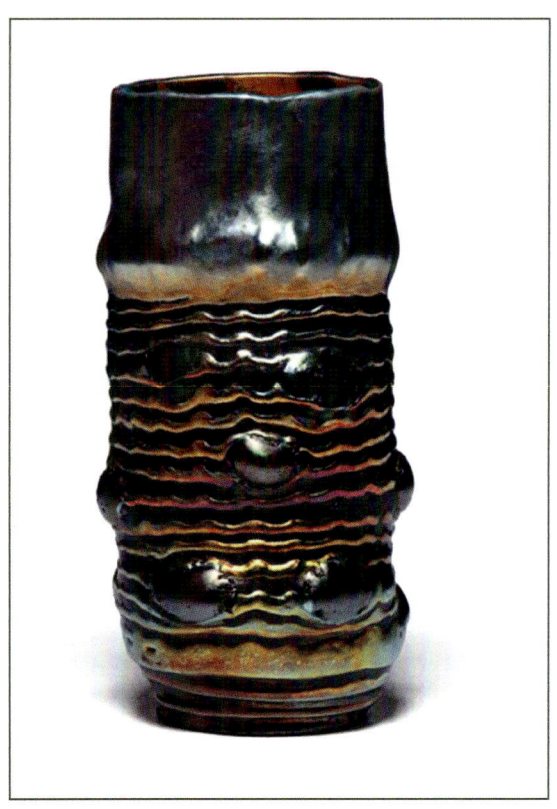

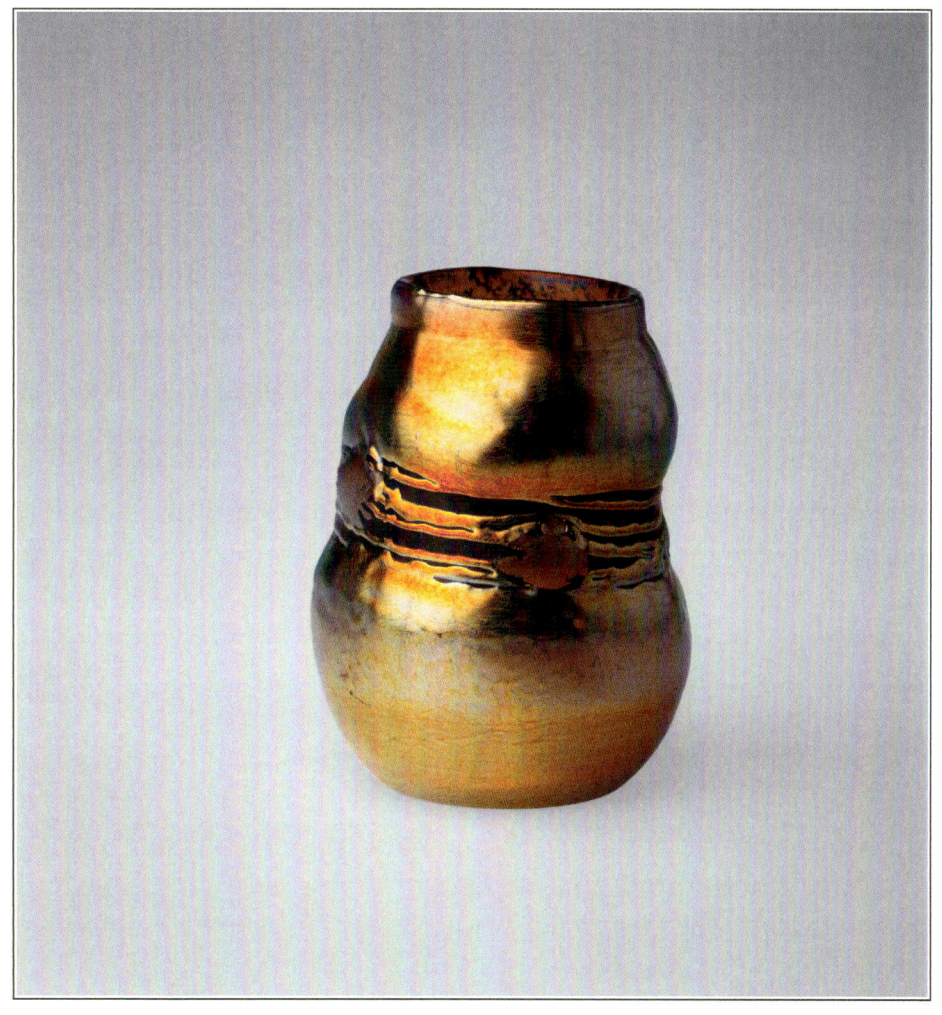

Do we need a moment of relaxed enjoyment? It is near at hand. There was a Golden Age of children's book illustration in the years from 1900 to the aftermath of World War I. I know it largely through English book illustration, but there were parallel developments on the continent. The central figures in the English-speaking world were the overwhelmingly brilliant Arthur Rackham (1867 – 1939) and the overwhelmingly brilliant Edmund Dulac (1882 – 1953). It was commonly understood at the time that Rackham resembled a gnome; or maybe a banker or accountant. Balding head, rather plain features, steel-rimmed glasses, the dress and manner of a proper Victorian householder. The few portrait photos I've seen reveal something more—a mix in his eyes of clarity and insistence, and an artist's strong, shaping attention. Like many artists of preceding centuries, he would occasionally insert himself into his pictorial worlds, always just as he was or comically worse. In the first illustration here, where King Edward VII strolls through Kensington Gardens and returns the greeting of an animated elderly bramble who salutes him with a leafy wreath, Rackham makes an appearance at the base of the tree among other gnomes. You can tell which one he is, he is wearing glasses.

It takes time to become oneself. Rackham was initially an undistinguished illustrator for English magazines and newspapers when opportunities in the mid-1890s in book illustration gave him the chance needed to develop his gifts. His illustration of Edward VII, unaware of the consternation he is causing among the little people, appeared in J. M. Barrie's *Peter Pan in Kensington Gardens* (1906). The image is nearly a thesis statement, a summation of Rackham's art. Many of the creatures in Rackham's visual theater appear here: gnarled trees with concealed faces, humorous or frightening; winged Art Nouveau fairies, miniature versions of ideal feminine beauty in that period; bald gnomes and I suppose elves at various sizes, some with knitted toques, others—quite scary—in the hollow of the tree; and then mice and maybe a cat. Rackham's imaginative world is completely, sweetly, terrifyingly alive. All of its creatures from svelte fairies to droll gnomes are part of the same pulsing world, and they seem to have worked out their little multicultural kingdom quite well. All are very pleased and curious to catch a glimpse of the monarch, taking his constitutional in rather formal attire and top hat. The image of Edward is a true likeness: this is indeed the immensely popular king who gave his name to the Edwardian era in British history and fashion.

The thesis statement here is the juxtaposition of fantasy and the proper, steady world. Edward has the merit of taking in stride the salute of a wintry bramble, but he does seem somewhat sealed off. His gesture is both greeting and shield. He would be surprised to learn how many other creatures were scrutinizing him. Rackham is measuring the distance between his endlessly rich world of fantasy and the correct world in which he actually lived from day to day, and which he addressed through his art. Was it his mission to create communication between worlds resident in us all? There are both dreams and science in us.

As you can see, he was a brilliant draftsman, often using thin washes of watercolor to enliven his images. There is something here of the Japanese woodblock print tradition (see pp. 113–115), something also of the Northern Renaissance, recalling Albrecht Dürer's treatment of deep forest in certain engravings. But influences can't account for all that much in Rackham; he offered a new vision—entertainment and education for children, yet sophisticated art that speaks to adults.

A further illustration you will surely enjoy captures a dramatic moment in the Scottish ballad of Young Bekie, a hero who goes forth, falls under a spell, and is about to marry the wrong woman when his true love and fiancée is alerted to the situation by a fascinating member of her house staff. A gnome or "brownie" awakens her and insists that she ride to the rescue. Again, two worlds. Through an abundance of luxurious, colorfully patterned fabric and precious furniture, Rackham gives his vivid princess a very special world—but the gnome has his place in it. It may be that only a creature of this kind, a little magical, can know afar what good or bad awaits. The princess is lucky to have such a loyal and concerned servant, although admittedly he is a little odd. One further point: it is not unlike Rackham to hint at sexuality. Underclothes strewn over a chest and the princess's chaste beauty send a subliminal message. In art-historical terms, the scene recalls Dutch genre painting of the seventeenth century and something of the luxurious settings and beautiful people of Pre-Raphaelite English painting, an impressive mid-nineteenth-century movement we haven't visited in this book. But all of that is absorbed and made Rackham's own. These illustrations, and much else in Rackham, are iconic. They skillfully draw elements from earlier art into an original world of fantasy, delight, and story. Rackham's art is a permanent invitation to realize that just beyond the confining fence begins. . . much else.

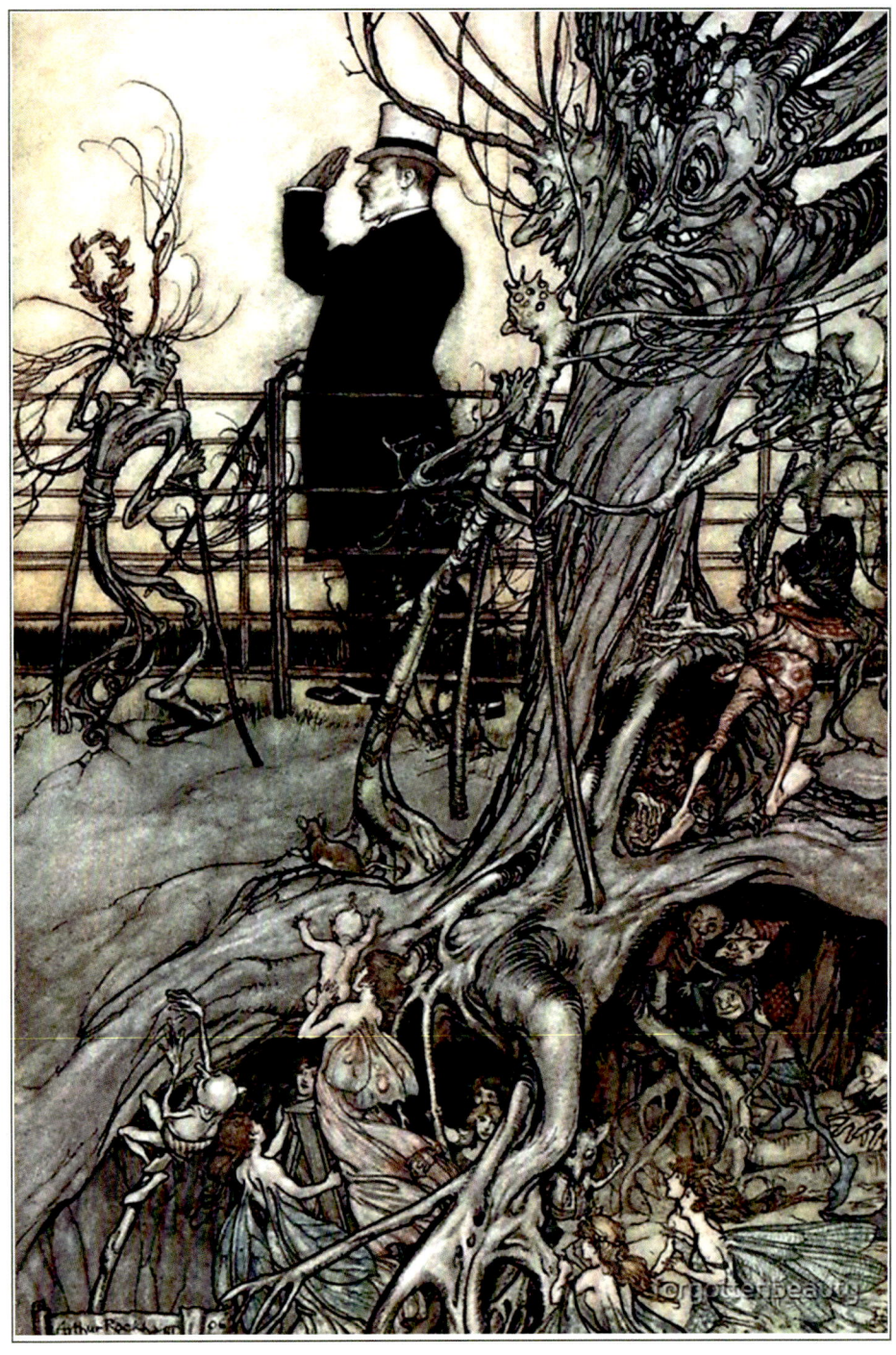

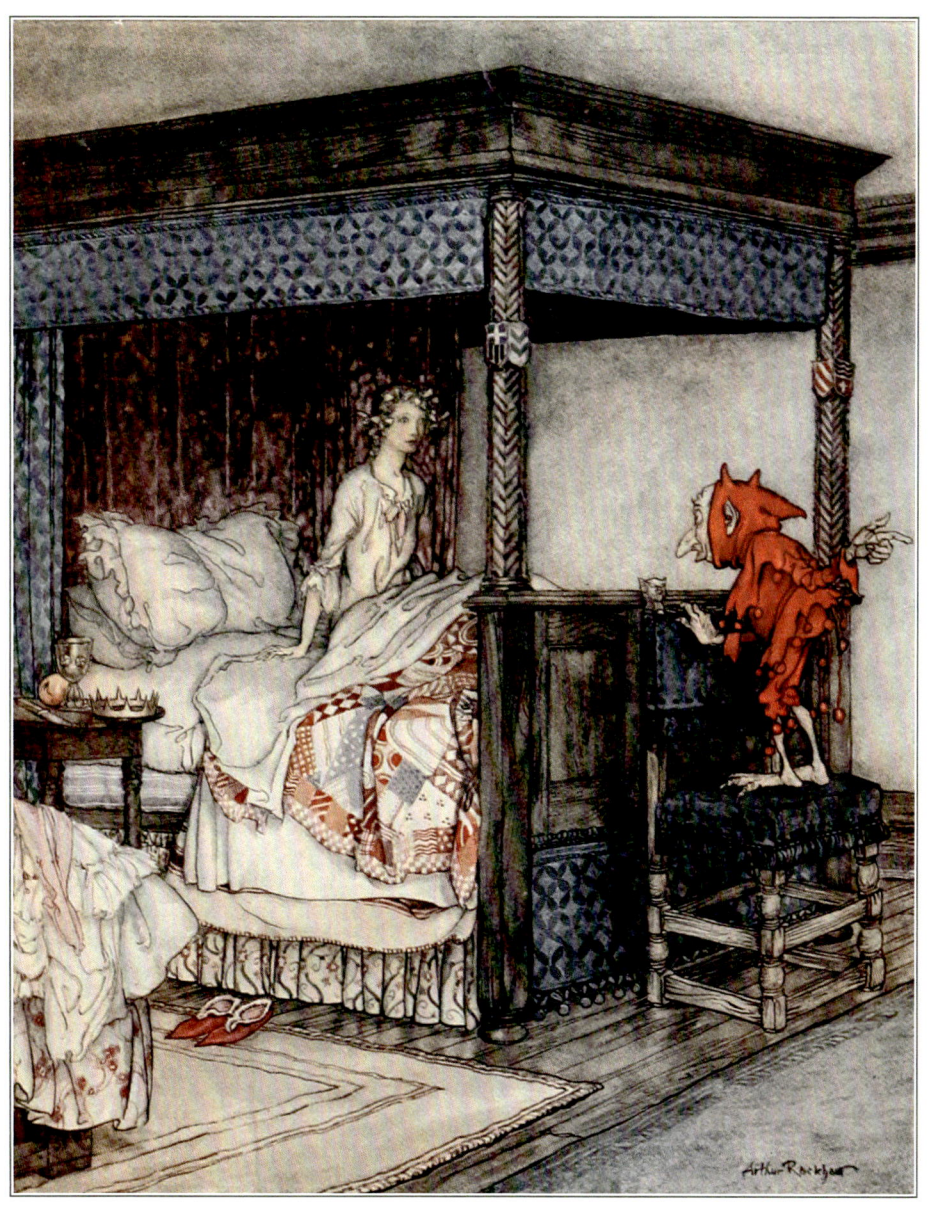

Edmund Dulac's work as an illustrator is easier to find than Dulac himself. A good many books preserve his work. Internet resources show his full range from the period when he was the worthy rival of Arthur Rackham to later years when he drew the "Night on Bald Mountain" sequence for the Disney film *Fantasia* and, still later, designed postage stamps for the coronation of Elizabeth II. But the only biography, excellent, is more than 40 years old; it's surely time for new work on this gifted, complex individual.[62] He had a nearly lifelong friendship with the poet W. B. Yeats and cooperated with him on theater works and much else—but his side of the decades-long correspondence with Yeats is not yet well published.[63] So be it. We can know him through his work.

No single page can fully exemplify his many and varied book illustrations, but the one chosen here, the dazzled alchemist in *Stories from Hans Andersen* (1911), is representative and often reproduced. It has found a place among my icons as the very image, sweet and foolish, of our unquenchable hope and frequent delusion. It is deeply and unstoppably funny and sad; further, its richness of color and detail call one back into its little world again and again to notice something more. The story it illustrates, "The Wind's Tale about Waldemaar Daa and his Daughters," is in keeping with Andersen's taste for sad tales. A prosperous castle-dweller with a beautiful family as the story opens, Waldemaar unwisely takes it upon himself to build a three-decked wooden war ship for the king, whom he expects to buy it. But an admiral who demands a bribe interferes, the king does not make the purchase, the investment is lost, and the family is soon impoverished. "Waldemaar Daa was proud and conceited, but he was also learned. . . . Many whispers went about as to his learning. The fire blazed in his stove even in summer, and his chamber door was locked. . . . He would soon discover the best of everything, the red, red gold!" On an Easter morning, he felt at last that he had attained the alchemist's dream. "Look at the alchemist's glass! Something twinkles in it; it is glowing, pure and heavy. He lifted it with a trembling hand and shouted with a trembling voice: 'Gold! Gold!'" Waldemaar rushes to show the flask to his daughters—and drops it. It "shivers into a thousand atoms."[64] All is lost.

Dulac chose to illustrate the moment of Waldemaar's greatest hope and astonishment. Dressed in something of a tattered Rembrandt outfit, surrounded with the tools of his alchemical trade, the books and vessels and stoves, the exquisitely detailed astronomical amillary at left and ragged bales of who knows what in the rafters, Waldemaar is a fully tragicomic figure. Dulac brings to bear a most sophisticated mind, pen, and brush. Like Rackham at the

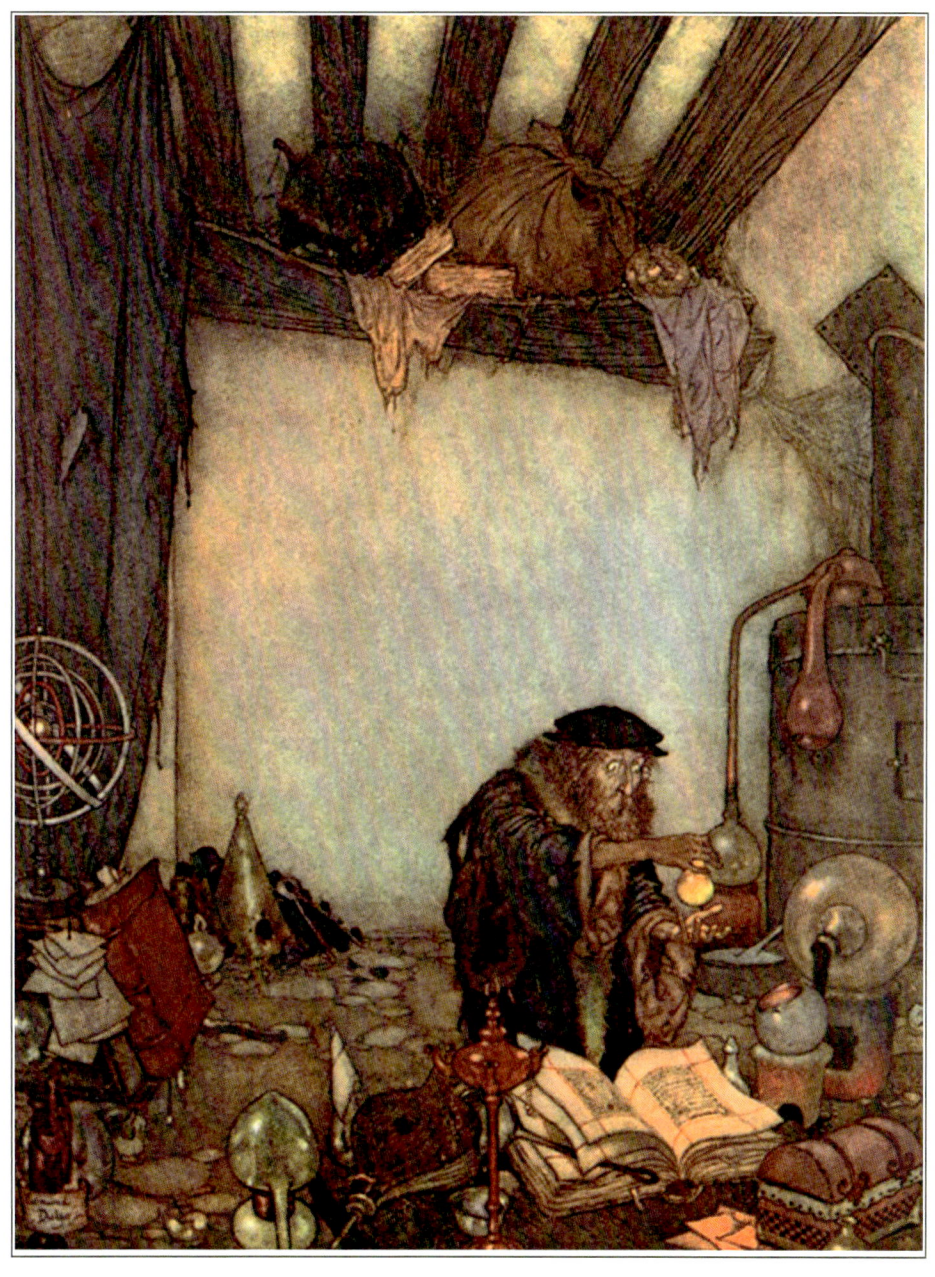

same moment, he draws on the Japanese print tradition and Dutch domestic interiors, and beyond that he is familiar with a colorful Flemish-Dutch repertory of images of alchemists in cluttered laboratories, best exemplified by David Teniers the Younger (1610 – 1690). It all comes together exquisitely well, and it is his own.

Such were two brilliant moments of art in the early twentieth century: a little-known repertory of glass work from the well-known Tiffany Studios and pages from the Golden Age of book illustration. The wind that tells the tale of Waldemaar is somewhat obsessive. It interrupts its tale from time to time with these words: "Whew! Whew! Fare away!"

Return. Begin Again.

Henri Matisse (1869 – 1954)
Backs I – IV, 1909 – 1931
Bronze, each panel app. 6′ 4″ X 3′ 10″
The Museum of Modern Art, New York
Source: iStock

Isamu Noguchi (1904 – 1988)
Funerary Monument, early 1980s [?]
[material, size]
Isamu Noguchi Garden Museum, Japan
Source: Takashi Yasumura

Henri Matisse knew the history of art. It lived in him as nourishment or sub-soil for the immensely innovative art he practiced from his early years as a "Fauve" painter, a Wild Man, to the late years as a very gentle man, making paper collages—once seen, never forgotten—and designing all elements of a chapel at Vence in the south of France. In this chapel of a man who wasn't sure about God, pervasive light and glowing color invite the barest, brightest prayer. In the long period 1909 – 1931, he returned periodically to the theme of the female nude in large-scale, low-relief sculpture, initially modeled in plaster, cast in bronze in an edition of nine soon after his passing. There is such intelligence in these works. They never fail to stop me in the full sense of the word: in front of them, no more thought, only a kind of abiding and a sense of being spoken to.

In these works Matisse is simultaneously moving forward and backward in time—and depriving himself of his greatest asset, his mastery of color, to explore questions of form in an austere manner. The first and earliest relief is a reflection on the classical treatment of the figure. The pose and generalized fidelity to realistic treatment of the figure place this version closer to academic art of the nineteenth century than to its own century at a time when Cubism and his own defiant Fauve art were emerging. The second version

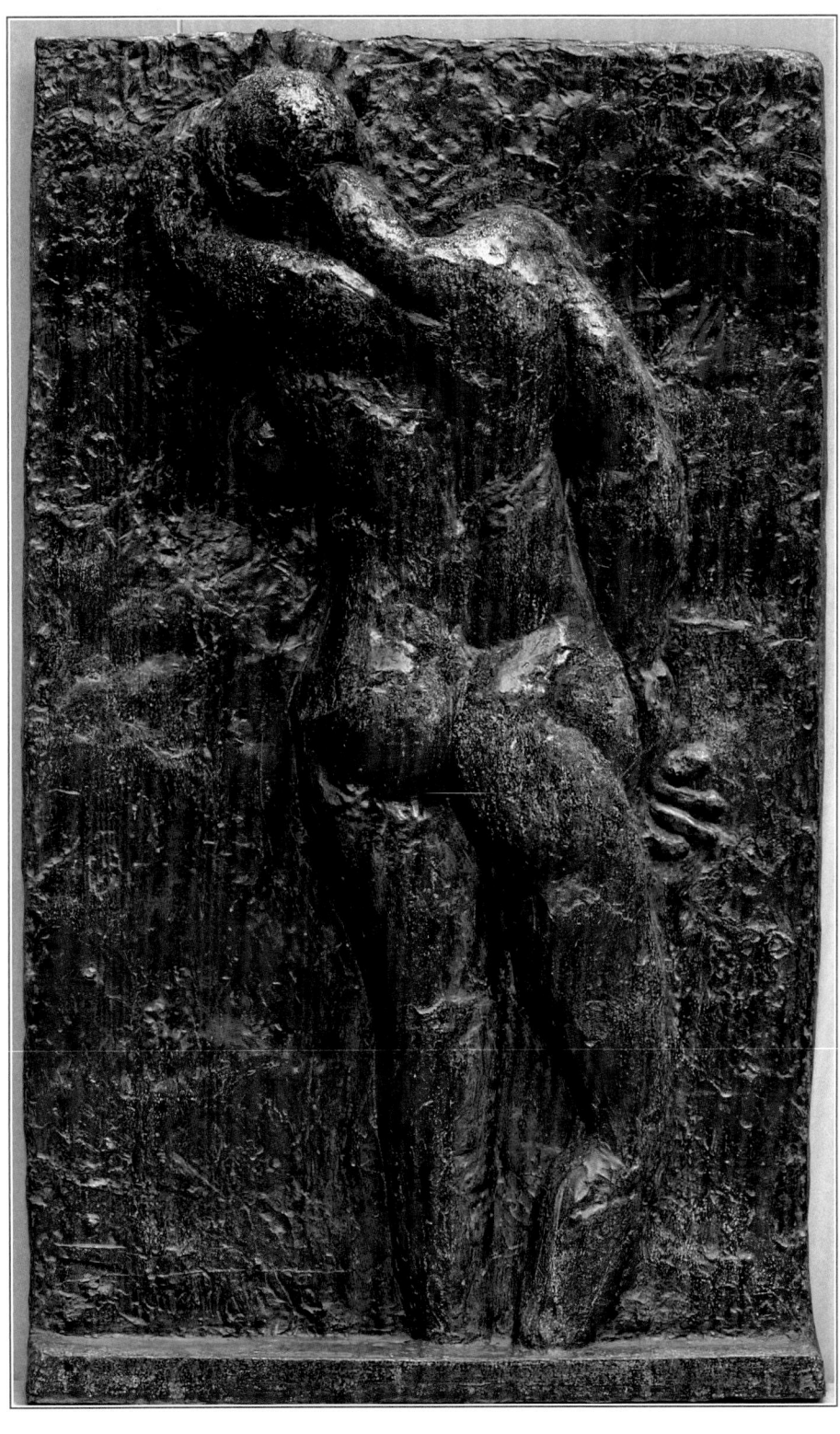

joins the twentieth century; its simplified planes, deep linear creases, and summary, almost brutal rendering of the head suggest that Matisse is looking for a new, more abstract vision. The subsequent version moves farther in that direction: we are likely to experience the figure as "mass and volume" quite abstractly, although the bearing leg / flexed leg tradition from classical sculpture still persists. And finally the magic of the fourth and last Back, which to my eye returns us to the simplicity and uprightness with which this book began, the so-called Hera of Samos (p. 4). There is a photograph of Matisse in his middle years, I suppose at the Louvre sketching a kouros, a sixth-century BCE fragmentary figure of a standing young man—the photograph an homage both to Matisse and to ancient models ever new. The Backs represent an extraordinary journey from what he had inherited as a French artist born in the nineteenth century to what we all potentially have as an inheritance: a feeling for humanity without detail, without time or place, archaic and enduring. This return to origins, so thoroughly performed by Matisse over a period of more than twenty years, is characteristic of some of the most impressive chapters in the art of our own time. It is not a turning away from what we are now; it is a turn toward what we are now and

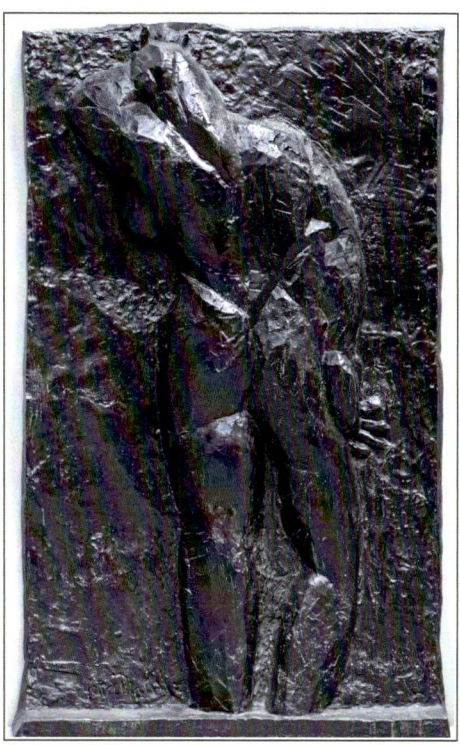

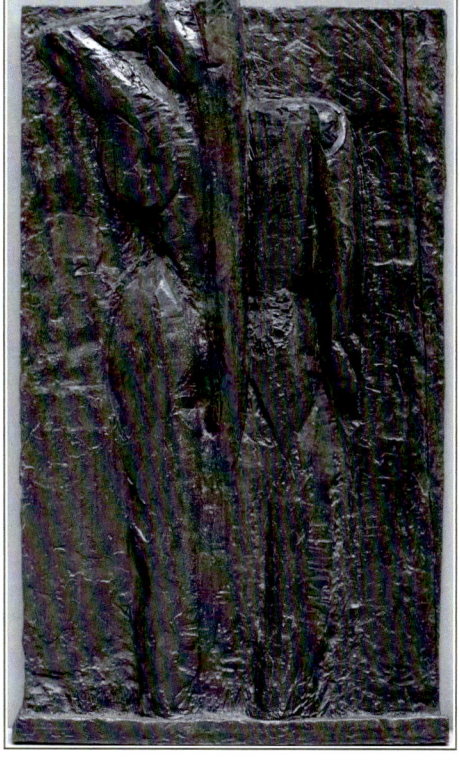

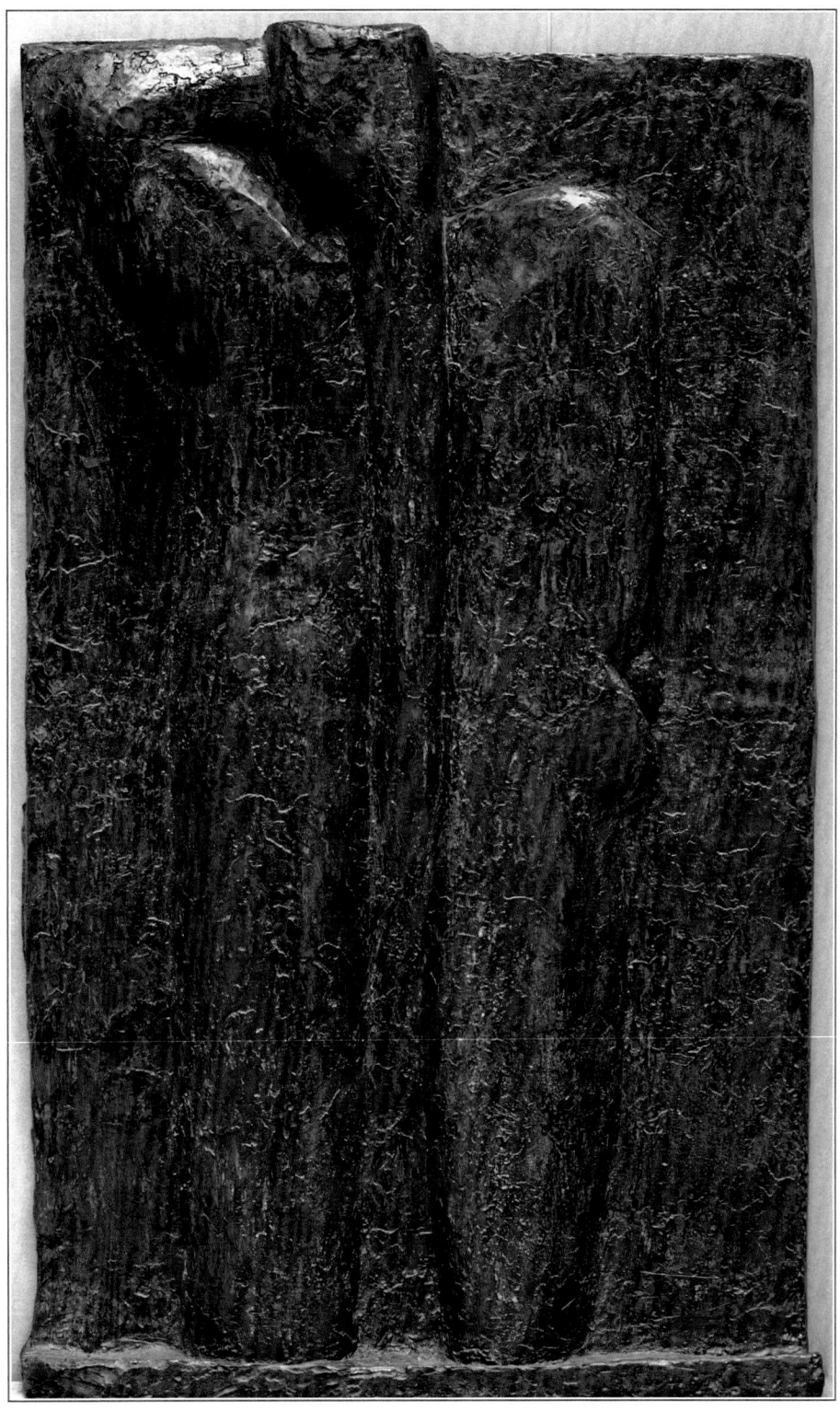

always. And for this we needed and continue to need artists with deep minds and skilled hands.

To the Japanese-American sculptor Isamu Noguchi we owe a comparable journey to a different province of ancient time. Though many of his later stone sculptures carry the theme, there is one—unfamiliar to me until recently— that is perfection itself in its presence and simplicity: his funerary monument. In his long and continually interesting career, Noguchi proved himself a master of complex form. But in later years he was drawn to simplicity inspired in part by the traditional Japanese stone garden. What we see here is a massive stone shaped by the sculptor without diminishing its presence as stone of the earth, on which he recorded a row of small recesses—a modest signature of humanity, of measurement, of touch. In the context of this icon collection, Noguchi's return is to the era of the Neolithic stone-carving at Gavrinis (see pp. 47–49). There he could rest, there we can rest.

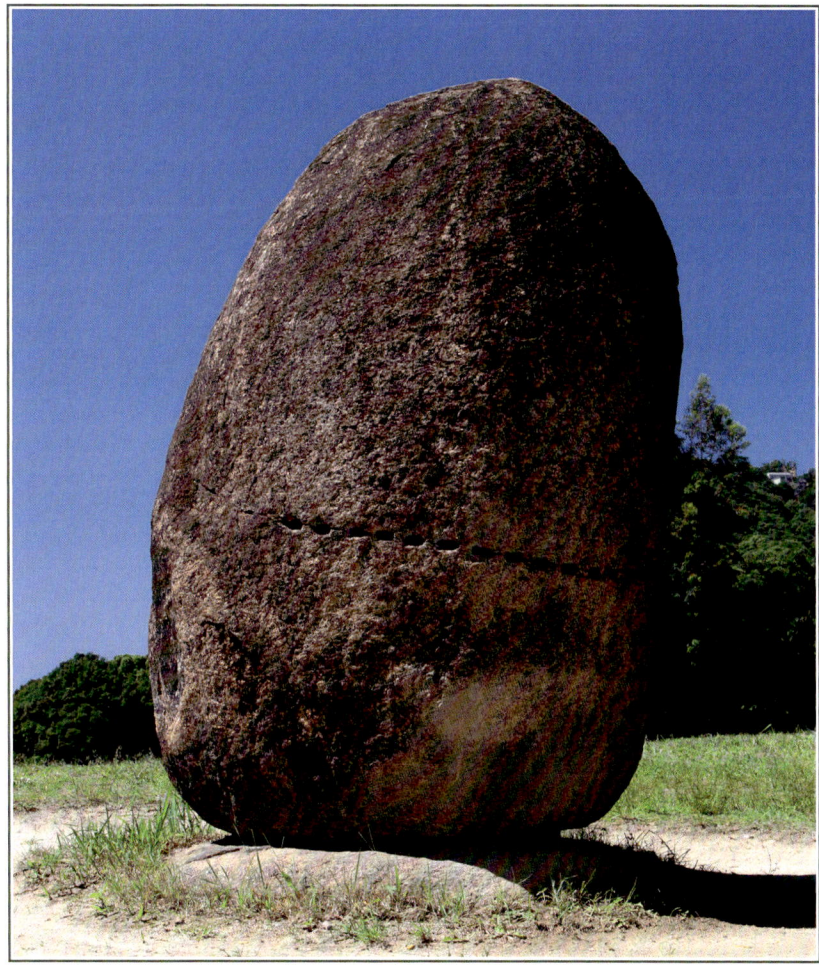

What moved these two returns—to the quiet dignity of early Western figural art, to the primordial era when human beings began applying shallow, rhythmic patterns to stone? There was a sense, there is still a sense, that we need to return to fundamentals and begin again. The need to return, to pare back to fundamentals, is itself ancient. One of the most compelling passages in the Brihadaranyaka Upanishad, dating to ca. 700 BCE, stages a conversation between a sage and a king, who asks, "What light does a person here have?" Ensues a sequence of deletions. "He has the light of the sun, O King, for with the sun as his light one sits, moves around, does his work, and returns." The king isn't satisfied with that answer. What happens when the sun goes down? The sage responds that moonlight will do. Again a deficient answer. Prodded anew, the sage proposes that fire is our light. No, that won't do. Well, then speech is our light: "O king, where one does not discern even his own hands, when a voice is raised, then one goes straight toward it." The courageously inquiring king asks yet again. At last, cornered as he must have wished to be, the sage provides his ultimate response: "The soul [atman—soul or Self] is our light, for with the soul, indeed, as our light one sits, moves around, does his work, and returns."[65] With that, the king is content.

We are not king and sage in the Axial Age, as that period of religious and philosophical renewal has come to be called. Circumstances have changed immeasurably, but the process hasn't changed. The need to return to fundamentals is characteristic of our period and frame of mind. Artists of genius have anticipated and echoed this need; they have given it an appearance. Thanks to their work, we can literally stand in front of that need, vividly experience it, know that it is not a stray concern of certain artists but fully shared. In the "art of our own," as I once wrote, there is a question of our own. In his wartime journal, Antoine de Saint-Exupéry, author of *The Little Prince*, put the question as simply and powerfully as possible: "Who am I? Who are we together?"[66] The question is not abstract, it is existential.

In our discussion of Islamic calligraphy (see pp. 119–122), I quoted a few lines from a remarkable book published in the year 1606: *Calligraphers and Painters—A Treatise* by Qadi Ahmad, Son of Mir-Munshi. Among much else, it reproduces a teaching text, an account of his own apprenticeship and advice for the next generation of calligraphers, written by Maulana Sultan-Ali Mashhadi, "whose writing is among other writings as the sun among the other planets. . . ."[67] At one point the maulana remembers the many students who came to work with him: "They were all my friends and brothers, / And all day long were with me." (The memoir is written in verse.) And then he writes the oddest, most beautiful thing about his attitude as he reviewed their work:

> I shut the eyes of the head and opened the secret ones,
> For looking with the secret eyes is not wrong.
> The eyes of the head look for faults and are defective,
> But what the secret eyes have seen becomes cherished.[68]

Here is another clue about return, useful for collectors of icons who wish to see with sensitivity. The eyes of the head, as he puts it, are defective; the judgments to which they give rise are flawed, lacking in love. They don't perceive what could be, fail to detect life within and promise emerging. But there are other eyes, secret eyes that allow us to cherish and encourage, to look toward the future and already to belong to that future because we care. This suggests another return, the return to oneself. That possibility is not obvious or lightly granted; it is nonetheless a birthright that can be recognized and claimed again and again. The maulana had understood that there were two in him: one the authentic teacher with prodigious knowledge to share, the other probably a cranky older man who had better things to do than look at student work. Which was it to be on any given day? The question, and challenge, must have made life interesting.

May we all find, and find again, our secret eyes.

NOTES

[1] Ananda K. Coomaraswamy (1877 – 1947) was a curator and later research fellow at the Museum of Fine Arts Boston from 1917 until his passing. A pioneering historian of Indian and Sri Lankan art in his earlier years when he lived both in South Asia and in the rural Arts and Crafts community in England, and later an immensely capable interpreter of the museum's South Asian and Muslim collections, he went on to become a polymathic scholar of art East and West, and of scripture and commentary East and West. His writings remain in print for the most part, and for good reason.

[2] Ananda K. Coomaraswamy, "The Nature of Buddhist Art," in Roger Lipsey, ed., *Coomaraswamy 1, Selected Papers: Traditional Art and Symbolism* (Princeton: Princeton University Press, 1977), 147.

[3] In the Louvre Collection online, she is referred to both as "Héra de Samos" and in another entry as "Kore [maiden] from the Chcramyes Group."

[4] See Ziony Zevit, "The Common Origin of the Aramaicized Prayer to Horus and of Psalm 20," *Journal of the American Oriental Society*, Vol. 110, No. 2, 213 – 28.

[5] D. H. Lawrence, *Etruscan Places* (London: Martin Secker, 1932); accessed April 2021 through The Gutenberg Project, http://gutenberg.net.au/ebooks09/0900381h.html#0900381h-07, where these entries appear in the chapter entitled "The Painted Tombs of Tarquinia."

[6] See Roger Lipsey, *Gurdjieff Reconsidered: the Life, the Teachings, the Legacy* (Boulder: Shambhala, 2019), 116 – 17.

[7] See the excellent Wikipedia entry at https://en.wikipedia.org/wiki/Diary_of_Merer, accessed 5/17/21; and Pierre Tallet and Gregory Marouard, "The Harbor of Khufu on the Red Sea Coast at Wadi al-Jarf, Egypt, *Near Eastern Archaeology*, Vol. 77, No. 1 (March 2014), 4 – 14. Most recently, a new book by Pierre Tallet and Mark Lehner, despite its publicity-seeking title, offers a full and exacting study of the context and documents from the harbor, with Ankhhaf at his place: *The Red Sea Scrolls: How Ancient Papyri Reveal the Secrets of the Pyramids*, London: Thames & Hudson, 2021.

[8] P. D. Ouspensky, *In Search of the Miraculous: Fragments of an Unknown Teaching* (New York: Harcourt, Brace, 1949), 27.

[9] Mary B. Moore, "Satyrs by the Berlin Painter and a new Interpretation of his Namepiece," *Antike Kunst* 49, 2006, 17 – 28.

[10] Mary Beard, *Pompeii: The Life of a Roman Town* (London: Profile Books, 2010), 131.

[11] Peter Mark Adams, *Mystai: Dancing out the Mysteries of Dionysos* (London: Scarlet Imprint, 2019).

[12] Françoise Henry, *Irish Art in the Early Christian Period (to 800 AD)* (Ithaca NY: Cornell University Press, 1965), 15, 218

[13] Ananda K. Coomaraswamy, «Bhakta Aspects of the Atman Doctrine,» in Roger Lipsey, ed., *Coomaraswamy 2, Selected Papers, Metaphysics* (Princeton: Princeton University Press, 1977), 396.

[14] The Koralek team's work is in Sirarpie Der Nersessian, *Aght'amar: Church of the Holy Cross* (Cambridge: Harvard University Press, 1965). A more recent publication with impressive color photographs is Step'an Mnasts'akanian, *Aghtamar* (Etchmiadzin: Erebouni, 1986).

[15] Thomas Merton, *New Seeds of Contemplation* (New York: New Directions, 1963), 296 – 97.

[16] Ananda K. Coomaraswamy, "The Dance of Shiva," in *The Dance of Shiva: Fourteen Indian Essays* (New York: Noonday Press, 1957, revised edition), 66 – 78.

[17] Stella Kramrisch, *The Presence of Śiva* (Princeton: Princeton University Press, 1981), 439 – 41.

[18] Thomas Merton, *The Asian Journal of Thomas Merton*, eds. Naomi Burton, Brother Patrick Hart, and James Laughlin (New York: New Directions, 1973), 233 – 35.

[19] Eileen Hsiang-ling Hsu, *Monks in Glaze: Patronage, Kiln Origin, and Iconography of the Yixian Luohans* (Leiden: Brill, 2017).

[20] The best source for Ikkyu is James H. Sanford, *Zen-Man Ikkyu* (Chico CA: Scholars Press, 1981). For freely interpretive translations of Ikkyu's poetry, see Stephen Berg, *Crow with No Mouth: Ikkyu, Fifteenth Century Zen Master* (Port Townsend, WA: Copper Canyon Press, 1989).

[21] For somewhat competing views, see Herbert Plutschow, *Rediscovering Rikyu and the Beginnings of the Japanese Tea Ceremony* (Folkestone UK: Global Oriental, 2003), and Morgan Pitelka, *Handmade Culture: Raku Potters, Patrons, and Tea Practitioners in Japan* (Honolulu: University of Hawai'I Press, 2005). A source for Rikyu anecdotes and a wealth of other information easily missed is A. L. Sadler, *Cha-No-Yu: The Japanese Tea Ceremony* (Rutland VT: Tuttle, 1962 [first edition, 1933]).

[22] My preference among the many translations available is J. C. Mardrus, trans. Powys Mathers, *The Book of the Thousand Nights and One Nights* (New York: St Martin's Press, 1972, in four volumes). A more recent engaging translation is Husain Haddawy, trans., *The Arabian Nights* (New York: Norton, 1990), based on a 14th-century Syrian manuscript. See also André Clot, John Howe, trans., *Harun al-Rashid and the World of the Thousand and One Nights* (London: Saqi, 2005).

[23] A *hadith* or saying attributed to the Prophet Mohammad, in V. Minorsky and T.

Minorsky, trans., *Calligraphers and Painters: A Treatise by Qadi Ahmad, Son of Mir-Munshi (circa A.H. 1015 / A.D. 1606)* (Washington, D. C.: Freer Gallery of Art Occasional Papers, Vol. 3, No. 2), 49, and internet site hadeethenc.com.

[24] A page much like the one in my study and of similar date is likely to be visible online by typing in the italicized words.

[25] *Calligraphers and Painters*, 52, presented as a truism or proverb.

[26] *Calligraphers and Painters*, 108.

[27] Ananda K. Coomaraswamy, "Two Passages in Dante's *Paradiso*," in *Coomaraswamy 2,* 246.

[28] Ananda K. Coomaraswamy, "Primitive Mentality," in *Coomaraswamy 1*, 296.

[29] For example, Jon Thompson, *Oriental Carpets from the Tents, Cottages, and Workshops of Asia* (New York: Penguin, 1993).

[30] Henry Beveridge, ed., Alexander Rogers, trans., *The Tuzuk-i-Jahangiri or Memoirs of Jahangir* (New Delhi: Munshiram Manoharlal, 1978, consulted in the edition of 2003); vol. 2, 108, offers an example.

[31] See Milo Cleveland Beach, *The Grand Mogul: Imperial Painting in India, 1600 – 1660* (Williamstown: The Sterling and Francine Clark Art Institute, 1978), 137 – 143, for Mansur and Jahangir. The translation of the marginal calligraphy was available online 5/17/21 in the Victoria and Albert Museum's entry: https://collections.vam.ac.uk/item/O16756/painting-mansur/.

[32] *Jahangir*, vol. 2 (bound with vol. 1), 111.

[33] W. R. Paton, trans., *The Greek Anthology* (Cambridge MA: Harvard University Press, 1916), vol. 1, including Book VI, entry 194.

[34] *Greek Anthology*, Book VI, entry 199.

[35] *Greek Anthology*, Book VI, entry 31.

[36] *Greek Anthology*, Book VI, entry 40.

[37] Linda Stone-Ferrier, "The Engagement of Carel Fabritius' *Goldfinch* of 1654 with the Dutch Window, a Significant Site of Neighborhood Social Exchange," *Journal of Historians of Netherlandish Art*, Winter 2016 (accessed online 2/22/2021).

[38] See Walter Frisch and Kevin C. Karnes, *Brahms and His World* (Princeton: Princeton University Press, 2009), 427. I am grateful to my neighbor Prof. Michael Musgrave for documenting this memorable statement.

[39] Giorgio Vasari, *The Lives of the Painters, Sculptors and Architects*, in 4 vols., trans. A. B. Hinds (New York: Dutton, 1963, revised edition), vol. I, 263.

[40] C. Jean Campbell, "Simone Martini, Petrarch, and the Vernacular Poetics of Early Renaissance Art," *Studies in the History of Art*, vol. 74, 2009, pp. 219 – 20, n. 19. Retrieved 03/08/21 from JSTOR.

[41] Vasari I, 69.

[42] Vasari I, 263 – 64.

[43] Vasari I, 268.

[44] *The Poems of Emily Dickinson: Reading Edition*, edited by Ralph W. Franklin (Cambridge, MA: The Belknap Press of Harvard University Press, 1998).

[45] Excerpt from the manuscript autobiography of Constantijn Huygens, Koninklijke Bibliotheek, The Hague, published in *Oud Holland*, 1891, trans. Benjamin Binstock. A more accessible source: Gary Schwarz, *Rembrandt: His Life, His Paintings* (New York: Viking, 1985), 73 – 77.

[46] For an extraordinarily rich and perceptive account of *The Night Watch*, see Simon Schama, *Rembrandt's Eyes* (New York: Knopf, 1999), 488 – 500. Schama's book overall is an invaluable resource.

[47] Charles Ford, ed., *Lives of Rembrandt: Joachim von Sandrart, Filippo Baldinucci, Arnold Houbraken* (Los Angeles: J. Paul Getty Museum, 2018), 39.

[48] Ford, 86.

[49] Ford, 78.

[50] Ford, 58.

[51] For the inventory of the bankruptcy sales, see Schwarz, 283 – 91.

[52] While I don't mean to assemble exhaustive endnotes for this freely interpretive book, new literature of high quality about Piranesi and his moment should be noticed: Carolyn Yerkes and Heather Hyde Minor, *Piranesi Unbound* (Princeton: Princeton University Press, 2020), and Susan Stewart, *The Ruins Lesson: Meaning and Material in Western Culture* (Chicago: The University of Chicago Press, 2020).

[53] Although there are other editions of Diderot's *Salons* commentaries, the most trusted and comprehensive French edition in several volumes, *Diderot: Salons*, is owed to Jean Seznec and Jean Adhémar for the first volume (*Salons 1759, 1761, 1763*) and to Seznec for subsequent volumes. Under conditions of pandemic confinement I have had access to a mix of editions, Seznec and others.

[54] Denis Diderot, *Oeuvres de Denis Diderot*, vol. 8 (Paris: J. L. J. Brière, 1821, reproduced in facsimile by Elibron Classics), vol. 8, Salon of 1765, 182.

[55] *Oeuvres de Denis Diderot* (the 1821 facsimile), Salon of 1767, 158.

[56] Pierre Rosenberg, *Chardin* (London and New York: The Royal Academy of Arts and The Metropolitan Museum of Art: 2000), quoting Diderot, 288. You will find the French text in Seznec and Adhémar, Vol. 1, 2nd edition, 222.

[57] Rosenberg., 27.

[58] Rosenberg, front matter, quoting Charles Nicolas Cochin's recollection dating to 1780.

[59] Shambhala Publications, 1988, now available from Dover Books under the subtitle.

[60] Martin Eidelberg and Nancy A. McClelland, eds., *Behind the Scenes of Tiffany Glassmaking: The Nash Notebooks, including Tiffany Favrile Glass* by Leslie Hayden Nash (New York: St. Martin's Press in association with Christie's Fine Arts Auctioneers, 2001.

[61] While I have found in a Sotheby's auction catalogue a reference to Ms. Spillman's suggestion, I haven't been able to locate her text. See *Dreaming in Glass: Masterworks by Tiffany Studios*, Sotheby's, 23 May 2019.

[62] Colin White, *Edmund Dulac* (New York: Scribner's, 1976).

[63] See Diana Poteat Hobby, *William Butler Yeats and Edmund Dulac; a correspondence: 1916-1938* (Houston: Rice University, doctoral dissertation, 1981, accessed online 4/23/2021).

[64] Accessed online, 4/08/21, at www.thefreshreads.com/the-winds-tale/.

[65] Robert Ernest Hume, *The Thirteen Principal Upanishads* (Oxford: Oxford University Press, 2nd edition revised, 1931), 133.

[66] I no longer know where to find these few words, I believe in Saint-Exupéry's *Ècrits de guerre*. Better readers than I, please advise!

[67] *Calligraphers and Painters*, 101 – 02.

[68] *Calligraphers and Painters*, 111.